The Catholic Church
in Modern China

The Catholic Church in Modern China

Perspectives

Edmond Tang and Jean-Paul Wiest,
Editors

ORBIS BOOKS

Maryknoll, New York 10545

The Catholic Foreign Mission Society of America (Maryknoll) recruits and trains people for overseas missionary service. Through Orbis Books, Maryknoll aims to foster the international dialogue that is essential to mission. The books published, however, reflect the opinions of their authors and are not meant to represent the official position of the society.

Copyright © 1993 by Edmond Tang and Jean-Paul Wiest

All rights reserved
Published by Orbis Books, Maryknoll, NY 10545
Manufactured in the United States of America

Acknowledgment is gratefully extended for permission to reprint the following:

"Is There Religious Freedom in China?" by Julia Ching, "In China, Appearances Can Be Different" by Thomas Gahan, and "A Church in Transition" by Edward J. Malatesta are reprinted with permission. Copyright 1990 by America Press. "A Schismatic Church?—A Canonical Evaluation" by Geoffrey King is reprinted with permission of *The Jurist*. "The Role of the Patriotic Association" by Bishop Aloysius Jin Luxian (English translation) is reprinted with permission of the China Department of the Council of Churches for Britain and Ireland. "My Vision of the Patriotic Association" by an underground bishop and "Who Is Not Loyal to the Church?" by Father Joseph Yao Tianmin are both reprinted with permission of China Catholic Communication in Singapore. *"L'Eglise clandestine en Chine"* by Jean Charbonnier and "The Language of Reconciliation" (originally entitled "The Task of Reconciliation in the Chinese Church") are reprinted with permission of Echange France-Asie, 128, rue du Bac, 75341 Paris. Copyright 1990 and 1991 by Echange France-Asie. "The Local Church in China" by Hans Waldenfels is reprinted with permission of the Holy Spirit Study Centre, 6 Welfare Road, Aberdeen, Hong Kong.

Library of Congress Cataloging-in-Publication Data

The Catholic church in modern China : perspectives / Edmond Tang and
    Jean-Paul Wiest, editors.
        p. cm.
    Includes bibliographical references.
    ISBN 0-88344-834-3
    1. Catholic Church—China—History—20th century. 2. Freedom of
religion—China—History—20th century. 3. China—Church
history—20th century. I. Tang, Edmond. II. Wiest, Jean-Paul.
BX1665.C382   1993
282'.51'09045—dc20
                                                        93-14944
                                                        CIP

Contents

Preface   ix
  Janet Carroll

Chronology of the Catholic Church in China   xiii

Map of China   xviii

Introduction   1
  Jean-Paul Wiest

PART I
Through a Kaleidoscope—The Catholic Church Today

1. **The Church from 1949 to 1990**   7
   John Tong

2. **The Church into the 1990s**   28
   Edmond Tang

3. **Is There Religious Freedom in China?**   43
   Julia Ching

4. **The "Underground" Church**   52
   Jean Charbonnier

5. **The Formation of New Church Leaders**   71
   Maria Goretti Lau

6. **A Schismatic Church?—A Canonical Evaluation**   81
   Geoffrey King

PART II
Tower of Babel or New Pentecost?

7. **Perspectives on the Government-approved Church**   105

   In China, Appearances Can Be Different   105
   Thomas Gahan

The Role of the Patriotic Association   112
Bishop Aloysius Jin Luxian

My Statement   120
Bishop Ma Ji

My Vision of the Patriotic Association   126
An Underground Bishop

8. Perspectives on the Underground Church   **135**

Who Is Not Loyal to the Church?   135
Father Joseph Yao Tianmin

Thirteen Points   142
Attributed to Bishop Fan Xueyan

The Present Chinese Church   146
A Priest from Northern China

9. A Church in Transition   **153**
Edward J. Malatesta

10. The Local Church   **158**
Hans Waldenfels

11. The Catholicity of the Chinese Church   **164**
Maria Goretti Lau

**PART III
Looking Toward the Future**

12. Learning from the Missionary Past   **181**
Jean-Paul Wiest

13. The Need for Reconciliation   **199**
Jeroom Heyndrickx

14. The Language of Reconciliation   **209**
Anonymous

15. Fundamental Attitude of the Bridge Church   **222**
Aloysius B. Chang

16. China and the Future of Hong Kong   **231**
Luke Tsui

17. **Contextualization of the Chinese Church**   **243**
   Edmond Tang

Selected Bibliography   **256**

Contributors   **259**

Preface

Christianity first arrived in China over a thousand years ago and although it never fully flowered, neither did it completely disappear. Today a resurgence of religious expression in the People's Republic of China accompanies a desire on the part of Chinese Christians to authentically root the Christian gospel in the ethos of the Chinese people. This means that the Christian religious tradition must truly incarnate itself in Chinese cultural and social traditions in a way that is both meaningful and appropriate. In a word—and this is equally true in the West—the church as an institution must be *relevant* to the socio-political realities of its context. In China, the church's greatest challenge, therefore, is to bring its moral and religious influence to bear on the rapidly changing social milieu gripping its one and a quarter billion people.

In this last decade of the twentieth century, the political and economic climate that has charted China's course remains volatile. Given this climate of continuing change and crisis, it is often difficult to understand events in China, and particularly those that affect the inner lives of the Chinese people. It has been pointed out, however, that the Chinese characters for "crisis" contain elements of the characters for both "danger" and "opportunity." After forty years of extreme internal and external pressures, the "danger" for the church is to succumb to fragmentation or factionalism. The "opportunity" for the church consists in seizing this moment to reform and renew itself in the spirit of Vatican II.

This book deals with both of these dimensions—the dangers and the opportunities—facing the Catholic church in the People's Republic of China. The editors have sought to present a carefully nuanced and balanced perspective by interweaving a broad spectrum of viewpoints and interpretations. The essays include a historical perspective, views of what is happening today, and possible scenarios of how the Chinese church might contextualize itself in the future.

Edmond Tang and Jean-Paul Wiest have done a great service by collecting a wealth of material for study and reflection on the multifaceted reality that is the Catholic church in today's China. In addition to providing basic information about developments in the church, this material can heighten our awareness of the paramount need for reconciliation and unity, internally as well as in communion with the Holy See. John Paul II has repeatedly urged all those concerned—both within and without China—to seek reconciliation and harmony. His pleas, now strongly echoed by many leaders of the Chinese church, remain the fervent prayer and hope of the vast majority of the Chinese Catholic community.

Pluralism, diversity, and even contradictions are germane to all human existence, but rarely more so than in modern Chinese society. While the church has not been spared these contradictions and confusion, there are many signs that point to hope and promise for a new tomorrow. Despite four decades of severe repression and persecution (which even today has not fully abated), when new policies of "reform and openness" were promulgated in the 1980s, the world was astounded to find that a strong and vibrant Chinese Christianity had not only survived, but flourished. Christianity continues to attract Chinese of all ages and stations in life, so much so that even Communist party literature refers to the phenomenon of "Christianity fever."

With other religious institutions in China, the Catholic church faces the demanding challenge to become a courageous partner in dialogue with the social reality of the People's Republic on the eve of the twenty-first century. The dialogue must take place in many milieus: the ideological/political arena, the quest for economic modernization and human development, and certainly the existential level of the religious and spiritual orientations of the Chinese people. As in other countries, the church must be both servant and prophet.

The heroic struggle of the Chinese Catholic church to remain faithful and to chart a path to a viable future in its own social and cultural context has many lessons to offer other local churches. Its quest for reconciliation and unity may become a graced moment for the universal church, bonded in the spiritual leadership of the Holy Father. In the end, we may all experience a more mature unity, truly reflective of the salvation history unique to peoples of vastly diverse cultural and social traditions.

Empathetic understanding and generous support offered by Christians of other lands must show respect for the autonomy of the Chinese church. The American missionary movement, originally sparked by the desire to share the gospel message with the Chinese people, is presented anew with an opportunity to serve. As Edward Malatesta points out in his essay, a new moment of cooperation is dawning that promises to be even more fruitful, since the Chinese will be the "creators of an authentically Chinese church and the inspiration and guide to foreign friends they invite to collaborate with them. . . ." Those of us in other local churches who wish to take on these supporting roles must first develop an informed understanding of what has happened in the past and of the contemporary reality of the Chinese church today. Friends outside China should avoid taking sides on the divisions within the church, nor should they naively promote simplistic resolutions for problems and difficulties that are rooted in generations of tragic misunderstanding and unjust relationships.

For a variety of largely political reasons, American Catholics at present are lagging far behind their Protestant colleagues in taking up the call to be in mission with their Chinese sisters and brothers. This book will hopefully go a long way to rekindling that missionary fervor, while sobering our understanding that we shall all be evanglized in new and unsuspected ways in the process.

Sister Janet Carroll, M.M.
Executive Director
U.S. Catholic China Bureau

Chronology of the Catholic Church
in China

635 Alopen, a Syrian monk, introduces Nestorian Christianity in China. Founding of several monasteries and churches. Gradual disappearance after persecution in ninth century. Brief resurgence in the fourteenth century under the Mongol Yuan dynasty.

1294 John of Montecorvino, Franciscan, begins evangelization of the Mongols in Peking. At least 30,000 converts. Disappearance after the ousting of the Mongol Yuan dynasty in 1368.

1583 Arrival of Matteo Ricci. Conversion of scholars.

1645 Decree of Propaganda Fide forbidding "worship" of Confucius and of the ancestors.

1654 Ordination of first Chinese priest at Manila; in 1685 he becomes bishop of Nanjing.

1704 The Holy Office forbids the Chinese "rites."

1724 Edict of the Yongzheng emperor: preaching is forbidden under death penalty; however some Jesuits and Lazarists remain at the court for almost a century.

1842 Opium War. The Treaty of Nanjing gives legal sanction to Christian missions in the ports.

1860 Treaty of Tianjin: the missions are protected by France.

1900 Boxer revolt, an anti-foreign movement; mass killing of Christians.

1924 Plenary Council of Shanghai. Archbishop Celso Costantini, first apostolic delegate.

1926 Ordination of six Chinese bishops in Rome. In 1940 there are twenty-three Chinese bishops.

1939   Propaganda Fide abolishes the oath against the "rites."

1949   Communist victory: intense atheistic propaganda.

1950   Korean War. The movement of Three Autonomies of the Catholic
        church is launched in Sichuan province.

1951   Creation of regional Chinese Catholic Patriotic Associations and
        Committees for Church Reform. Expulsion of Archbishop Anto-
        nio Riberi, the internuncio. Arrests of Catholics, nationalization
        of religious institutions (schools, colleges, hospitals).

1954   Pius XII condemns the "Three Autonomies" (*Ad Sinarum Gen-
        tes*).

1955   Catholic resistance loses its leaders: the bishops of Shanghai, Bao-
        ding, Taizhou, Hankou, and other areas are arrested.

1957   Repression of opponents after the "Hundred Flowers" (1956) and
        creation of the national Chinese Catholic Patriotic Association
        (CCPA). First democratic election of a bishop at Chengdu
        (Sichuan).

1958   The first two illicit ordinations of bishops (April 13). They are
        condemned by Pius XII on June 29 (*Apostolorum Principis*) and
        followed by eleven other ordinations.

1962   Second congress of Chinese Catholic Patriotic Association.
        Another seven illicit ordinations; there are now forty-five bishops
        not recognized by Rome.

1966   A decade of chaos during the Cultural Revolution: churches are
        closed, priests and religious are secularized and sent to prison or
        forced labor.

1970   Liberation of Bishop James E. Walsh, the last Catholic missionary
        in prison, as a preparation for the normalization of Sino-American
        relations. From Hong Kong, Paul VI addresses a message to
        China: attempt dialogue.

1972   Reopening of the Nantang church in Beijing.

1978   Two Catholic bishops and fourteen leaders of other religious
        groups are delegates to the Political Consultative Conference.

1979   Election of the bishop of Beijing, Fu Tieshan. He is ordained in December. Liberation, and in many cases rehabilitation, of priests from prison or work camps. In August the pope expresses hope of re-establishing relations with the church in China. In September a Chinese religious delegation participates in the Third World Congress of Religions for Peace in the United States. Only Protestants are represented.

1980   Third National Assembly of the Catholic Patriotic Association (May). Creation of Chinese Catholic Bishops' Conference and the Chinese Catholic Church Administrative Commission; these two are "church" associations as distinguished from the Patriotic Association, which is political. Protestants create China Christian Council as distinct from the Three-Self Movement. Liberation of Dominic Tang, bishop of Canton, after twenty-two years of imprisonment.

1981   Manila message of Pope John Paul II to the Chinese people, appealing for dialogue. Press conference of Cardinal Agostino Casaroli, the secretary of state, in Hong Kong, implying ways of reconciliation. Patriotic Association accuses Vatican of creating an underground church. John Paul II nominates Dominic Tang as archbishop of Canton unilaterally; strong reaction from the Patriotic Association and the Chinese government. More ordinations of bishops in China. International China conference in Montreal with ecumenical Chinese delegation, including three Catholic leaders.

1982   Letter of John Paul II to the bishops of the world, asking for prayer but also stating Roman primacy. New Chinese Constitution includes clause against foreign domination of Chinese churches. First reopening of major seminary near Shanghai. New arrests of Catholic priests in Shanghai for being in contact with the Holy See. Visit of archbishop of Canterbury.

1983   Joint national conference of Catholic Patriotic Association and Church Administrative Commission. Twenty-fifth anniversary of first popular election of bishops; ceremony attended by high government officials. Priests arrested in Shanghai receive heavy sentences. Pope John Paul II renews appeal for dialogue. Inauguration of Catholic seminary in Beijing with sixty seminarians; total of four Chinese seminaries. First reopening of a convent of sisters.

1986   In May police clamp down on clandestine seminary and novitiate in Hebei. In November the joint national conference of the Chinese Catholic Patriotic Association and the Church Administrative Commission establishes new statutes that emphasize the principles of independence and self-governance.

1987   Five Asian bishops and Cardinal Jaime Sin of Manila visit China.

1988   Death of Bishop Zhang Jiashu, president of the government-approved Bishops' Conference and the Catholic Patriotic Association. Bishop Zong Huaide of Jinan is named interim president. Bishop Jin Luxian replaces Bishop Zhang as the government-approved bishop of Shanghai.

1989   Shanghai diocesan center "Guangqi" begins translation of major Vatican II documents. Some Chinese and foreign priests residing outside the PRC are allowed to teach for short periods of time in seminary near Shanghai. Persecution against underground church intensifies. In March the Bishops' Conference meets in Beijing and decides 1) to recognize the pope as the spiritual head of the church; 2) to assume the control of church affairs; 3) to exclude married bishops from the conference. In April Youtung incident in Hebei province between Catholics and police forces: two dead, three hundred and fifty wounded. Arrests of Christians are on the rise. A modern Catholic printing house is inaugurated in Shanghai. In November underground bishops establish their own episcopal conference. The officers of that conference are all arrested.

1991   Rome reveals that Vatican-appointed bishop of Shanghai since 1950, Bishop Gong Pinmei, was made a cardinal in 1979.

1992   In April deaths of Bishops Fan Xueyuan and Li Zhenrong, two prominent officers in the underground episcopal conference. In September the three Catholic organizations hold their fifth national Catholic Representatives' Congress. Bishop Zong Huaide is elected president of the government-approved Bishops' Conference and the Catholic Patriotic Association. The episcopal conference is officially placed above the Church Administrative Commission and on an equal footing with the Patriotic Association.

In 1992 *Yi China Message*, a publication in Hong Kong, published statistics on the government-recognized Catholic church released by the fifth national Representatives' Congress.

Catholics	3,900,000
Bishops	68
Priests	800
Sisters	900
Dioceses	113
Churches	3,900
National seminaries	1
Regional seminaries	11
Preparatory seminaries	12
Major seminarians	700
Minor seminarians	190
Ordinations	106
Sisters' convents	30
Novitiates	37
Sisters in formation	370

Underground church statistics are, understandably enough, difficult to obtain or to verify. "China-church" experts usually estimate the total number of Catholics frequenting both the open and the underground churches at more than ten million.

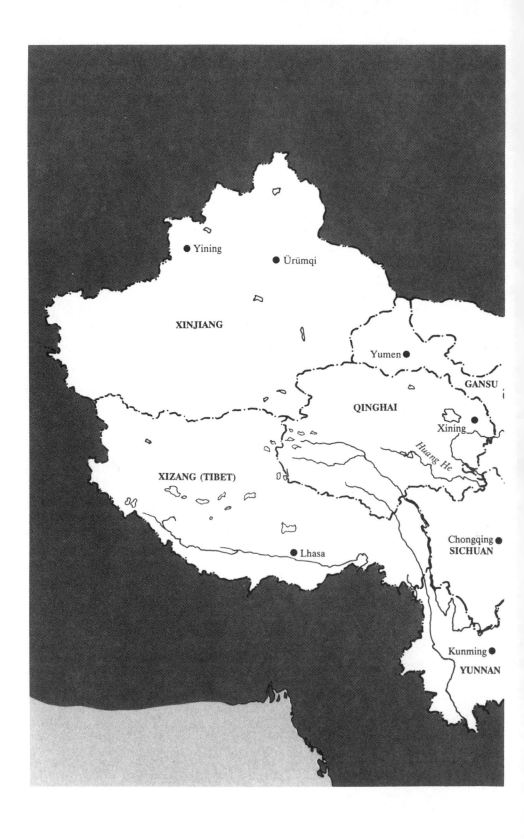

Introduction

JEAN-PAUL WIEST

Friends who know of my interest in the Chinese Catholic church often confess their puzzlement at what they read in the press concerning the present state of Christianity in the People's Republic of China. They wonder in particular about the various factions within the Catholic church, especially the government-recognized public group and the hidden underground church communities.

Their questions touch on a broad variety of topics that may often be shrouded in a heavy cloak of political, economic, social, or theological antecedents. Thus, our conversations can easily expand into discussions of issues such as imperialism and colonialism; nationalism and patriotism; religion under communism; schism, excommunication, and reconciliation; and, of course, that of the relationship between universal church and local church.

When asked to recommend a book on these topics, I am at a loss. I have looked, but in vain, for a well-balanced, accessible volume on the intricate yet fluid situation of the Catholic church in the People's Republic of China. Many of my fellow researchers, Chinese as well as Westerners, also deplore this lacuna, but at the same time they stress that, given the present situation, the task of writing such a book is too difficult to be successfully undertaken by a single author.

Meanwhile, excellent testimonies, interviews, articles, and research papers on the Catholic church in China exist, but they are scattered and not always accessible to an English-language audience. Edmond Tang and I, therefore, decided to review these materials and to gather as broad as possible a selection, which resulted in this single volume.

Although this book deals specifically with the Catholic church in the People's Republic of China, the reader will also find ample references to the Protestant church. However, the primary objective of this book is to focus on the particular problems of the Catholic church and not to ignore other expressions of Christianity in China.

The book is divided into three parts. Part I, "Through a Kaleidoscope," looks at transformations within the Chinese Catholic church since the founding of the People's Republic of China in 1949. The six essays in this part deal with the Catholic church's successful struggle to survive, its various

1

responses to the Communist regime and its ensuing internal divisions, its canonical status with Rome, and government policies toward religion.

Part II focuses on the present conflict within the Chinese Catholic church and includes an array of differing perspectives. Entitled "Tower of Babel or New Pentecost?," it provides divergent opinions regarding the part of the church that functions with the permission of the government and the other part that is banned by the regime and thus operates underground. The ferocious attacks and counterclaims in some of these selections attest to a profound chasm between these two parts of the church. At the same time, however, other more heartening perspectives describe a church in transition, searching to define parameters for its own selfhood and uniqueness in communion with Rome and other local churches.

Part III, which turns to the future of the church, considers elements essential to its continuance and growth in the modern milieu of the People's Republic of China. This process of "contextualization" cannot take place without a critical study of past encounters between China and Christianity to identify what worked best and to avoid repeating past mistakes. At present, divisions within the Chinese Catholic church and tensions with the church of Rome are major threats to its survival and its future as a local church in communion with the universal church. Achieving reconciliation internally and externally is, therefore, identified as the most pressing need. The role of nearby churches in facilitating reconciliation at various levels is also explored. The church in Hong Kong, in particular, is given special attention because in 1997 the People's Republic of China will regain control of that territory.

The reader should always remain aware that the selections in this book express a variety of viewpoints; they were written for different purposes and at different times during the past four to five years. Through careful editing, Edmond Tang and I have tried to eliminate repetitions and to reconcile many inconsistencies. Nonetheless, it is important for the reader to keep in mind that each selection reflects a *particular situation* and should be read in that context. In addition, a variety of names has been used by different authors to designate the Catholic church in China: on the one hand, "underground," "clandestine," and "secret" commonly refer to churches that are not registered with the government; on the other hand, "government-approved," "public," and "open" refer to churches that are recognized by the government.

Edmond Tang and I sincerely attempted to be as impartial as possible in our selections and to include as many points of view as possible. The task was more challenging with materials from within the People's Republic. Understandably, it was easier to identify reliable sources from the government-approved church than from the underground church communities. Our goal is not to force upon the readership a ready-made one-sided opinion about the Catholic church in China. On the contrary, by providing divergent views and analyses, we want to impart an accurate sense of the seriousness and the complexity of the situation faced by the Chinese church.

We hope that from reading this book Christians outside China will gain a greater respect and empathy for their brothers and sisters at this critical stage in time. Some readers may even respond to the call of becoming— individually or collectively—instruments of reconciliation or bridge-build-ers.

But most of all, Edmond Tang and I wish that this book, in some way, will encourage our Chinese sisters and brothers to continue steadily on the bitter but salvific path of reconciliation that leads to a vibrant self-assured unified Chinese local church in full communion with the universal church.

Part I

Through a Kaleidoscope —
The Catholic Church Today

1

The Church from 1949 to 1990

JOHN TONG

The four decades that span the establishment of the People's Republic of China on October 1, 1949, and the Tiananmen incident of June 4, 1989, are one of many volatile and tumultuous periods in Chinese history. These decades had a profound impact on the political, social, and religious reality of the country. Four stages can easily be identified, each bringing its own challenge and leaving a distinct legacy. The fragmented picture of the present Catholic church of China is the direct result of what took place during those forty years.

1949-1956: Establishment of Communist Control

Social and Political Background

Many factors led to the rapid fall of the Nationalist government in China in 1949. A major cause was the ineffectiveness of the Nationalist government in solving the problems of social reconstruction after the Sino-Japanese War, a crisis accentuated by severe inflation and attractive Communist propaganda about land reform.

Since China was essentially an agrarian country, it was inevitable that both contending armies, the Nationalists and the Communists, were largely composed of farm boys. Communist propaganda about land reform persuaded these farm boys that under the Communist regime their families' economic situation would be improved and that their parents who had been landless their whole lives would become landowners. Consequently, the

Father John Tong wrote this essay in 1988 as a conference paper. He revised and updated it in 1991 for publication.

Communist army penetrated the entire country without encountering too many large battles or too much violent resistance.

At that time, convinced by the very successful land reform propaganda, many Western observers regarded the Chinese Communists more as a party of agrarian reformers than a genuine Communist party. However, as soon as victory had been achieved, Mao Zedong proclaimed his "Lean-to-One-Side" policy, a policy which meant that China would not maintain a neutral position between the Communist world and the non-Communist world, but would seek unity with the Soviet Union and the rest of the Communist world.

The nationwide land reform movement launched in 1950 aimed first at eliminating the rural ruling class (landlords and money lenders), and then focused on developing agricultural production. These two steps were considered essential for paving the way for the industrialization of the New China. As a result, almost all landlords were deprived of their power and privilege; some were even sentenced to imprisonment or death. At the same time, indoctrination courses, lectures, and discussions on the subject of land reform were imposed throughout China.

Shortly after the inauguration of the land reform movement, anti-imperialistic campaigns were intensely accelerated by the beginning of the Korean War and the "Oppose America — Aid Korea Movement." On June 25, 1950 the Korean War broke out after North Korean forces crossed the Thirty-Eighth Parallel in a large-scale attack upon South Korea. Hostilities continued for over two years before an uneasy peace was negotiated. China entered the war in October 1950 when U. N. forces under the leadership of General Douglas MacArthur threatened to cross the Yalu River into Chinese territory. On December 29, 1950, "Regulations" were issued within China that required all institutions receiving foreign funds, including religious ones, to register with the government. A Religious Affairs Division, later renamed the Religious Affairs Bureau, was established in January 1951 and entrusted with the supervision and regulation of all religious activities throughout the country. Religious groups, many of whom were subsidized from abroad, were required to follow a policy of complete independence and become self-supporting. In 1953 the Korean War finally ended in a stalemate.

The Response of the Catholic Church

This period was a time of turmoil, confusion, and reorganization for both Protestants and Catholics. Immediately prior to U. N. intervention in Korea in June 1950, several Protestant church leaders from Shanghai held three meetings in Beijing with Zhou Enlai, the premier. At the beginning of the land reform movement, Communist propaganda about land redistribution had appealed to some leading Christians who were actively involved in preaching the social gospel. They believed that the Christian gospel could be combined with the gospel of Chinese communism, especially the teaching on serving the poor. At the last of these meetings in May 1950, a "Christian Manifesto" that had been drafted by church leaders was approved by Zhou. When it was published, this manifesto bore the names of forty prominent Protestant church leaders from various Christian churches in China. About a year or two later, the number of signers reached 400,000 — almost half of the total Protestant membership in China. The manifesto constituted a blueprint for future church action and also prepared for the coming into being of independent Chinese churches.[1]

The Catholic response did not come until November 30, 1950. In north Sichuan, a group of Catholics under the leadership of a Chinese priest, Wang Liangzuo, was said to have issued its own manifesto, calling for the severance of all church ties with the forces of imperialism and the establishment of a self-supporting, self-governing, and self-propagating church. The document essentially condemned the way in which the imperialists had used the church in the past as an instrument of colonial aggression, and it called on Chinese Catholics to cut off connections with imperialism so as to build up the "Three Autonomies." Later on, a second manifesto was published in Chongqing. This latter manifesto, signed by 14 priests, 7 religious sisters, 1 brother, and 695 lay Catholics, used language similar to the north Sichuan manifesto.[2]

On January 17, 1951 some Catholic leaders requested a meeting with Premier Zhou Enlai in order to clarify the government's insistence on an independent Catholic church. Because nothing of substance was reported in the Chinese press, little was known about this meeting except for the premier's remarks on the relationship between the Vatican and the Catholic church in China. Premier Zhou Enlai knew very well that continued relations between the Chinese church and the Vatican had to be tolerated temporarily. Therefore, he stated that as long as there was no opposition to the political power of the Chinese people and no support within the church for American imperialism, relations with the Vatican could be maintained. Zhou also called for the Catholic church to support the patriotic movement known as the Three Autonomies. He added that "A true patriot would have nothing to do with the enemies of his country."[3]

When the Communists had come to power in 1949, there were about 35 Chinese bishops out of the 146 bishops or monsignors throughout the country. The general reaction of the Catholic bishops in China to the manifestos and to the meeting with Premier Zhou was published in an official church document, entitled *The Church in China: Declaration of Principles*,[4] issued in February 1951. This document was circulated to Catholics and to government officials alike. Condemning the so-called "national" or "independent" Catholic church as "schismatic," it began with a statement of the traditional Catholic position that Catholics who willingly separate themselves from the Holy See also separate themselves from Jesus Christ and from the Catholic church. The bishops insisted that since no alliance existed between the Catholic church and imperialism, there was no imperialist connection to sever. However, criticism of the pope as an imperialist or as a tool of imperialists was totally unacceptable to the Catholic clergy.

This church document also attempted to clarify the bishops' understanding of the implications of the Three Autonomies. "Self-governing" meant that the Catholic church would gradually establish an indigenous hierarchy, but according to ecclesiastical regulations rather than according to Communist principles. "Self-supporting," in the bishops' understanding, included support of the church by Catholics of any country; only subsidies with political implications—whether from abroad or from within China—would not be accepted. "Self-propagating" meant that foreign missionaries would propagate the faith to serve the interests of local churches, not the interests of foreigners. The importance of developing an indigenous hierarchy was affirmed, as was the right to continue using foreign missionaries until the number of Chinese priests was adequate. Obviously, the bishops' understanding of the Three Autonomies was not acceptable to the Communists.

During the Oppose America—Aid Korea Movement, almost all missionary institutions and properties, such as universities, hospitals, orphanages, and so forth, were taken over and nationalized or confiscated by the government. Catholic and Protestant seminaries generally were able to survive longer than other Christian higher educational institutions, yet additional government regulations eventually closed them down as well. By the end of 1951 the majority of Protestant missionaries had left China, while the majority of Catholic missionaries, in spite of working under difficulties, were still at their mission stations. Because of the continuing presence of Catholics and because of the definite stand of the Catholic church against communism, the Communists persecuted a larger number of Catholic missionaries than Protestants during the Oppose America—Aid Korea Movement.

In the summer of 1951 a fierce campaign was launched against the Catholic church. The Vatican internuncio, Antonio Riberi, was placed under house arrest and then expelled from the country. The city of Shanghai, which had been the main center of opposition to the independent church movement, was especially targeted. There was an Oppose America—Aid Korea indoctrination course particularly directed at the Catholic church. Accusation meetings were held and pamphlets were widely circulated, particularly in Shanghai, accusing Catholic priests, the Legion of Mary, and other Catholic organizations of anti-government activities. Some five hundred Communist students were sent daily to Catholic families to persuade them to support the government's political campaigns.

In Beijing Catholic resistance was weaker than in Shanghai. After mass arrest of missionaries and Chinese priests on July 25, 1951, the Religious Affairs Bureau set up "Catholic reform committees" to govern the parishes and lay the foundation of a national Catholic church. These committees were gradually established in all major cities. They helped prepare documents or manifestos for Catholics to sign and denied that any schism was involved in their activities. They also maintained that they were only carrying out their patriotic duty and bringing needed reforms to the church. Obviously, some priests cooperated with this reform movement, yet during the period from 1951 to 1954, many Catholics shunned the movement because they considered it to be schismatic.

Meanwhile, in January 1952 Pope Pius XII issued the apostolic letter *Cupimus Imprimis*[5] in which he compared the situation in China with that of persecutions in the early church and praised Chinese Catholics for their faithfulness. He also addressed the inappropriateness of setting up particular national churches that could destroy the unity established by Christ.

By 1954 a change of emphasis had begun to take place in the movement for reform of the Catholic church in China. "Progressive" Catholics now stressed the "patriotic" elements of the movement instead of speaking of the "independent church" or "reforming the church." The year 1955 was a turning point. Resistance was suppressed by mass arrests, and the terms Three Autonomies and Three-Self Movement were gradually replaced by the more persuasive and appealing use of "Patriotic Association." One could oppose the Three Autonomies on the basis that they affected the traditional structures and the nature of the Catholic church, but no Chinese Catholic could resist loving his or her country.

The government also showed a milder attitude toward the Catholic church. Unfortunately, in October of 1954 Pope Pius XII's encyclical *Ad Sinarum Gentes* (*To the People of China*) refueled the fires of persecution. In this encyclical addressed to the bishops, priests, and laity of China, Pope Pius XII defended the missionary enterprise, distinctly rejected the independent church movement, and affirmed the necessity, on the basis of Christian charity, of allowing ties of mutual support in the Catholic church throughout the world. He encouraged the faithful to remain firm and called upon those who had erred to repent. This strong, public criticism of communism by the pope deeply offended the Chinese Communists, who prepared to confront the Catholic church even more boldly.

In September 1955 Shanghai Bishop Ignatius Gong Pinmei, with a large number of other priests, sisters, and lay Catholics, was arrested. Bishop Gong was one of the strongest opponents of the Catholic independent church movement, and his diocese of Shanghai was the main stronghold of opposition. By the end of November 1955 fifteen hundred Catholics had been arrested, including several seminarians and about fifty priests. During that time, similar arrests took place in Guangzhou where Bishop Dominic Deng Yiming was put in prison.[6]

1956-1966: The Hundred Flowers Campaign and the Anti-Rightist Campaign

Social and Political Background

By 1955 China's first Five-Year Plan (1953-1957) for national construction, including land reform, had all the appearances of a success story.

Fueled by a phenomenal rate of industrial growth, the Chinese economy outpaced that of any Asian country. Testing how well the socialist foundation had been grounded in China's soil, Mao Zedong felt confident enough to propose a campaign of "letting a hundred flowers bloom and a hundred schools of thought contend."

This Hundred Flowers movement was a campaign of historical importance, because it was the first major example of a Communist party in a socialist state encouraging massive criticism from outside the party. Critics came largely from the professional and educational sectors of the population, with only a small number of workers. Such an unexpectedly overwhelming criticism shocked Mao and some party leaders, who became aware that they still had a long way to go to establish a Chinese Communist state. In order to suppress the outburst of the Hundred Flowers, a counter-criticism campaign called the Anti-Rightist movement was initiated by Mao and the Communist party. These two campaigns—the Hundred Flowers and the Anti-Rightist movements—were carried on from 1956 to the end of 1957. The Anti-Rightist campaign was renewed again in the later part of 1959 when the Great Leap Forward and the commune system failed.

Although the first Five-Year Plan achieved the results anticipated by Mao Zedong, Mao also realized that proceeding with more of the same would invite disaster. The Soviet model of taxing agriculture to build industry and repay Soviet loans had put too heavy a burden on the Chinese peasants. Mao, who opposed the Soviet "revisionism" of Khrushchev, realized that if China desired to become a modern power, China "had to walk on its own legs rather than depend on someone else's car." To turn China into a strong nation during Mao's own lifetime would require a "Great Leap Forward" into self-sustaining economic growth. This Great Leap Forward (1958-1959) was an overall effort to transform Chinese society by lessening the gap between town and country, between intellectual and manual worker and peasant, between those in authority and the mass of the people.

The establishment of people's communes and the reorganization of rural life served a number of purposes: they facilitated planning on a large scale of both the utilization of land and water and the use of labor; they freed women for work in the fields and factories by establishing communal dining halls and nurseries; and they provided the structure for developing industry in the countryside.

From 1959 to 1961 exceptionally bad weather struck many of the Chinese provinces, causing extensive damage to agriculture. Moreover, in July 1960 Khrushchev ordered all the Soviet experts (some fifteen hundred persons) to withdraw from China, and he terminated the contracts for supplying equipment to some of China's largest undertakings. This pullback, along with serious damage caused by bad weather and the mistakes committed by the Communist party leadership in the formation of people's communes and in the Great Leap Forward program, slowed down the revolutionary tempo. From 1959 onward, increasing complaints led to a strong political and ideological reaction on the part of Mao and the Communist party. This reaction reached its apex in 1962 and paved the way for the disastrous Cultural Revolution that began in 1966.

The Response of the Catholic Church

During the Hundred Flowers period, the Communist government made every effort to establish a Catholic Patriotic Association on a national scale, although the Patriotic Association had already existed in some cities. In July 1956 thirty-six Catholics, including four bishops, were invited to meet with the director of the national Religious Affairs Bureau and some other government officials in Beijing. This week-long meeting established a preparatory committee charged with the responsibility to draft a constitution for a national Catholic Patriotic Association. On the day following the final session, Premier Zhou Enlai received the delegates, encouraged them to lift their patriotic spirit high, and to lead their churches along the road to socialism. Because of sharp criticism from several Catholic bishops and priests during the Hundred Flowers campaign, the government released some previously arrested lay Catholics, bishops, and priests as a friendly gesture to the church.

In the middle of June 1957 the director of the Religious Affairs Bureau convened a follow-up meeting that brought together 241 Catholics and a number of government officials. After a month of off and on discussions, the delegates established the national Chinese Catholic Patriotic Association (CCPA), with Shenyang Archbishop Pi Shoushi as its chairperson. The participants denounced the Vatican because the pope had not recognized the new bishop elected in Shanghai to replace Bishop Ignatius Gong Pinmei. Moreover, Communist officials present at the meeting strongly suggested electing and ordaining bishops independently of Rome. Yet, in spite of the fact that some of the bishops attending the conference disagreed with the suggested policy of ordaining bishops without Rome's approval, the local election of bishops was soon underway.[7]

On December 16, 1957 Father Li Xiying of Chengdu was chosen as the first locally elected bishop. Although Li's election was the first, his episcopal ordination did not take place until after that of two Franciscans in Wuhan, Fathers Dong Guangqing and Yuan Wenhua. The reason for the local election of bishops put forth at the time was pragmatic. Since expelled bishops were not allowed to return to their sees, and since some Chinese bishops were in prison, new bishops had to be chosen from among the "patriotic" priests to fill episcopal vacancies. On April 13, 1958 Bishop Li Daonan of Puqi ordained the two Chinese Franciscans. Shortly before the ordination ceremony, their names were sent by cable to Rome; however, the Congregation of Propaganda Fide replied that the election was illegal and threatened the ordaining bishop, Li Daonan, and the two priests with excommunication. Between April 20 and July 20 of 1958 thirteen more "patriotic" bishops were ordained in six different Chinese dioceses without Rome's approval.

Rome received this news with great sadness. On June 29, 1958 Pope Pius XII issued another encyclical, *Ad Apostolorum Principis* (*At the Tomb of the Leader of the Apostles*), addressed to the church in China. The pope expressed his disapproval of the Catholic Patriotic Association and did not recognize the ordination of bishops whose nominations had not been confirmed by the Holy See.[8] By mid-1958 the reported number of illicit episcopal ordinations ranged from twenty-three to thirty-two. All these consecrations were "valid" but "illicit." By 1962 about twenty Chinese bishops who had been appointed by Rome remained, while the number of illicitly ordained bishops appointed by the government reached forty-two. Among these government-appointed bishops, some had been ordained by "illegitimate" bishops.[9]

In order to suppress the overwhelming criticism voiced in Catholic circles during and after the Hundred Flowers campaign, the government set up a new program of indoctrination meetings to deal with Catholic "rightists." Catholics attending these indoctrination meetings were asked to condemn "rightist" Catholics, to denounce the Vatican, and to discuss the establishment of a national hierarchy as well as the socialist, independent, autonomous nature of Catholicism in China. Some opposition came from bishops and priests who supported Bishop Ignatius Gong Pinmei and who refused to cut off relations with the pope. Some bishops even threatened clergy with excommunication if they joined the Catholic Patriotic Association. Although the resistance was not as strong as it had been in 1950 to 1955, this resistance by a minority of Catholic clergy called forth a more intensive indoctrination program, which lasted from August 1957 to February 1959.

This brief review of the Catholic church in the 1950s prompts a question: Why have a Chinese Catholic Patriotic Association? First and foremost, it was the manifest aim of the Chinese Communist party to assert leadership over the church, replacing papal rule with a new structure. Similar organizations have been established in most Communist-controlled countries. A second reason is that China's revolt against centuries of Western exploitation and colonialism and its decisive move toward independence exerted a strong influence on a number of Chinese priests and lay Catholics. Many of them were motivated by deep feelings of nationalism to join the newly formed Patriotic Association. Of course, there were those who claimed to be "patriotic" but who joined out of fear of reprisals or those who were opportunists and joined for personal gain. However, many were genuine patriots.

A third reason might be laid at the doorstep of the legacy of China's missionary history. Even though throughout the four-hundred-year history of Catholicism in China, foreign missionaries were generally accepted and genuinely loved by their Chinese Christians, who were grateful for their contributions, some directly or indirectly retained strong ties with their countries of origin and their colonial policies. Foreign missionaries were often identified—whether fairly or unfairly—with imperialistic powers, and this caused resentment among many of the more nationalistic Chinese Catholics.

1966-1976: The Cultural Revolution

Social and Political Background

The Cultural Revolution, which was carried on from 1966 to 1976, was primarily a revolution aimed at the superstructure of the Chinese Communist state. Although Mao claimed that Chinese communism was a unique model, it could not be properly understood when isolated from the international Communist movement. In fact, what was new in Maoism was that Mao combined Marxism and Leninism with his own patriotism.

In 1966 the Cultural Revolution, seen as an ideological struggle as well as a power struggle, moved from the stage of purging the "Black Gang" of intellectuals and writers, to the stage of "rectifying" party leaders and the educational system, and, finally, to the stage of the rise of the Red Guard crusade.

One dimension of the 1966 split was the conflict between those who saw the Great Leap Forward as the policy that had brought China to the point of collapse by 1961 and those who saw it as a historic step toward communism. This struggle between radicals and moderates can be traced back to 1959 and the failure of the Great Leap Forward with its commune system. In September 1959 Peng Dehuai, a member of the Politburo and minister of defense, was dismissed from his ministry for having led an attack on the Great Leap Forward and the commune system.

From 1960 to 1964 a group of writers closely associated with the city administration of Beijing published a series of attacks on the leadership of Chairman Mao, the Great Leap Forward, the people's communes, and in defense of leaders such as Peng. These writers also demanded that leadership should be handed back to the former professional experts.

In September 1965 a working conference of the Central Committee was held. Mao raised the question of the danger of revisionism arising within the Central Committee itself. From May to June 1966 a rectification campaign in literature and arts spread across the country. More than one hundred sixty-five prominent artists and writers were purged.

As momentum gathered, some thirteen million Red Guards—mostly teenage students—went to Beijing in the fall of 1966 for a succession of mass rallies in support of Mao. They then dispersed throughout China to carry out their own "long marches" and to attack the "four olds" (old ideology, thought, habits, and customs). Some young teachers and workers also became involved in the Red Guard organization. A reign of terror and destruction ensued in most parts of China.

In 1973 the Cultural Revolution suddenly turned moderate. A travel ban was imposed on the Red Guards and students were ordered back to school. However, the Red Guard movement had turned the entire country upside down and the Liberation Army was called in to restore social order and to help stabilize transportation, finance, internal trade, agriculture and industry.

The Cultural Revolution did the most damage to the younger generations who, when they awoke from the nightmare, discovered that they were without cultural roots. Traditional Chinese culture had been denied but the new Maoism had been an inadequate substitute. Young people were bewildered by both old and new value systems. Even today, a continuing search for ultimate meaning and existential value is a characteristic of Chinese youth in mainland China.

The Effect on the Catholic Church

While the destructive storm of the Cultural Revolution raged across the country, all religions as institutions disappeared in China. As the campaign against the "four olds" raged, the writings of Confucius were burned and all publications of a religious character were prohibited. All churches— official or unofficial, approved or not approved—went underground in order to survive. The Religious Affairs Bureau and the Catholic Patriotic Association both ceased to function. During this period of great violence, some seminarians and clergy were sent to labor camps. Groups of Red Guards marched into churches to tear down crosses and to break windows. Sometimes they forced old pastors to kneel on the broken glass. Many pastors and their families were harshly treated. Churches were closed and locked or were converted to assembly halls for the Red Guards. Through beatings and torture, Christians were forced to give up their faith. Red Guards searched Christians' homes and confiscated books, records, jewelry, and family letters. Despite persecution and suppression, devout Christians continued to worship and pray individually and in groups in their homes. To avoid detection, they met infrequently and at irregular hours.

By the end of August 1966 news of the deportation from China of eight French sisters shocked Catholics in Hong Kong. These French sisters, who belonged to the Franciscan Sisters of Mary, had been allowed to remain in China to operate their school because diplomatic personnel demanded an adequate education for their children. They travelled by rail from Beijing to Guangzhou under an armed guard, and crossed the border at Lowu on August 31, 1966. A large group of Red Guards gathered at the railway station on the Chinese side of the border and shouted slogans at them. An eighty-five-year-old nun collapsed as she crossed the bridge. She was taken to a hospital in Hong Kong and died the following day.

1976-1990: The Four Modernizations

Impact of the Change in Leadership

In 1976 China experienced one shock after another. The claws of death trapped the Communist party's top leaders, including Premier Zhou Enlai and Chairman Mao. Accompanying these political earthquakes, the worst earthquake in centuries took about 700,000 lives and devastated the major industrial city of Tangshan. Shortly after Mao's death on September 9, 1976, the ultra-leftist Gang of Four — Mao's widow together with three Shanghai leaders — was arrested and charged with plotting a civil war.

The ten-year nightmare of the Cultural Revolution came to an end. Many party leaders formerly denounced as "bourgeois rightists" during the Cultural Revolution returned to power. Deng Xiaoping's re-emergence as the most influential leader of the Chinese Communist party captured world-wide attention. Deng had been purged as the "Number Two Capitalist-Roader" from 1966 to 1968, along with Liu Shaoqi, the "Number One Capitalist-Roader," both primary targets of the Cultural Revolution. In 1973 Deng had been restored as a possible successor to Premier Zhou. He was toppled again after Zhou's death in 1976, and then officially rehabilitated in July 1977.

In spite of the fact that Deng obviously preferred "economy" to "ideology," "revisionism" to "dogmatism," and "expert" to "Red," under Deng's leadership, China remained a socialist country. Deng would not violate Mao's and Zhou's anti-imperialist principles in foreign policy, although he considered that a detente with Russia would benefit China more than if China continued to depend only upon its friendship with the United States.

In the post-Mao era, a full commitment to the implementation of the "Four Modernizations" policy[10] was necessary for China to achieve economic growth, improved living standards, and a viable military defense against external attack. The vehicle for moving forward was called the United Front. Unlike the United Front formed by Communists and non-Communists in order to defeat the Japanese invaders during the Sino-Japanese War, the new United Front was an alliance forged by people from all walks of life to effect the socialist modernization of their country. The present relationship between "religion" and "politics" in China can best be analyzed in light of this new United Front. Its general policy is summed up in the phrase: "seeking unity, preserving differences." It is a matter of fact that this United Front policy has been used by politicians as a basic principle to interpret the Communist government's attitude toward national minorities, religion, and intellectual and cultural activities.

For pragmatic reasons, the complete ban on religious belief and practice was relaxed. The Communist party stated that toleration of religion was justified by the continued existence within China of significant groups of believers, by the influence of religious philosophies on Chinese culture, and by the importance of religion in world affairs. Yet religion was not granted the same liberal concessions as was the economy. In economic affairs, the Communist party took an active interest in learning from the best of foreign economic practices. Technical literature of every kind was imported and given wide distribution. However, religion was not treated so positively and the importation of religious books into China is still strictly controlled.[11]

It is significant, however, that the Chinese Communist party has distinguished the "major" world religions from "popular" religion, which is very influential in rural areas. The government's policy of religious freedom applies primarily to the major world religions, while popular religion, seen as a form of superstition, is prohibited. In order to take the major world religions seriously, an Institute for the Study of World Religions was established in Beijing in March 1978. The aim of the Institute for the Study of World Religions is to study these world religions seriously from a Marxist-atheist viewpoint and to deal with them more effectively on an intellectual level.

Freedom of Religious Belief and Activity

Article 36 of China's new Constitution (1982) makes a clear distinction between freedom of belief and freedom of religious activity.

The Citizens of the People's Republic of China enjoy freedom of religious belief. No state agency, public organization or individual may compel citizens to believe in, or not to believe in, any religion; nor may they discriminate against citizens who believe in, or do not believe in, any religion. The state protects normal religious activities. No one may make use of religion to engage in activities that disrupt public order, impair the health of citizens or interfere with the educational system of the state.

According to the Constitution, all citizens enjoy freedom of religious belief and the country has the duty "to protect normal religious activity." Although the term "normal" has never been clearly defined, a clue to its interpretation is found in the "bottom line" of the government's policy; this, apparently, is whatever the government itself allows. What the government permits is considered "normal"; what it does not permit is not only considered "not normal," but can even be construed as illegal. The bottom line is whatever the dictatorship of the Communist party decides and whatever does not hinder the achievement of the Four Modernizations. Whatever conflicts with this is "forbidden territory." By examining some important documents published by the Communist party and the central government of the People's Republic, it is possible to discover the bottom line for all religious activity in China.

In 1980, when speaking about training of religious leaders and the restoration of churches and other places for religious activity, Li Weihan, the former Chinese Communist party's head of the United Front department, said:

In order to safeguard the people's freedom of religious belief, we must not intrude into the normal religious life of believers. Moreover, we must allow them to have places for religious activity and a certain number of religious professionals. If we have been remiss in these two matters and people are dissatisfied, we must make the necessary corrections. It is most important for us to train persons within the religious world who are of high caliber, patriotic and who have a profound knowledge of their religion. We need religious intellectuals to collate and study documents on the history of religions and also to implement the policies of the international United Front. Religious leaders of high standing must train successors who will know how to handle themselves in international situations.[12]

It is Li's opinion that the church had opened too many churches before Liberation, but that too few were left open during some of the past political campaigns and the Cultural Revolution. By using the principle of "avoiding two extremes and keeping the middle way," he drew the "bottom line." He allowed a "certain number" of churches to be opened and a "certain number" of seminarians and sisters to be trained. At the same time, Li Weihan, though only by hints, established another bottom line. He said that while "winning over and uniting the greatest number of religious persons to serve socialism, we must also isolate the few reactionaries among them." This foreshadowed pressures that would later be brought to bear on the key leaders of the "underground" church.

A third "bottom line" was established in "The Basic Viewpoint and Policy on the Religious Question in China during This Period of Socialism," known popularly as Document 19 (March 1982), a policy statement of the Central Committee of the Chinese Communist party. This statement is concerned with relationships with foreign churches and the acceptance of foreign funds as contacts gradually increased during China's open door policy of the 1980s.

Religious persons may and should develop mutual relationships with religious persons from other countries. They should maintain good communication with them and promote academic cultural exchanges on religion. However, while carrying out these various exchanges, they must firmly maintain the principle of the independent and autonomous administration of church affairs. They must firmly resist all attempts by reactionary forces within foreign churches, which are seeking once again to control the Chinese church. They must firmly refuse to let any foreign church or religious person meddle in or interfere with the affairs of our Chinese church. They must refuse absolutely to allow foreign religious organizations (and this includes the agencies which they control) to use any means whatsoever to return to China for missionary purposes, or secretly to send in large quantities of religious propaganda for distribution.[13]

Consequently, churches must adhere to the principle of the independent and autonomous administration of their own affairs. They must not permit any foreign religious body to come to China to do missionary work and they should oppose the diffusion of religious propaganda from abroad. In order to avoid outside interference and control by foreigners, the religious policy designed for Catholics and approved by the Chinese government is to uphold the principles of independence and self-governance of the church. In line with this policy, the primacy of the pope is not officially recognized, and more than forty bishops have been elected and ordained without the approval of the Holy See.

Regarding funding from abroad, Document 19 states:

Religious organizations and individuals [in China] are not allowed to seek funds from any foreign organization or person. All Chinese religious organizations and religious personnel, as well as any other organization or person in China, must not accept any subsidy or financial assistance from any foreign religious organization. If overseas Chinese and our Hong Kong and Macau compatriots, as well as other foreign believers, according to religious custom, wish to make an offering or give alms to temples, mosques, or churches in China, these religious bodies may accept them. Before accepting very large offerings or donations, however, a person or organization must first seek the approval of the concerned provincial, city, or autonomous district's government or responsible central department in charge of these affairs. This must be done even if it can be attested that these large sums of money are given out of religious fervor with no strings attached.[14]

The bottom line for accepting foreign funds is clear. Foreign donations must be given without any strings attached. Small sums may be accepted, but large donations may not be accepted without government approval. It is reported the government considers "large sums" to be anything in excess of 10,000 RMB (around $1,925 in 1988 and $1,370 in 1992).

Administration of Religious Activity

In China today, the United Front department and the Religious Affairs Bureau are two related organizations whose duty is to carry out the official religious policy of the government. The original meaning of the United Front is based on the words of Lenin: "One should unify lesser enemies in order to struggle against the most important enemy." However, the United Front has moved with the times, and its meaning and direction have both changed. It now works to mobilize all positive elements, unify all possible strengths, and change negative elements to positive ones. It also has the task of uniting political affairs, strengthening the legal system, and completing the unification of the country. The United Front department is the organization of the Communist party that is responsible for establishing religious policy.

The Religious Affairs Bureau is the executor of religious policy set by the United Front. Its former director, Xiao Xianfa, has identified the bureau's functions as follows:

> to put in good order organizations of religious works, and revitalize already existing religious groups in order to have organized guidance and planned expansion of religious activities; to rectify all mistakes in the religious field that were manufactured during the Cultural Revolution; to promulgate the principle that citizens have the "freedom to believe or not to believe" according to the religious policies of the constitution of China; to renovate and reopen some temples and churches; to protect peace and contribute to the modernization of China.[15]

After the end of the Cultural Revolution, the national Religious Affairs Bureau in Beijing was restored and the Catholic Patriotic Association became active again. They have been responsible for the reopening of churches and for other public religious activities. In May and June of 1980 the Third Assembly of the Chinese Catholic Patriotic Association was held in Beijing. This conference was followed by an even larger meeting of the National Catholic Representatives' Congress. These two meetings were convened to discuss how the Catholic church could effectively contribute to the "modernization" of China. Two new national organizations were established to administer Catholic church affairs: the Chinese Catholic Church Administrative Commission and the Chinese Catholic Bishops' Conference. Both organizations function as agencies to facilitate church unity and to make decisions on national church affairs. Relationships between these two organizations and the Catholic Patriotic Association were not clearly defined.

According to Article 2 of its constitution drawn up at the assembly in 1980, the Chinese Catholic Patriotic Association is composed of the Chinese Catholic clergy and laity who love their country and their church. Their aims are to unify all clergy and laity under the leadership of the government of China, to observe government policies and decrees on religion, to play an active role in the country's socialist reconstruction, to increase relation-

ships with international Catholic groups, to oppose imperialism, to safeguard world peace, and to assist the government in carrying out its policy
on religious freedom.

The Chinese Catholic Church Administrative Commission is responsible
for the internal affairs of the Catholic church. Article 2 of its constitution
states that the commission is:

> to continue and develop the traditional spirit of Jesus Christ, to pro-
> mote the endeavor of glorifying God and saving souls, to lead the
> clergy and laity in observing God's commandments, to uphold the
> principles of independence, self-governance, and democratic admin-
> istration, to deliberate and decide major questions of church affairs
> and to manage the Chinese Catholic church satisfactorily.

It should be noted that many members of this commission are also members
of the Patriotic Association. It is explained that this commission is related
to the Catholic Patriotic Association as "two hands of a body."[16]

No doubt, the importance of the Patriotic Association and the Church
Administrative Commission in terms of the Communist party's policy
toward religion is obvious. What is less clear is the importance of such
organizations in the lives of local Christians. To say that the Catholic Patriotic Association and Church Administrative Commission are merely tools
of the government seems not quite fair, but the issue of their influence on
Christians is quite ambiguous. Today the question remains: To what extent
do these organizations represent the interests of ordinary believers? And
how much freedom will these organizations be given in the future to engage
in genuine religious activities?

Development of the "Underground" Church

As mentioned above, the emergence of the Chinese Catholic Patriotic
Association and an independent Catholic church in China was the result
of government policies in the 1950s. However, at that time, the vast majority
of Catholics rejected the government-sponsored church, preferring to pray
privately at home. They became known as the "underground" church. Even
in this post-Mao era, some members of the underground church have continued to maintain an uncompromising and uncooperative attitude toward
the Communist government and the Catholic Patriotic Association.

Why an underground church? How did such a phenomenon arise? After
the establishment of the Patriotic Association under Communist rule, some
clergy and lay leaders attempted to compromise with the association, but
very soon the Communists gave notice that this was not satisfactory and
continued to exert even greater pressure. Many of the clergy and lay leaders
then decided to stand firm in their opposition to government pressure. In
doing so, they gained the support of a majority of local Catholics. Bishop

Joseph Fan Xueyan of Baoding diocese in Hebei province became a leading figure of the underground church. He was arrested in the 1950s and sentenced to fifteen years in prison. Finally released in 1979, Bishop Fan, in response to basic needs in his diocese, took the initiative in training clergy and even ordaining some bishops. This was done without any mandate from Rome. At that time, his friend Bishop Zhao Weidao of Fengxiang diocese in Shaanxi wrote to admonish him about ordaining bishops without papal approval. Bishop Fan replied that in this extraordinary situation canon law grants such a faculty. His reply eventually reached Rome, where the pope, after hearing Bishop Fan's position, agreed with what Bishop Fan was doing. The pope indicated privately that as long as grave reasons existed and the candidates' qualifications were examined and proved satisfactory, the ordinations were licit. After three years, Bishop Fan was arrested again. The charge against him was the performance of private ordinations of priests and bishops and with maintaining contact with foreign powers. He was sentenced to twenty years of imprisonment, but was released on parole on November 27, 1987.[17]

The Church at the Beginning of the 1990s

In 1989, a year marked by global dialogue, Sino-Vatican relations began to move away from confrontation. As China sought international dialogue, it realized that it needed to delineate a new policy toward the Catholic church. Accordingly, the party's Central Committee and the State Council promulgated Document 3 (February 1989), "Directives of the Party on How To Deal with the Catholic Church in the New Situation." Its contents outline four new "bottom lines":

1. Catholics are permitted to "maintain purely religious relationships with the Holy See." This means that Catholics can acknowledge the pope as head of the church and can publicly pray for him. However, Catholics cannot have direct contact with the Holy See, and the Chinese church must continue to choose and ordain its own bishops.

2. The document allows for a reorganization of the Patriotic Association giving the Bishops' Conference the highest authority,[18] thus bringing the conference in line with other bishops' conferences throughout the world.

3. The document proposes further steps to implement the policy of returning church property. The aim is eventually to make the church completely self-supporting and thereby eliminate the state's financial liability for it.

4. The document spells out a policy to deal with the underground church. The masses must be won over and united while the minority is to be isolated and suppressed:

Those individual underground leaders [must] be dealt with who, despite the many patient efforts on the part of the government, stubbornly cling to their hostility and their tactics of confrontation and who, by stirring up believers, create public disturbances and disrupt public order. Their crime must be clearly determined and fully unmasked before the whole community. The law must deal with them severely.[19]

Looking back on how such a complex situation has developed, it is important to note that there have been some abuses on all sides (and this is particularly true in certain areas in China), including use of the faculty in canon law to ordain bishops under extraordinary circumstances. Although underground Catholics remain faithful and loyal, their isolation fosters a closed mentality where rumors flourish and misinformation can lead to further divisions and separations. The hardening of conflicting positions results in serious obstacles to eventual unity within the whole church. Such a situation also tends to breed superstitious activities where religious expression is no longer directed and tempered by sound doctrine.

Besides the Catholic Patriotic Association and the underground church, there is a third group of Catholics active in China. During the present period, where there is a more relaxed atmosphere and greater tolerance toward religion, some clergy and lay Catholics who had been imprisoned in the past for their unswerving loyalty to the faith and the pope and who had refused to have any relationship with the Patriotic Association are now more willing to come forward and work together with the association for the future of the whole church in China. They feel that there is a genuinely new political climate and that they must avail themselves of the opportunity it offers to restore Catholic life. In some instances, they minister to the pastoral needs of Catholics in churches officially displaying the plaque of the Patriotic Association. Among this group, there are even some persons who actively seek to secure higher positions within the authority structure of the association in order to more effectively influence its decisions and to serve as an inhibiting factor on a tendency in the association toward unilateral control. These people continue in their loyalty to both the church and the pope. Local Catholics are well aware of their efforts in this delicate situation and love them for it. This phenomenon is seen mostly in southern China.

It is impossible to draw a complete picture of the Catholic church in China. However, many priests, sisters, and laity who have visited the People's Republic have been deeply moved by the strong living faith of the Catholics there. According to statistics given by the Chinese Catholic Patriotic Association, the number of Catholics in 1991 is estimated to be 3.6 million, which is higher than the figure of 3.3 million for 1949. There are about one thousand priests and seventy bishops, whose average age is seventy years. About three thousand Catholic churches and prayer centers have been reopened, along with sixteen seminaries and some twenty convents. Seminarians now total more than eight hundred.[20]

The church in China is pluralistic. On the surface, bishops, priests, and laity are divided into two groups: those who join the Patriotic Association and those who belong to the underground church. Some "patriotic" bishops and priests live in a very uneasy situation because their relationship with the pope has been severed. Some also face psychological problems, spiritual problems, problems because of their marriages, and problems regarding theological updating. On the other hand, many of the bishops, priests, and laity who did not join the Patriotic Association are heroic figures, faithful to their religion and to the Holy Father, and worthy of admiration. According to their estimates, Catholics number between five and six million persons. Some young men and women are being trained privately to be priests and religious sisters. However, they tend to be isolated and in danger of being out of touch with the church's current thinking.

In reality, however, there is a wide variety of Patriotic Association Catholics and underground church members, and even among the groups of Catholics in between. Outsiders should be slow to pass judgment on them or attempt to categorize them, or even worse, to lump them together in a well-meaning effort to simplify a situation that is extremely complex.

Many Catholics in the underground church play a *prophetic* role, grounded in the Holy Scriptures, by their refusal to participate in a government-sanctioned organization. They dare to challenge government policy regarding human rights and religious freedom from a Catholic standpoint. In so doing, they play the role of a loyal opposition within the established system. Their struggle to obtain religious freedom will be long and painful, but, hopefully, will prevail in the end.

At the same time, not a few members of the Catholic Patriotic Association play a *priestly* role, equally grounded in Scripture. They work within the social system to minister to the spiritual needs of Catholics, administering the sacraments to them, teaching them, and furthering the love of God among them within the boundaries of the public church. They are also involved in works of social service, through which they gain respect and share in the responsibility of the government to its people.

Conclusion

China's social and political situation is in a continual state of flux. As a result, the situation of the Chinese Catholic church is also continually changing. China is a large and complicated nation and it is difficult to paint a clear and complete picture of the church that will include all its variations. This pluralistic church faces, at one and the same time, both crises and opportunities. It has suffered many deep wounds and has experienced great pressures, but at the same time it continues to receive abundant graces. Since the "June 4th" (1989) crackdown, the Catholic church of China has been under even greater pressure. The government has adopted even stricter measures in its dealings with the underground church. However, the Holy Spirit is always with the church, breaking through barriers erected by systems and continuing its divine action in leading the church forward. The church continues to add many new members to its ranks each year, due to catechetical instruction and the witness of many Catholics. Vocations to the priesthood and religious life are also increasing. Many priests, sisters, and laity who have visited the People's Republic of China have been deeply moved and edified by the strong living faith of Catholics there.

Besides praying for the church in China, Catholics throughout the world should seize the moment to show their concern in concrete ways. They should foster a balanced and prudent attitude, which is neither fearful nor naive, and through appropriate means, always avoiding unfortunate misunderstandings, offer Chinese Christians both spiritual and material support. In this way, Catholics can help the Chinese church attain reunification with the one, holy, catholic, and apostolic universal church and, at the same time, help it to strengthen its foundations so that it will become a flourishing local church.

It is interesting to note that in Pope John Paul II's three speeches directed to the Catholic church in China during the past decade (Manila in February 1981, Seoul in October 1989, and to the bishops of Taiwan in Rome in December 1990), he made no distinction between members of the Patriotic Association and underground Catholics. Rather, he addressed the Catholic community in China as a whole. In the concrete, it is impossible to see the church in China as a "whole" church, because of the divisions resulting from history and the on-going demands and policies of the government regarding religion. In relations with Patriotic Association members, Catholics outside the People's Republic must voice their disagreement with the way the government has imposed the Patriotic Association structure on the church, dividing the faithful by insisting that relations with Rome be severed. On the other hand, in contacts with underground church members, Catholics must also be aware that there are aspects of the underground church that need to be corrected. A lack of a spirit of forgiveness exists on both sides of the division. And even if relations between the Vatican and the Chinese government can be improved, the bitterness and unwillingness to be reconciled may well remain. There is a need to work through different channels in order to achieve complete unity, both internally in China and with the universal church. The ever increasing spirit of concern shown by Catholics the world over, be they Chinese or non-Chinese, is most moving and should be encouraged. It is certainly much appreciated by those who long to see Catholics of China one in the Lord and one in the communion of the church.

Notes

1. The text of the "Christian Manifesto" appears in *Tian Feng,* 233-34 (September 30, 1950), pp. 146-47.

2. The texts of the Sichuan and Chongqing manifestos appeared in *China Missionary Bulletin* 1 (January 1951), pp. 149-51.

3. Richard C. Bush, Jr., *Religion in Communist China* (Nashville, TN: Abingdon Press, 1970), pp. 105-107.

4. The text and some of the reactions in the Chinese press appeared in *China Missionary Bulletin* 4 (May 1951), pp. 384-88.

5. Elmer Wurth, ed., *Papal Documents Related to the New China* (Hong Kong: Holy Spirit Study Centre, 1985), pp. 32-37.

6. Bush, pp. 121-124; see also *Papal Documents Related to the New China,* pp. 38-45.

7. Bush, pp. 132-135.

8. Wurth, pp. 48-61.

9. Bush, pp. 139-157.

10. The targets of the "Four Modernizations" are agriculture, industry, the armed forces, and science and technology.

11. Leo Goodstadt, "Atheism and the Chinese Communist party after Mao Zedong" in *Tripod* (Hong Kong: Holy Spirit Study Centre), 1981, no. 3, p. 43.

12. Li Weihan, *The United Front and the Question of Nationalities* (Beijing: Beijing People's Press, 1980), pp. 508-509.

13. Mainland China Studies (Taipei) 1983, no. 10, p. 90.

14. Ibid.

15. John Tong, "Selected Resources for Reference" in *Tripod*, 1981, no. 5, pp. 59-64.

16. Ibid., pp. 61-63.

17. The Union of Catholic Asian News (UCAN) reported on May 1, 1992 that Bishop Fan Xueyan of Baoding, Hebei, died in mid-April at the age of 85 but added that the exact date and place of his death were yet to be determined. Other reports suggest that he died much earlier and that the body was brought back in April 1992. — Eds.

18. This directive has not been fully implemented. At the fifth national Catholic Representatives' Congress held from September 15 to 19, 1992 in Beijing, the Bishops' Conference received a new constitution that confirmed its authority over the Administrative Commission. At the same time, however, Bishop Zong Huaide, the newly elected president of the Bishops' Conference and the Chinese Catholic Patriotic Association, said that these two remaining "official" Catholic bodies were "equal in status." — Eds.

19. *Tripod*, 1989, no. 52, pp. 73-76.

20. By comparison, Protestant Christianity has increased even more from an estimated 700,000 in 1949 to the official figure in 1990 of 6.5 million.

2

The Church into the 1990s

EDMOND TANG

When I was asked in early 1989 to draft a report on the situation of the Catholic church in China, I gave it the following title: "The Catholic Church in China—Seen Through a Kaleidoscope." The players in the field were clearly distinguishable, but their positions were constantly changing and none of them had yet to dominate the field of action. The picture of the Catholic church was very different—depending on the angle from which the viewer looked at the situation.

There were, first of all, the "patriotics" and the "faithfuls." However, more and more of the "patriotics" were openly declaring their allegiance to the pope, and among the "faithfuls," many found working with the government-sponsored Patriotic Association an acceptable *modus vivendi*. On the other hand, a new group, calling itself the "underground" church was emerging with a clear confrontational posture. The Vatican, worried about the unbridled growth of the underground hierarchy, tried to moderate its posture and sought with a new urgency to normalize the situation. Also, for the first time a group of bishops acceptable to both the Chinese government and the Vatican was increasing in number and becoming an important factor in solving the long-standing Sino-Vatican conflict. Even well-placed observers admitted there was confusion:

> Even the closest observers of the church in China are bewildered by the strange and contradictory stories which they are hearing. In one place a church which had been destroyed is being rebuilt, thanks to government money; elsewhere Christians are building a church and reject government assistance; in still another place Catholics refuse to accept a bishop without papal approval. In some churches believers will make their confession to one priest but refuse to accept another. Some bishops of the independent church, which refuses to accept the

authority of Rome, openly attack the authority of the successor of Peter; other bishops of the same independent organization send secret messages of loyalty to the pope. Certain elderly priests work together with official bodies; others choose to return to prison rather than join a church which they consider apostate. A married "patriotic" bishop dies and his priests refuse to give him a religious burial. In a provincial city, one priest preaches loyalty to Rome; in another city a priest is frightened to receive foreign visitors. In some areas only the priests know who the bishop is: the believers are not told for fear that someone will betray him.[1]

Another commentator notes that "three bishops visited on the same day may represent three realities of the church: the underground, those approved by both the Holy See and the government, and the open, official one—realities that are part of the complex spectrum of the church in China."[2]

Amidst this confusion certain patterns were emerging but the whole situation was also fluid and changing in the midst of hopes and inherent dangers. On the one hand the establishment of relations between the Vatican and China was said to be imminent. The visit of Cardinal Jaime Sin of Manila to China in November 1987 and his high level discussions with Zhao Ziyang, the premier and secretary general of the Communist party at the time, led many to ask how much longer it would be before China established normal diplomatic relations with the Vatican, the only state in Europe which still does not recognize the People's Republic? In fact, low-key official conversations had been going on for some time.

This speculation was reinforced by the changes in China itself. A new religious law was drafted and circulated that would eventually normalize the rights of religions in Chinese society. The hierarchy of leadership in the Catholic church was redefined in a series of declarations that put the authority of the Bishops' Conference and the Church Administrative Commission above that of the Chinese Catholic Patriotic Association (CCPA).[3] The latter had always dominated the internal as well as the external affairs of the church since its creation in 1957. These changes seemed to meet one of the Vatican's conditions—that to establish normal relations the Catholic church in China must be directed by a proper religious authority. Although it may be questioned whether this transfer of authority was as effective as it sounded, it cannot be denied that many bishops had openly asserted their authority in the previous couple of years. Institutionally pastoral and theological concerns had also been taken up by the Bishops' Conference and commissions were established to study the reform of the liturgy, theological concerns such as "inculturation" of the faith, theological training of future priests, and so forth.

It is important to mention that in the same declarations, both by the government and by the church, it was recognized for the first time that spiritual affiliation with the Holy See did not necessarily contradict loyalty to the country. In fact some bishops, illicitly ordained in the past, had been privately reconciled with the Vatican.

Despite this rosy picture we have just painted, dark clouds were never completely absent from the horizon. The growth of the underground church was troublesome. After years of silence it had surfaced with an organized strength that could not be underestimated. Its style was becoming openly hostile and its influence was spreading, creating confusion among Catholic communities. To counter this "disruptive" development, the CCPA was returning to repressive measures.

In 1989 many still believed that there was some hope of changing the situation through dialogue and bridge-building by moderate groups both inside and outside China. The Vatican, too, after years of encouraging the development of the underground church, became concerned about the negative developments and sent a series of directives with the hope of clarifying the situation.

1989: A Year of Confrontation

By spring 1989 events in China had taken a dramatic turn and the pattern that emerged was more and more one of open confrontation. At a time when a solution seemed to be at hand, schism also became a real possible outcome. The determining factor seemed to be the growth of an underground Catholic church whose strength and tenacity had, up to this point, been underestimated.

Throughout 1989 there were a number of large and small confrontations and the underground church was involved in almost all of them. For the purpose of illustration, it suffices here to mention only two.

In April 1989 in a place called Youtong, about thirty kilometers south of Shijiazhuang in Hebei province, a group of underground Catholics had taken over a local school campus and erected a tent for use as a church. The school was built on property where a church had once stood before it was destroyed.

After a series of fruitless exchanges, the government raided the place on April 18. It was reported that two persons were killed in the melee and three hundred and fifty were wounded, with thirty arrests. The Youtong Catholics then disseminated pamphlets in Tiananmen Square in Beijing with the help of university students from Shandong province, accusing the government of violating their religious freedom and using force against them. On June 23, three hundred armed police went to the campus and demolished the tent.

Since November 1989 there have been several waves of arrests. One immediate cause was a secret meeting in Zhangerce, Shaanxi province, on November 21 that brought together a number of underground bishops. The purpose of the meeting was to set up an alternative bishops' conference. This was a direct challenge to the legitimacy of the official Bishops' Conference created in 1981. From December 1989 to February 1990 there was a sequence of arrests. Among the thirty or so clergy detained were six bishops from Gansu, Hebei, Shaanxi, and Inner Mongolia.

These arrests signified a different level of confrontation between the government, the Patriotic Association and the so-called underground church. The arrests could no longer be considered as individual cases of conscience or as individuals having trespassed the official line. What was involved was a growing campaign by a group of Catholics in a series of coordinated actions against the open churches under the administration of the Patriotic Association.

These incidents, given their scale and significance, should have attracted greater attention from the international press, which reported them only in passing. This is not surprising, since these incidents took place either during the turbulent pro-democracy movement in China or in its aftermath. They were also overshadowed by the dramatic turn of events in Eastern Europe.

Several questions come to mind when we try to analyze the growing conflict.

1. To what extent are the confrontations involving the Catholic church, especially the arrests since November 1989, related to the crushing of the pro-democracy movement of June 1989?

2. Does this concern only the Catholic church or are the Protestant churches equally affected?

3. To what extent does this represent a shift of the government's religious policy, not so much in theoretical terms, but in its practical application?

4. Why did those confrontations come to a head in 1989? What are the likely scenarios for the Catholic church if the number of conflicts continues to increase?

Repercussions of the June 4 Incident

The events of June 4 did not leave the churches untouched. First of all, with the growing identification of the churches with the social problems of the country, some Christians and theological students took an active part in the pro-democracy movement, both in Beijing and Nanjing. Some Christian leaders were involved, too, with some giving support to the cause of the students and joining with other members of the People's Congress to oppose the declaration of martial law.

After June 4 all organizations in China were under pressure to support the government. Understandably, both Catholic and Protestant official institutions issued public statements supporting the government's actions, if not directly denouncing the pro-democracy movement. Some church leaders had to reinterpret their earlier statements. All over the country, churches felt obliged to hold prayer services for the victims of the June events, "victims" here referring to the soldiers who died on duty. Donations were also collected for the soldiers' families. Seminarians were asked to sign statements concerning their whereabouts and attitude vis-à-vis the pro-democracy movement; some refused to sign and were denied ordination.

The June events were not taken lightly by the Chinese authorities in spite of reassuring statements to the contrary. Throughout the latter half of 1989, party/security officials were sent from Beijing to all provinces to settle accounts with cadres and work units that were suspected of sympathizing with the students. Important cadres, including those in the churches, were said to be under internal criticism for their stance during the June events. Although the policy of religious freedom was officially maintained, it is questionable whether the leaders of the church who were sympathetic to the pro-democracy movement could still exercise effective leadership. It is also clear that there were divisions within the churches regarding the proper attitude they should assume.

In short, even if the official policy had not changed and, in fact, the government did allow more overseas visits of Chinese church leaders, it is certain that the reins on religion have grown tighter in China. Unofficial activities, such as those of some house gatherings, as well as those of the underground Catholic church, will no longer be tolerated. The official tone has become harsher as well.

The Underground Catholic Church

On the other hand it is not possible to make a direct link between the June events and the growing conflicts involving the Catholic church. In fact these conflicts have a history dating back to before the rise of the pro-democracy movement. The harsh response of the Chinese authorities had also been expressed in an earlier policy document (as I will mention below). The single most important factor that brought the confrontations to a head was the emergence of a militant underground Catholic church.

Before attempting to discuss the situation any further, it may be useful to provide a few details about the so-called underground church and its evolution in the past few years. What, or more exactly, who is the underground church? When speaking of the underground church, it is perhaps useful to distinguish between two moments of its history.

There are, first of all, Catholics who, in the 1950s, following the instruction of the Holy See, refused to join or recognize the leadership of the Chinese Patriotic Association. They refused to go to the open churches or to accept the sacraments administered by pastors who had joined the association. These Catholics, therefore, practiced their faith privately in homes and were served by itinerant priests. Although hostile to the open churches, their attitude was more defensive in character.

Many Catholics emerged from the Cultural Revolution accepting the more open government policy and recognizing the changes within the Patriotic Association itself. Some changed their attitudes and agreed to work within the framework of the Patriotic Association—although they did not share its extreme position toward the Vatican.

The underground church that is often talked about in the 1980s or early 1990s is of a different character; it is more organized and more aggressive. The concern of its leaders is not limited to the pastoral concerns of seeking alternative ways of serving Catholics who do not want to worship in open churches. Activities of its leaders become more and more daring and seem to suggest that they seek a confrontation with the existing authorities. Secretly ordained priests have been sent all over China, denouncing others who joined the Patriotic Association and instructing Catholics not to receive sacraments from the latter since they are considered to be invalid. Many communities have become confused and divided by actions of these priests and their denunciations.

It is undeniable that the present underground church took shape in late 1979 when the Vatican gave a series of exemptions to underground pastors so that religious life could be practiced without following the canonical laws of the church. Most of the exemptions concerned the canonical regulations for the effective celebration of the sacraments. However, following repeated requests from the aging bishops and priests who were worried about their succession, the Vatican also granted permission to ordain priests without the required seminary training. Permission was also given to aging bishops to nominate and ordain their successors, and this power was even extended to the selection of bishops for neighboring dioceses with vacant bishoprics.

This extra-canonical permission was seen by some as a green light to build an opposition church. The first secret bishops were ordained in 1981. According to a confidential document, there were at least fifty such ordinations by the end of 1989: eight in 1981, thirteen in 1982, four in 1983, five in 1984, three in 1985, one in 1986, five in 1987, one in 1988, and ten in 1989. In fact, the real figure might be much higher because there were ordinations that only came to the notice of the Vatican much later on. Numerous priests were also ordained secretly. It seems that the ordinations of priests and bishops were already far beyond the original pastoral intentions of the Vatican permissions.

Even persons close to the Vatican's position have expressed their disquiet regarding recent developments. They acknowledge that some of the newly ordained bishops do not have sufficient pastoral experience, and in some cases they do not have a good working relationship with other priests. As for the privately ordained priests, many are very young and have received minimal doctrinal instruction. Some are known more for their zeal for denouncing others than for their pastoral skills. The result has been the birth of a militant opposition that puts the new atmosphere of dialogue in jeopardy.

Divisions in the Church

What characterizes this new underground church? Not only is it antagonistic to the open churches, but it is more and more open and aggressive in its tactics. The "little black priests," as they are often called because of their operation in secret, have been sent to different provinces from Hebei up to the remotest parishes to mobilize the faithful against the open churches. They say that the Patriotic Association is the work of the devil ("love your enemies but not the devil," they would teach), and that the sacraments administered by priests belonging to it are invalid and ineffective. In fact, they advise, it would be better to abstain from the sacraments than commit another mortal sin.

The source of this information about the underground church is contained in a document called "The Thirteen Points" attributed to Bishop Joseph Fan Xueyan of Baoding.[4] Bishop Fan had always been a staunch opponent of the Patriotic Association and had endured long imprisonment and police surveillance for his beliefs. His closeness to the Vatican also lends authority to his views. Since its circulation in September 1988, the effect of "The Thirteen Points" has been devastating. Churches once full are now empty. And the faithful have been thrown into confusion.

An example is the diocese of Xianxian in Hebei province. Xianxian is a traditional Catholic stronghold as are many dioceses in Hebei. Hebei Christians suffered a lot during the Boxer Uprising of 1900 and the Sino-Japanese War. The conflicts of the 1950s also left their mark on these Catholics.

After the Cultural Revolution, many of the priests who had formerly been imprisoned for their opposition to the Patriotic Association welcomed the new movement toward religious freedom. They recognized the positive developments in the association, especially those which did not follow the position of the national association in Beijing. In some places, such as Xianxian, a *modus vivendi* was found that allowed pastors faithful to the Vatican to operate within the framework of the association. This, however, was not acceptable to the underground group of Christians.

Recently Xianxian diocese was visited by a Catholic bishop from Taiwan, himself a native of Hebei. It was his first visit since the change of regime in the People's Republic. In a report written after the visit, he expressed his painful observation of the division in the diocese:

> In the diocese of Xianxian, the church is very much alive. In the diocese there are 26 priests and 100 sisters. There is also a seminary with 60 seminarians from 18 to 20 years of age. Between 1985 and 1989 70 churches had been built.

The major problem of the area, according to this Taiwan bishop, was the dissension sown by the underground priests.

His Excellency, Joannes Liu Dinghan and all the priests (11 Jesuits and 15 diocesan priests) work very hard, even if they have been constantly misunderstood by the neighboring diocese of Baoding.[5] The latter says that Bishop Liu Dinghan belongs to the "patriotic" church. Bishop Joannes Liu and his priests have, nevertheless, publicly declared their obedience to the Holy Father. Moreover, in every church of Xianxian diocese, the faithful pray for the Holy Father, for all bishops, priests and the universal church.[6]

In the same diocese there was also an underground bishop, a Rev. X, who refused to cooperate with Bishop Liu and accused Liu of having been excommunicated by the pope, without knowing that Liu had, indeed, been legitimized by the Vatican. This bishop, isolated from other priests and Christians, ordained on his own some ten young priests after only a few months of study. These young priests were more specialized in acts of denunciations and "knowledge" about excommunications than in the doctrine of the church or pastoral work among the faithful. They publicly denounced other pastors and preached that sacraments administered by the "patriotics" were invalid. As for those who had been baptized or married by "patriotic" priests, they must be re-baptized and re-married.

This state of affairs is not limited to Xianxian or Hebei. In fact, the influence of the underground church is widespread, from Gansu and Inner Mongolia to Shaanxi, Shanxi, and Hebei, to Liaoning in the northeast and Fujian in the southeast. The Taiwan bishop's report concluded that the Holy See must establish sanctions and regulations to ensure that underground bishops do not unnecessarily ordain new bishops and priests who do not meet the requirements for the priesthood. These "little black priests" do not spread the gospel; instead, they foster hate among the faithful. They do not preach God's word; instead, they engage in namecalling and labelling of other people. Obviously, the church is divided; hence, the Christians are scandalized and have no wish to go to church. This sad situation exists in several places.[7]

The situation, indeed, is not limited to Hebei province. For example, a certain diocese of Inner Mongolia has three bishops, each claiming legitimate authority over the same territory. One is a secret bishop only recently known to the Vatican. Another is a bishop who had reconciled with Rome without the knowledge of the underground bishop. The antagonism that exists between the protagonists has practically paralyzed the whole diocese and has divided the Catholic community.

Government Responses

Officially the Catholic church in China is an independent church, and the Chinese Constitution stipulates that no religious body can be dominated by a foreign power. Yet it is commonly acknowledged that over the last couple of years in many churches, including those in Shanghai and other prominent cities, Christians pray openly for the pope. More and more church leaders have declared themselves united with the Holy See without necessarily attracting the ire of the authorities. In the case of Xianxian, it is common practice. The residing bishop has been reconciled with the Vatican. Pictures of John Paul II are exhibited in the churches of the diocese and prayers are said for him. Does this development represent a change of position in the government's policy in dealing with the Catholic church?

A recent document seems to suggest this possibility. "Document 3: Directives of the Party on How To Deal with the Catholic Church in the New Situation," promulgated by the party's Central Committee and the State Council in February 1989, recommends to the cadres a policy of differentiation in dealing with Catholics. Article 4 of the document says: "Pay attention to differentiate the underground forces from those clergy who are separated from us because of their faith in the pope."[8]

The "new situation" that the document refers to could be promising negotiations leading up to the eventual establishment of diplomatic relations with the Vatican. For some time, a moderate or intermediate group between the staunch "patriotics" and the "underground" Catholics has been accepted and even promoted in view of this "new situation." In the same document, the authority of the Bishops' Conference is recognized over that of the Patriotic Association.[9] The rights of the churches to their former property have also been extended from the actual church buildings to their land and associated buildings. On the other hand, the "new situation" may also be referring to the growing strength of the underground church. The document recommends that cadres deal sternly with all underground activities. This is in line with the regulations issued by provincial authorities in areas such as Guangdong, Hebei, Yunnan, and Xinjiang. These regulations gave exclusive rights to groups recognized by the government, while calling for "the elimination of Catholic underground religious activities." The Hebei regulations stipulate that only clergy (and their religious activities) recognized by the national Bishops' Conference and the provincial Catholic Church Affairs Commission will be protected by law; unrecognized clergy will not be allowed to conduct religious activities. In the same vein, only the training centers officially run by the dioceses are protected; those without such permission are to be dissolved.

Many analysts interpret Document 3 as having two objectives: 1) to eradicate the influence of the underground church, and 2) to give exclusive legal rights and financial support to an autonomous Catholic church and to make this a *fait accompli* before the establishment of relations with Rome. Whatever the major objective of the directives of Document 3, it is certain that the underground church will become the target of mounting pressures from the government. The use of force in the Youtong incident in April 1989 and the resurgence of arrests of dissident clergy since December 1989 seem to bear this out.

New Attitudes of the Official Church

On the other hand the official church is also positioning itself for the "new situation." A meeting of the Bishops' Conference was held in March 1989 in which certain new positions were adopted, namely:

1. The pope must be recognized as the head of the church and Catholics must be allowed to pray for him.

2. The Bishops' Conference should assume the leadership of the church and not the Patriotic Association, which should function only under the Bishops' Conference.

3. Bishops who are known to be married should no longer be members of the Bishops' Conference or the Church Administrative Commission.

Similar questions were raised at a meeting of the Church Administrative Commission held at the end of April. In that meeting the bishops reaffirmed their position that it was the Bishops' Conference that was the primary holder of responsibility for the administration of the dioceses.

As for relations with the Holy See, the bishops had this to say: "Our faith relationship with the Holy See has never been cut off. What has been cut off is the political relationship which prevents us from having the external contacts with the Holy See. Our faith remains the same as before."

This affirmation of the spiritual leadership of the pope is in line with some of the statements made by individual bishops in the past few years. Instead of looking for alternative theological arguments, which was the case in the early 1980s, the same bishop theologians are returning to the traditional ecclesiological position of the Catholic church.[10] ·

Some China analysts are skeptical about the ecclesiological assertion of the bishops' authority, knowing the past domination of the Patriotic Association in the affairs of the church. However, it should not be forgotten that a similar trend is taking place in the Protestant churches as well. The China Christian Council is also asserting its authority over the Three Self Movement and this seems to have received the support of the United Front itself.

It is questionable, of course, whether the Patriotic Association has changed its fundamental attitude. On the other hand, it cannot be denied that some internal changes have taken place in these last years. First there is a growing difference between the national association in Beijing and the provincial ones. Some of the latter have gradually moved to more open positions and under their umbrella religious activities have returned to normal. In some places they have been openly criticized and discarded by the local bishop. In other instances they were challenged by the local bishop to revise their views and strategies in order to catch up with the changing moods of the majority of Christians. Despite certain attitudes manifest in Beijing, it is no longer feasible to treat the Patriotic Association(s) as a monolithic bloc that does not respond to the changing tide.

Concluding Observations

It should become clear from the above account of the recent developments of the Catholic church in China that the emergence of the underground church has tilted the traditional balance and holds the key to any solution in the future. It must be remembered here that the emergence of the underground Catholic church finds a certain parallel in the Protestant house gatherings. Although not as militant and organized as the Catholic underground, there are groups in the Protestant churches that escape the jurisdiction of the China Christian Council and would prefer to remain so. This suggests an important consideration: that the division in the Catholic church cannot be reduced simply to a dispute over loyalty to the Holy See. There must be sociological factors that are common to both these Catholic and Protestant dissenting groups.

There are a number of questions that are of particular interest:

1. To what extent has the Cultural Revolution changed the organizational patterns or power relations within the church and made the growth of dissenting or parallel groups possible?

2. How far is the emergence of these groups related to the revival of popular religions now documented by social scientists? In fact, popular Christianity is characterized by practices of healing, miracles, and so forth that echo some of the practices of the folk religions. Are there common aspects in their rural background, figuration of deities, and emphasis on "magical" rituals?

3. What are the patterns of conversion and what are the determining factors for the growth of underground or parallel groups? Why are they more effective, in some cases, than the official churches?

4. Can the reluctance of these groups to accept central authority be attributed to historical forms of Christianity, or are there social determinants?

In the early 1980s it was forbidden to talk about the divisions inside the church, be they Catholic or Protestant. To do so was considered an "unfriendly" gesture and, worse, a divisive tactic introduced from the outside. As a result, the divisions were not recognized as such and practically no objective study of the situation was done.

This partly explains the poverty of our knowledge about Christianity in China today. On the other hand, the study of Christianity in China has too often been undertaken from only an ecclesiological or missiological point of view. Christianity as a social reality cannot become a feasible object of study until empirical data can be gathered—without the theological trappings.

Our knowledge about Christianity in China remains fragmentary. We are still far from understanding the patterns of its development, the laws governing its expansion, the underlying issues that make reconciliation difficult. More research, with the cooperation of social sciences, will be necessary before a more coherent picture will emerge, both for our own understanding and for relations with Christians in China.

Postscript

Since 1990 a number of important developments have affected the religious situation in China. A general tightening up, already discernible after June 4, 1989, is now evident. The role of ideology is again being emphasized in education, including in seminaries and training centers for clergy and religious personnel, although the reasons for this may have less to do with the suppression of the pro democracy movement than was first thought. Two other factors have emerged that appear to be playing an equally important role—if, indeed, not more important—in determining the present religious policy of the Chinese government.

The first is the collapse of the Soviet system in the former U.S.S.R. and the Eastern European states. The steady disintegration of these regimes no doubt confirmed the Chinese government's view that it had acted wisely in 1989 to stem the tide of political change before China also plunged into chaos. It seems that the Chinese government attributed the general collapse of the system partly to the active role played by the churches. In Poland, Romania, Czechoslovakia, and former East Germany, the dissident churches allied themselves with unions or groups of intellectuals in confronting the state, and they played a very visible role in the final stages in the downfall of these governments.

Although this view may not stand up to an objective analysis and although China's booming economy is in stark contrast to the impoverishment of the former Eastern European states, nevertheless the Chinese government sees the threat as very real. The government has orchestrated a series of speeches and documents warning the Chinese people of the danger of "peaceful evolution," a term that describes a conspiracy of Western liberalization and the infiltration of foreign values and ideas. The Christian churches as well as Muslim organizations are the targets of these warnings.

A second factor that has nourished the government's fear of religion grows out of internal developments in Chinese society. For many years it was thought that religions in China had been brought under the government's control and that their role had been safely circumscribed. However, in the late 1980s the government came to realize that religions not only underwent a revival after the Cultural Revolution, but were growing at an unprecedented rate.

In the case of Christianity, government and church authorities put the number of Christians at six to seven million Protestants and three million Catholics. Other estimates made by observers both inside and outside China put the numbers much higher: fifty to sixty million Protestants and ten to twelve million Catholics. With even the most conservative estimates, this represents an increase of more than 1,000 percent over the last fifteen to twenty years.

Government documents do not hesitate to talk about a so-called "Christianity fever," especially in reference to some provinces such as Henan and Zhejiang. Scholars are still speculating as to the reasons for this sudden, spontaneous expansion. It is quite clear, however, that the government is alarmed. Control is particularly difficult when these groups are widely dispersed and do not necessarily come under the administration of the open church authorities. Since 1989 a number of measures have been introduced to deal with the situation, with the emphasis on "administrative control," meaning stricter government measures to control the membership, place, and leadership of religious activities.

Since 1989, in general, it appears that the government is demonstrating better cooperation with the open churches while keeping a much tighter control at the grassroots level. In 1992 and the beginning of 1993 activities and structures of the open churches are more liberalized, acknowledging the legitimate authority of churches to regulate their internal matters. Facilities have improved for building new churches and for running training institutions, and the role of religion in social development is increasingly recognized.

On the other hand, strict measures have been introduced to control the spread of Christian groups, including the requirement that they be registered. The government officially recognizes some twelve thousand Protestant and Catholic churches, but this number falls far short of meeting the needs of the widely spread and growing Christian communities. Protestants have tens of thousands of "meeting points," some of which, if not registered by the government, will become illegal and subject to closure. Registration measures equally affect Catholic churches, particularly in the countryside where there are few churches and priests.

During the period from 1989 through 1992 the Catholic church could be seen evolving and adapting in this new policy framework defined in Document 3 issued by the government in April 1989. This document already recognized the authority of the bishops over the affairs of the Catholic church. When the Fifth National Catholic Representatives' Congress met in September 1992, it established new structures based on this shift in authority. The congress approved a constitution for the Bishops' Conference, which it had not had in the past. Inaugurated in 1980, the Bishops' Conference had existed only under the Church Administrative Commission, which directed the bishops in their duties. Within the new structures the Bishops' Conference has sole authority over the church, and the Church

Administrative Commission, placed under the bishops, continues to exist only as one of several commissions. Equally important is the placing of the Bishops' Conference on an equal footing with the Catholic Patriotic Association.

It is still too early to predict the efficacy of the new structures, but there are already signs that many bishops are taking new initiatives in the areas of pastoral work, training of clergy, and in the social apostolate of the church. More students can be sent overseas for theological training to meet the need for qualified teachers in the seminaries. Lecturers from Hong Kong and Taiwan as well as other countries can be invited to teach in the two national seminaries of Beijing and Shanghai. Other commissions on liturgical renewal and theological training show signs of vigor and new initiatives.

What effect does this new government policy emphasizing both cooperation and control have on underground Catholics? Document 3 states very clearly that underground Christians must be brought within the official fold or suffer punishment by the law. In November 1989 a group of clandestine Catholic bishops met in the village of Shangyi in the province of Shaanxi in north China. The aim of this meeting was to establish a parallel Chinese bishops' conference that would be in full communion with the pope. In a statement about their meeting, the clandestine bishops claimed that they wished to be a continuation of the Synod of 1924[11]; this posed a direct challenge to the open Catholic church recognized by the government.

This meeting provoked a sharp response from the government and a wave of arrests and detentions took place during November 1989 and early 1990. Bishop Fan Xueyan, regarded as the leader of the underground Catholics, died in mysterious circumstances in autumn 1991 and his body was returned to his family only several months afterward.[12] Observers outside China attribute this crackdown to the excess of local government officials, while others in China were perplexed because it did not follow any of the patterns of the government. The death of Bishop Fan and the continued detention of others, still numbering some seventy on the list of Amnesty International, will no doubt reinforce the clandestinity of underground Catholics. On the other hand, the threat of division has also convinced some to seek dialogue and cooperation.

Observers of China must be prepared for change and sometimes sudden change. The danger is to remain rooted in old clichés and ideologies. The developments of the last three years are encouraging in many respects and troubling in others. As Chinese society changes rapidly, new ideas and new accommodations will come about. But the vision must always be turned toward the future with openness and humility.

Notes

1. Laszlo Ladany, "Réflexion sur l'Eglise en Chine" in *Commentaire*, 1988, p. 640.

2. Ismael Zuloaga, "The Actual Situation of the Catholic Church in China," paper presented to the European China Meeting, Rhondorf, Germany, November 16-18, 1988.

3. See note 18 in the previous chapter.

4. Different versions of this document circulate in China. An English translation can be found in the transcript of Radio Veritas broadcasts (undated). See also pp. 142-45 of Chapter 8.

5. The diocese of Bishop Fan, who was supposed to have issued the "Thirteen Points."

6. An unpublished report widely circulated in English.

7. Ibid.

8. *Zhonglian* (English), January 1990, pp. 3-5; *Tripod* 4 (1989):70-76; 6 (1990): 83-86.

9. However, see note 18 in the preceding chapter.

10. The latest issue of the Catholic prayer book for the laity published by the Shanghai Catholic diocese in December 1991 includes prayers for the pope.

11. The First Plenary Council of China was held in Shanghai from May 14-June 12, 1924 under the direction of Archbishop Celso Costantini, the apostolic delegate to Chine.

12. The Union of Catholic Asian News (UCAN) reported on May 1, 1992 that Bishop Fan Xueyan of Baoding, Hebei, died in mid-April at the age of 85 but added that the exact date and place of his death were yet to be determined. Other reports suggest that he died much earlier and that the body was brought back in April 1992. — Eds.

3

Is There Religious Freedom in China?

JULIA CHING

The role that religion and religious people played in the events of June 1989 in Tiananmen Square is still unclear. What is known and clear is that religious people in each of the major religions in China joined demonstrations and supported the students. The uprising in Tiananmen Square raises two important questions: How important is religion to the Chinese people? Is there religious freedom in China?

In today's China, there are five officially recognized religions: Buddhism and Taoism are so-called native religions, even though Buddhism came originally from India and Central Asia; Catholicism and Protestantism, both introduced from outside, and Islam, which came to China earlier. In the language of political ideology, Buddhism and Taoism have been associated with imperialistic powers. Islam defies labels, but is usually considered to be more on the feudal side.

Among the various *living* religions present in China, Islam and Tantric Buddhism are both associated with particular ethnic groups: Islam, with the Hui population dispersed in various regions (descendants of Arabs, Persians, and other converts to that religion) and with the Turkic peoples of Chinese Central Asia or Xinjiang (Uighurs, Kazakhs, Uzbeks, Kirghiz, and others); Tantric Buddhism, with the Tibetans and Mongols. It is difficult to give correct statistics for these peoples — perhaps two million Tibetans and ten million Muslims altogether, though the latter figure is definitely on the low side.

Islam started early in China, probably in the mid-seventh century, although the exact date is difficult to establish. Over the course of centuries, Chinese Islam absorbed certain features of Confucian philosophy, especially its ethics and cosmology, with ideas of good and evil as well as *Taiji*,

This essay, published in *America*, June 9, 1990, pp. 566-570, is reprinted with permission.

43

yin and *yang*. Both the Sunni and Shi'ite traditions are present in Chinese Islam, and Sufism has been active in special regions. Under Communist rule, a Chinese Islamic Association was established in 1953 as a parallel to the Chinese Buddhist Association and to the Christian counterparts.

Muslims in China, as elsewhere, advocate "holy war" (*jihad*) for the defense of their faith; they have always given trouble to their Communist overlords. The Kazakh revolt (1950-1951) was put down with difficulty, and a great number of them later sought to flee China. Communists sought to infiltrate Islamic schools and to persuade Muslims to become party members. Sporadic insurrections took place in different parts of the country, for example, in Gansu (1952) and in Yunnan (1972), in each case with thousands of deaths and casualties along with the annihilation of whole districts or villages. Although socioeconomic grounds exist that cause discontent, religion is also a factor. Muslims, for example, are insulted if they are asked to raise pigs.

As such, none of these religions is desirable in a Marxist China and may be granted no more than tolerance by a regime that believes in the historical triumph of dialectical materialism. In actual practice, their treatment by the Chinese government has varied, depending on the religious body as well as various events in recent history. But here, too, a discernible pattern parallels—and is subordinate to—the pendulum swings of political history concerning greater tolerance of, or tighter control over, the thinking of the Chinese people.

The "Good Years"

During the period 1949 to 1966—that is, until the outbreak of the Cultural Revolution—the Chinese government made some efforts to honor the guarantee of freedom of "religious belief" enshrined especially in the 1954 Constitution, but without mention of "religious activities." Such freedom was extended to those who consented to collaborate with the authorities. To further that end, an official Religious Affairs Bureau was established in the 1950s and was directly affiliated with the State Council; each religious group was encouraged to set up its own "association." Such freedom, however, was limited and short-lived, and the Korean War subsequently furnished the occasion for all kinds of suspicions, while the Anti-Rightist campaign in 1957 put an end to many dreams.

Collaboration with the government meant accepting the "Three-Self Principles" (self-governing, self-supporting, self-propagating) by abandoning ties with the outside world. In 1951, many mainline Protestant denominations accepted these principles rather quickly in the "Three-Self Movement," although some more evangelical groups, like the Little Flock and the Jesus Family, resisted. It was especially difficult for Catholics, who regarded the Roman pontiff as the head of their church.

A clerical victim from Shanghai, Beda Chang, a Sorbonne graduate and highly respected Jesuit, died in prison in November 1951, three months after his arrest, possibly after torture. His tomb was not marked because the regime insisted that the word "convict" be attached to his name, even though he was never brought to trial. Four years later, Bishop Ignatius Gong Pinmei of Shanghai and about 1,500 Catholics, mostly lay people, were rounded up and taken to jail. Similar arrests took place all over the country. Under these circumstances the Catholic "Patriotic Association" came into being in 1957. (The term "patriotic church" is often used to refer to the Catholic church in collaboration with the state.) Since the expulsion or imprisonment of missionaries meant a decrease in personnel, the Patriotic Association proceeded in 1958 to request permission from Rome to consecrate bishops; eventually the Patriotic Association made pledges of loyalty to the Communist party and the government and ordained bishops without obtaining Rome's permission.

The conflict between the Catholic church and the Communist government in China was underscored by the Vatican when Pope Pius XII condemned the "Three-Self Principles" in two encyclicals, one in 1954 and the other in 1958, and forbade the more than three million Chinese Catholics from cooperating with the Communist regime, including holding membership in Communist organizations or reading Communist newspapers, magazines and books. Those bishops ordaining other bishops and priests without permission, as well as those who were ordained, were all excommunicated. This state of affairs persisted even after the end of the Cultural Revolution, and continues today.

Chinese Buddhists also experienced pressures from the government, and monastic life was infiltrated by cadres who persuaded monks and nuns to abandon a "parasitic" lifestyle. The Chinese Buddhist Association was formed in 1953, claiming to represent 500,000 monks and 100 million lay followers. It collaborated with the regime that proceeded to convert many temples to secular uses. The other native religion, Taoism, fared less well since it was regarded as less scientific and more "superstitious."

The "Bad Years"

With the beginning of the Cultural Revolution (1966-1976), all religious organizations and activities were suppressed, until it seemed as though China had no more religion. The Cultural Revolution had the designated aim of "Destroying the Four Olds" (culture, thinking, habits and customs). All ancestral tablets and domestic shrines in peasant houses were destroyed and replaced by pictures of Mao Zedong. Red flags were placed over Christian churches in place of crosses, objects of veneration were removed from the premises, and Bibles were burned, while busts of Mao Zedong were frequently installed in the middle of these places of worship. In the aftermath of Red Guard terror, all places of worship in the country were closed or put to other uses, and religious personnel were forced into labor, or sometimes even tortured and killed. On the other hand, people were made to demonstrate devotion to Mao Zedong, the great leader, rather than to God or Buddha. Throughout the country, a new "liturgy" was carried out as people paid respect to their portraits of Mao mornings and evenings, seeking daily instructions from him in a quasi-religious manner. These exercises took place especially in Tiananmen Square, where soldiers, workers, and Red Guards went at sunrise and to which they returned at sundown. Thus, Maoism became a surrogate religion offering a new faith, elucidated in the *Little Red Book*, and witnessed by Mao images, lapel buttons, posters, songs, and drama. The political leader had become a god.

While traveling in 1979 with a group of Americans associated with Sargent Shriver and the Kennedy Institute of Ethics, I was asked to locate the parish priest of the reopened Catholic church in Beijing. A group of us were taken to the church's parlor, where a very reluctant priest received us. He was obviously uncomfortable with our questions, including the one about what he had suffered during the Cultural Revolution. He said, for example, "I was made to walk on all fours in the streets, to show that I was a running dog of the imperialists."

The fall of the Gang of Four signaled the return of the "good years." As the country opened to the outside world, visitors to China were treated with stories of persecutions suffered during the "ten years of turbulence." It appeared that everyone had been a victim, the party member as well as the religious believer. For a while, it also appeared as if common suffering might create a bond of understanding and sympathy between the rulers and the ruled. As a new leaf was turned, however, outsiders learned that worship had never ceased; Christians, for example, had gone underground and held home services. This continues to take place in villages as well as in cities today. In the case of Catholics, I have heard of priests going around celebrating Mass here and there, reminiscent of Elizabethan times in England when Catholic activities also went underground.

I remember meeting a Chinese professor, a man in his late thirties who had no idea that I was a Christian. In the course of our conversation, however, he disclosed to me that he and his wife were married for more than twelve years before he found out that she was a Catholic. "She came from a Catholic family," he told me, "but did not dare tell anybody. Only at the end of the Cultural Revolution did she dare to come out in the open."

Believers are still very aware of political pressures suffered in the past and thus fear for the future, and some Catholics hesitate to go to confession to priests who have collaborated with the government; they prefer those who have not collaborated. People remain very loyal to Rome in their hearts, and even those serving in the Patriotic Association would like to settle things with the pope, in return for papal recognition of the People's

Republic of China, their own bishops, and church autonomy.

The past decade has seen the reopening of thousands of Christian churches and Buddhist temples, as well as the recruitment of religious personnel. I was told by a mainland researcher in 1986 that there are still more Christians who worship at home than there are those who worship in the open, even though the churches are always full.

As previously explained by John Tong,[1] the new constitution is very specific about the rights of believers to enjoy freedom of religious belief. In 1982, the official figure put Catholics and Protestants at three million each, which implies a large growth rate during the years of the Cultural Revolution. In 1987, Protestants claimed to have reached four million, a quick rise indeed, with new recruits coming especially from educated circles. Speaking generally, Protestants no longer have denominational divisions, although, in fact, sectarian loyalties remain. There is the prestigious Union Seminary for Protestants in Nanjing and twelve Catholic seminaries throughout the country, of which the best known is in Sheshan outside of Shanghai. Buddhists and Taoists each have a headquarters in Beijing for the advanced training of novices, while monasteries in the provinces are also known to be training recruits on their own.

An interesting question is that of "clerical celibacy," whether for Buddhists, Taoists, or Catholics. Buddhism has always been a monastic religion, whereas Taoism is represented in recent history by two sects: the southern Heavenly Masters sect, which permits a married clergy, and the northern Perfect Truth sect, which enforces celibacy. I have been told that many Buddhist monks and Taoist priests are known to have married during the Cultural Revolution. A large percentage of these have returned to active service in their congregations without always leaving their wives and families. When I visited the Jade Buddhist temple in Shanghai, I was told that some of the monks put on monastic garb at the temple in the morning and remove it to return home at night. It appears, however, that the Buddhist novices are trained to be celibate. Taoists seem to have decided in favor of "nature," without formal proscriptions. In the case of the Catholic church, some clergy, including some bishops, are known to have married. They are permitted now to help with church work, but not to celebrate the eucharist.

Opium of the People?

Ren Jiyu, the former head of the Institute of World Religions in the Chinese Academy of Social Sciences, has always defended an "orthodox" line—namely, that religion is the opium of the people. His basic assertion is that "all religions are superstitions, but not all superstitions are religions." In practice, this means that religion is superior to pure superstition. According to this view, atheism is superior to all religion, but some religions are superior to others. Christianity, for example, is often regarded as superior to Taoism, which is associated with "superstitious" practices like divination and exorcism.

In the 1980s, in a debate over the nature of religion, Ren Jiyu insisted upon pushing the "opium of the people" definition, while Zhao Fusan, the former vice–president of the Chinese Academy of Social Sciences, asserted that, in its functions, religion is *not* just the opium of the people. In the aftermath of the military crackdown on the pro-democracy demonstrations, Zhao Fusan did not return to China after attending a UNESCO meeting in Paris in July 1989. The irony of these debates about religion and superstition is that Marxism has served *both* as religious truth *and* as superstition for the people governed by the Communists. Chinese intellectuals are well aware of this irony. For this reason, too, they have shown a tolerance and openness toward religion, the enemy of militant atheism.

The Communist army first entered Tibet in 1950, and both the Dalai Lama and the Panchen Lama, the two highest spiritual leaders, received government protection and promises of religious freedom. A few years later, however, taxes were increased, estates confiscated, and land redistributed, while lamas were sometimes assaulted and killed. In the aftermath of a 1959 uprising, which was quickly squelched by the government, the Dalai Lama and his entourage escaped to India, where they still remain. Harsh repression followed in Tibet itself as monasteries were secularized and monks were rounded up and forced to work and marry.

Even very recently (1988-1989), the bloody repression of people, including monks, asking for more autonomy in Tibet alarmed world opinion. Calls for "real autonomy" were heard as well in Xinjiang. On this account, the Communist party secretary (*Saifuding*) there was transferred to Beijing. Interestingly, several students from ethnic minorities (Wu'er Kaixi, a Uighur; Nixi, a Tibetan) were elected by their fellows as leaders during demonstrations of the spring of 1989 in Beijing. A female student, Chai Ling, was also prominent in Tiananmen Square. Buddhist monks, including those in Tibetan costumes, are known to have participated in the demonstrations in Beijing, as did Taoist priests.

Ethnic conflicts and hostilities between the Han population and the others are real, especially in the frontier regions where there is little true autonomy, and where the minorities are rightly anxious about being overwhelmed by the forced influx of the Han. On the other hand, the unfolding drama in Tiananmen also revealed that the deeper cause for disunity was the repressive regime. With the process of democratization, many problems can be resolved with relative ease, not only with regard to Tibetan Buddhists and Turkish Muslims, but also with regard to Hong Kong and even Taiwan.

In the past, Chinese intellectuals have usually been proud of their culture's predominantly secular attitudes toward life and the universe. The names of contemporary philosophers and historians such as Hu Shih and

Ch'ien Mu (now both deceased) come to mind. It comes, therefore, as some surprise to hear words such as the following from Liu Xiaobo, a lecturer at Beijing University, who (before his arrest in June 1989) attracted thousands of hearers to his talks:

> The Chinese believe that they themselves are the center of the world, and that human beings are omnipotent. But to be omnipotent is actually to be impotent, as the human being is [really] limited. Whether physically or spiritually, the human being is not the center of the universe, and no nation can become the center of the world. . . . The tragedy of the Chinese is the tragedy of not having a God. Because of the lack of light from beyond, the darkness on this shore has been mistaken as light . . .[2]

After the religious repression of the Cultural Revolution, people have returned to their places of worship, even to practices of divination and faith-healing. Particularly impressive is the way children of religious parents, whether Buddhist, Taoist, Catholic, or Protestant, have returned to the practices of their respective religious heritages. But I have also found, to my amazement, that an immense number of people show an interest in the Christian religion—an interest that did not emerge from a Chinese sensibility. It is indeed ironic that the breast–beating of many ex–missionaries over cultural or religious "imperialism" has not found much echo in the country, except in official circles. In spite of the available literature in the People's Republic of China on this subject, people (especially the younger set) appear not to concern themselves with such accusations, but do express strong interest in *Western* religion. No doubt, they associate it in their minds with the modern (rather than the medieval) West. Protestant Christianity seems to attract the most people, but many find the Catholic liturgy appealing. The churches are full, especially at midnight masses every Christmas, so that priests have to devise ways of turning away non-Christians. One way is to ask people to give their Christian names. One young man wanting very much to get in declared: "My name is Maria." He didn't make it.

While we who live in the West are conscious of the diminishing statistics of our church attendance, Chinese visitors to our countries still manifest astonishment at the "strength" of religion in our societies. The dissident astrophysicist Fang Lizhi, for example, recorded his own impressions of an Advent service in Cambridge, England, in 1979, during which he kept asking himself: Why has Christianity been so influential in Western society? Why does it attract so many scholars and students? A student newspaper article on Fang Lizhi published at Beijing University in 1985, also printed the following:

> Our attitude toward the entire religious question bears rethinking. We naively assume that Western religions reveal ignorance, but fail

to realize that modern Western religion is a vigorous tradition infused with contemporary meanings. Western religion is also a means of experiencing such emotions as love, friendship and compassion.[3]

Conclusion

What next? An American teacher in China, John Shillington, reported the following experience that he presumably had on Sunday, June 4, 1989:

> As I walked into church I saw the young teacher at the altar. He was from our college, about my age, and wearing a black mourning arm band. The elderly church members were gathered around him in a heated argument. The young man had made a tape of a prayer he had composed for the students and soldiers who had died in Beijing. The people around him were urging him to sit down, begging him not to speak, for they knew he would certainly be arrested and possibly killed for asking prayers for students who are now referred to as hooligans and counter-revolutionaries. . . . Surrounded, silenced, the young man finally collapsed on the back pew of the church and wept convulsively. Intense sobs racked his whole body.
>
> As I went by the teacher I stopped and stared. I'd never witnessed such intense pain. The teacher wept so bitterly, sobs which did not sound human, as if the screams and cries of those in Beijing were carried inside his body. It was beyond grief, the sound of injustices so large that they could not be overcome or humanly forgiven. Sounds of such empathy bordered on the brink of insanity where humanity merges with God.
>
> A policeman waited outside of the church to take the teacher away.[4]

By June 27, 1989, the various officially recognized religious groups in China had all come out in support of the regime and its crackdown. They had no other choice. But what future can we forecast for the religious situation in China? Will the guarantee of religious liberty survive the tragic end to the student demonstrations? The answers to these questions are still being awaited. The mass arrests, the quick judgments, and the reports of torture indicate a return to the methods of the Cultural Revolution. The churches appear to be carrying on as usual, while reports have come through of a new crackdown on Catholic bishops and clerics who have Vatican links.

I am convinced that freedom of religion is an issue that cannot be separated from freedom of thought and expression, freedom of speech and association. The virtual suspension of these constitutional freedoms has now rendered the 1982 Constitution a dead letter. Has religion also entered a new dark age? I hope not, but fear the worst. I have witnessed the cycle of "good" and "bad" years in the past, and quite honestly the good years were never so good, whereas the bad years were very bad indeed. When will this cycle of repression be broken by democratization? This is the question on everyone's mind.

Notes

1. See pages 18-19 in Chapter 1 above.
2. *Ming Pao Monthly*, August 1989, p. 36.
3. *China Spring Digest*, March/April 1987.
4. *China News Update*, August 1989.

4

The "Underground" Church

JEAN CHARBONNIER

The brutal suppression of the democratic movement in June 1989, with its shocking pictures of the slaughter in Tiananmen Square, provoked a vigorous reaction on the part of world opinion, especially in France and North America. The repression of underground Christians in China, which has gone on for more than forty years, has failed to arouse the same indignation, except on the part of human rights organizations like Amnesty International, or religious groups keeping an eye on persecution in Eastern countries. Nor indeed is there any direct connection between the repression of the students in Beijing and that of the underground Christians.

The object of this report is not to heighten Western readers' dissatisfaction with recent Chinese policy. Instead, it seeks only to view the manner in which the Christians of China express their fidelity, and, at the same time, help the reader appreciate the unfortunate divisions that rend the church in that land. While mistrustful of outside interference, China's Christians are anxious to be known and understood.

The task, then, is to perceive the disparate elements of a complex situation. Is there really an underground church in China? What are the causes of its existence? Why can one speak of such a church today, when a policy of religious freedom has been applied in China for some ten years now? What hopes are there for peace and unity among the Christians of China?

The Existence of the Underground Church

In the early 1980s, Chinese authorities, both civil and religious, officially denied the existence of an underground church in their country. To speak

This essay was originally written in French and appeared as a supplement to *Eglises d'Asie* 85 (April 1990). Translation by Robert R. Barr.

of an underground church was an "unfriendly gesture" on the part of foreigners either seeking to divide the church of China, or simply understanding nothing of the Chinese situation.

It was not foreigners alone, however, who called attention to the sufferings of "underground" Catholics. Archbishop Dominic Tang of Guangzhou, who was released from prison in 1980 and authorized to seek medical attention in Hong Kong, traveled to various countries to reveal the existence of two Catholic churches in China, the one approved by the state and enjoying the benefit of subsidies and a certain freedom of worship, the other bearing witness to its loyalty to Rome and deprived of everything. He had nothing to hide. Severely criticized by "patriotic" authorities for having met the pope and received from him the title of archbishop, he now found it impossible to resume his pastoral task at Guangzhou. In 1990, he began publishing a short bimonthly newspaper in Chinese called *Sui Shing* (a name for Guangzhou), and a newsletter in English for distribution to his friends. In these he reports news of underground Catholics and their trials, while taking care not to reveal anything that could be used by the Chinese police. He speaks without bitterness, and always notes positive developments that might be signs of hope.

For two or three years now, patriotic Catholic leaders themselves have complained openly of the activities of the underground church, whose existence they thus admit. Foreign Catholic delegations visiting Beijing have frequently had to listen to accusations, either by Liu Bainian, a ranking official of the Patriotic Association, or by Bishop Fu Tieshan of Nantang Cathedral in Beijing, of undue interference on the part of the Vatican in the affairs of the Chinese church in authorizing the ordination of underground bishops. Rome, they say, seeks to divide China's Catholics. Similarly, Bishop Jin Luxian of Shanghai has often deplored the "untimely" activity of underground bishops in his diocese and the neighboring ones.

We should not conclude from this that there is an organized, loyal underground church operating in stubborn defiance of an official, quasi-schismatic one. There are a number of distinctions to be made, and in both directions. Indeed, it is surely false to speak of two churches. There is actually only one Catholic church—loyal on the whole—with an official face and a concealed one. The naturally conciliatory Chinese people see no contradiction between an outward submission to power and an inner loyalty to their local, religious, cultural, or even simply clannish communities. We must attempt to be precise, then, when it comes to the various subcategories of "underground" and "patriotic."

Quite a number of analyses carried out in recent years all agree as to the existence of an intermediate group—actually comprising a majority—that is neither underground nor patriotic. These members of the faithful practice their religion openly, and refuse to reject the authority of the pope. A good many nuances are distinguishable within this group, depending on the presence or absence of the Patriotic Association and the nature of its local requirements. In many regions of China, the Patriotic Association has never been put in place. This is often the case with entirely or nearly entirely Catholic villages in remote rural areas. There was a case, for example, of a Catholic village in Inner Mongolia where the priest was thrashed with sticks on his way out of the church because he had undertaken to flirt with the Patriotic Association. The unfortunate gentleman quickly made appropriate amends.

By contrast, it occasionally happens that Catholic minorities in large cities manage to strike a peaceable *modus vivendi* with civil authorities without having to form a Patriotic Association. The two hundred Christians of Urumqi in Xinjiang province have formed a committee to handle relations with the municipal Religious Affairs Bureau. True, the two priests of the church, released in 1979, were again imprisoned from 1983 to 1985, but this dynamic community has since built a new church. The post-Vatican liturgy is celebrated there in Chinese, with the commemoration of the pope in the eucharistic prayer. A new altar missal has been printed and the choir is one of the best in China.

More frequently, however, a local branch of the Patriotic Association has been formed in conformity with government policy, but the members of the association do not force the priests and faithful to declare themselves against the pope. The bishop of Wanxian in Sichuan province, Bishop Duan Yinming, maintains friendly relations with the head of the association without having to dissimulate his loyalty to Rome. In a number of provinces of China, bishops and priests themselves have taken charge of the association, thus lending it an orientation compatible with Catholic doctrine.

However, not everything works for the best, even in the best of worlds. There are determinedly underground Catholics who must either hide or face police investigations and arrests. Here again a distinction is to be made. In numerous dioceses, one finds elderly priests who are not authorized to perform their ministry openly. Having already spent thirty or more years in prisons or labor camps, they are prepared to return to prison rather than to compromise themselves. The faithful have a special devotion to them, and there are long lines at their confessionals, when they are permitted to hear confessions. Among these clergy, it is estimated that there are about fifty bishops who are "underground" in the strictest sense of the term.

There are also other priests, often younger, ordained clandestinely, who celebrate mass in private homes, even when the local church has been reopened by the Patriotic Association. The faithful may avoid a particular church because a priest has married or taken a position openly against the pope. Finally, there are points of concentration where underground Catholics are more organized and have their own seminaries and novitiates. These are found especially in southern Hebei, in Shaanxi, in southern Zhejiang, and in northern Fujian. At the other extreme, on the patriotic side, we likewise find bishops and priests who take an outright position against

Rome and actively support a completely independent church. These clergy have the support of the political authorities.

In a number of provinces of China, some bishops ordained clandestinely have later obtained the more or less tacit consent of the authorities for the exercise of their pastoral ministry. Conversely, a score of some sixty official, "democratically elected" bishops have discreetly obtained the approval of Rome, either before or after their episcopal ordination. Thus, there are underground bishops officially recognized by the government, and official bishops secretly approved by Rome. China watchers fond of the *chiaroscuro* in the Chinese landscape will perhaps see this as a sign of the inculturation of the church. Those who prefer contrasts will tend, instead, to despair.

Causes of Clandestinity

To understand the causes of clandestinity, we must refer to its historical genesis. In inflicting legal penalties on underground Christians, the Chinese Communist party has only resumed a policy that it has been applying since 1950, shortly after seizing power. The Patriotic "Three-Self Movement" (self-supporting, self-propagating, self-governing), first launched among the Protestants, then implemented with greater difficulty among the Catholics, proclaimed Chinese independence and the struggle against foreign imperialism. According to the interpretation of a Marxist-Leninist party, independence likewise meant atheistic propaganda and the gradual destruction of the religions. Beginning with the Anti-Rightist campaign launched in 1957, churches and temples were gradually closed and converted into schools, hospitals, factories, or hangars, or even completely destroyed. The Cultural Revolution of 1966 marked an abrupt end to the visible existence of the church; this remained so for an entire decade.

As all foreign missionary personnel bearing the "imperialist" label had been driven from the country in the early 1950s, most dioceses found themselves without bishops, and the number of their priests down by half. Chinese priests and bishops bore valiant witness to their loyalty to the church and the pope by refusing to join the Three-Self Movement. All efforts on the part of Archbishop Antonio Riberi, the apostolic internuncio, to obtain recognition by the government were to no avail. In May 1951 the *People's Daily* accused him of sabotaging the movement for an independent church. Shortly thereafter he was expelled from China.

In Rome, Pope Pius XII took a firm position in the face of events in China. His encyclical letter of January 18, 1952, *Cupimus Imprimis*, was later followed by another letter, *Ad Sinarum Gentes*, on October 7, 1954, in which he encouraged Catholics of China to bear witness to their faith, and criticized the Three-Self Movement. The bishops of China, for their part, took severe measures in the case of priests and Christians who joined Communist campaigns, even excluding them from the sacraments. After seven years of violent political repression, the Communist government managed to win a few priests and bishops to the Three-Self Movement, and on July 15, 1957 formed with them the Chinese Catholic Patriotic Association. The following year marked the beginning of the ordination of bishops without the consent of Rome. In June 1958 the encyclical *Ad Apostolorum Principis* condemned the "patriotic church" and the illegal election of bishops. The underground church was born of this confrontation, and made up of bishops, priests, and Catholics integrally loyal to the Catholic church and its pontiff.

Later events were to encourage the development of this underground church. From 1966 to 1976, ten years of Cultural Revolution plunged all Christians into a *de facto* clandestinity, with all places of worship closed and most priests and nuns in prisons or labor camps. Christians still prayed in the secrecy of their homes, but they had to keep their religious books hidden away and parents at times had reason to fear denunciation by their own children. Following Mao's death in September 1976 and the inauguration of the new policy of the United Front, most priests returned to their dioceses in 1978 and 1979. There they resumed their ministry, at first believing that they could exercise it in complete freedom.

However, the Patriotic Association also resurfaced, and soon asserted a strictly independent line. Deng Xiaoping put an abrupt end to the democratic movement expressed by the *Dazibao* posters in Beijing. He defined the cardinal, untouchable Four Principles: the socialist way, the leadership of the party, the dictatorship of the proletariat, and Maoist Marxism-Leninism.

Rather than yield on principles for which they had spent many years in prison, numerous priests now drew back into the shadows. Scattered, aging, and overwhelmed by the multitude of faithful they were called upon to serve, they sent desperate appeals to Rome asking for additional bishops and priests. Rather broad faculties were accorded the priests and bishops of China that they might supply the needs of Christians in their sacramental life. With Rome's approval, bishops were given the ability to name and ordain successors, and even designate qualified bishops for neighboring dioceses that were without bishops. Rome desired that these faculties be used only with the greatest restraint in order not to interfere with its effort to strike an accord with the Chinese government. Certain loyal bishops now made use of this faculty to confer episcopal orders on a number of priests, so that dioceses would not be left without shepherds in case of arrest or death. Some of these ordinations, conferred under the pressure of circumstances, were not always felicitous. At times, the new secret bishops had not had a great deal of pastoral experience, or else found themselves in conditions of isolation such that they were prevented from performing their ministry. In certain localities, several bishops were ordained for the same diocese. Conflicts of authority arose, and the common good of the diocese was sometimes sacrificed in the interests of ultra-loyal cliques, which, while vying with one another in their loyalty to Rome, also reflected the Chinese propensity to clannishness.

In most cases, underground opposition to official religious policy was in no way motivated by a will to political dissidence. It was primarily for reasons of faith that the underground felt itself compelled to live outside the law. However, elements of the conflict have evolved since the 1950s. The government slogan of imperialism is heard less frequently now (although this reactionary refrain has had a tendency to reappear since late 1989 or early 1990). The emphasis now is on the maintenance of an independent church, the need for political integration of the church, and the orientation of the religions to the service of modernization. The underground, for its part, stresses the unity of the church under the guidance of the successor of Peter. It fears a tampering with the faith if this link with Rome is broken. It knows the atheistic policy of the party to transform gradually religious teachings into an active service of social development. Underground Catholics are guided by a *sensus fidelium* steeped in persecution, and they fear any devaluation of the faith.

The Protestant Underground

For a better appreciation of the reasons for clandestinity, one must take account of parallel developments among the Protestants. It would be an oversimplification to reduce these reasons to the sole handicap of communion with Rome. Ever since the Communist regime came to power, the strikingly dynamic witness of the evangelical communities has collided with the administration of the Three-Self Movement, the Protestant equivalent of the Patriotic Association of the Catholics. The faith of the evangelicals is of a deeply devotional, pietistic mold, quite unlike that of the liberal Protestants, who seek more of a political and social contextualization of the faith.

Young Chinese evangelicals of Hong Kong, North America, and more recently, Taiwan, are particularly solicitous for the numerous small local communities scattered all across China. These groups, often made up of young converts, meet in homes and are not officially registered. Spirits are fired by itinerant "preachers," who take their own liberties as well. The large evangelical center in Hong Kong (Shatin) periodically lists arrests of preachers and nonaligned pastors in its weekly publication, *China News and Church Report*.

In July 1989 the Second Lausanne World Evangelical Conference was held at Manila, without a single participant from China. Invitations had been rejected by the Christian Council of China, the Protestant organ for pastoral supervision that corresponds to the Catholic Church Administrative Commission. The Christian Council faithfully follows the Three-Self Movement policy. The reason given for the refusal was the interference of

Lausanne II in internal Chinese affairs, along with a "divisive approach" to the question of Chinese participation.

> They have split the Church of China into two categories: what they call the "Church of the Three Autonomies (the "official church," or "church registered with the government") on the one hand, and the "domestic churches," "underground churches," or "unregistered churches" on the other. They ask that each party send 150 delegates, or 300 in all—else it will be obvious to all that there is no religious freedom in China. This is an effort to discredit our principle of the Three Autonomies, and is an attempt to divide the Church.[1]

The evangelicals reproach the Three-Self Movement for its tight control of their religious activities, and its secularizing orientations inspired by the ideology of the Communist party.

But as with the Catholics, the government seems to have loosened the reins a bit. A joint congress of the Three-Self Movement and the Christian Council of China was held in Shanghai on December 13-17, 1988. The respective constitutions of the two organizations were reaffirmed. However, it was stipulated that "the ingrained habit of reserving church administration to the Three-Self Movement should be changed. All church work should be seen to independently, at the various levels in question, by the Christian Council of China and by the churches."[2]

The witness of the evangelicals has surely been a help to the ensemble of the Protestant churches in maintaining the primacy of faith and requiring the government to respect their religious specificity.

Growth of the Catholic Underground during 1988 and 1989

The new wave of persecution of the underground since the end of 1989 is perhaps partly to be explained by the conservative rigorism of those in power since 1989. But, even more, it is a response to the assertiveness and daring of underground Christians over these last years. The declaration of Bishop Ma Ji of Pingliang merits special attention. In August 1988 he noted the growth of the underground movement in his province:

> This rent in the Catholic church is particularly apparent in Gansu province, where it is now widespread and growing even worse. Here the vitality of the underground church is revealed in broad daylight, inspiring an attitude of trust and support in the faithful. The self-styled "three Catholic organs" (the Patriotic Association, the Administrative Commission and the Bishops' Conference) see their authority dwindle by the day. Isolated, paralyzed, and deprived of any influence, these organizations are only very reluctantly tolerated.[3]

Bishop Ma Ji attributed this "rent" in the church to errors on the part of the Patriotic Association. He put the blame on a minority of patriotic bishops whose behavior he denounced. Some have married, some have rejected the authority of the successor of Peter, and others have subverted the role of a "bridge" that the Patriotic Association could have assumed to link the government and the church. Bishop Ma also reproached the Patriotic Association for stubbornly maintaining its outdated 1950s anti-imperialism, while current governmental efforts look to the construction of a Chinese socialism with the cooperation of everyone. Finally, he accused the association of ineffectiveness in performing its task of returning church properties.

The fact that Bishop Ma Ji made this declaration and published it in China is not without its suspicious implications. Ill at ease with the growth of the underground churches, officials of the United Front undoubtedly wished to call attention to the reasons for that movement and plan their strategy to deal with it. Bishop Ma's seemingly audacious declaration supplied them with justification for the corrective measures they proposed to apply in handling the religious question and in more effectively suppressing the underground. In order to ensure actual control over the Catholic church, United Front officials would have to be in minimal agreement with Rome and show a certain respect for church discipline.

Similar underground movements were spreading in neighboring provinces. In Shaanxi, Father Anthony Zhang Gangyi, who had been permitted to go on pilgrimage to Rome in 1987, returned to his Sanyuan diocese with a message from the pope. Exhibiting a photograph of himself with the Holy Father, he reported that the pope had declared to him that it was sinful to assist at patriotic masses. This news spread among Christians of the whole Chinese northwest, who now challenged pastors under the aegis of the Patriotic Association.

In September 1988 a document entitled *The Thirteen Points*, attributed to Bishop Fan Xueyan of Baoding, circulated in Hebei province and beyond.[4] The substance of its message was that Catholic faithful commit a grave sin in attending mass in patriotic churches. Laden with the authority of a universally respected confessor of the faith, this document had a devastating effect. The churches emptied. Shepherds of good will, unjustly labeled "patriotic," saw their flocks scatter. Patriotic directors and party officials were exasperated by this act of sabotage of their religious freedom policy.

The underground church publicized the reasons for its action in a document entitled "My Vision of the Patriotic Association" circulated *sub rosa*.[5] Written by an underground bishop from southern Hebei, it declared that bishops and priests who cooperate with the Patriotic Association are lying to themselves when they claim to do so in good conscience. They imagine that a purely external, formal accommodation does not engage their faith, he says, but the moment they compromise on papal primacy, they are committed, willy-nilly, to a process that leads inexorably to the gradual abandonment of the more essential articles of the Catholic belief. The bishop listed twenty-two reasons why it is impossible to tolerate any cooperation whatever with the Patriotic Association. Throughout, the document echoes the anguish of an elderly priest anxious to preserve the integrity of the faith, but also bitter at being victimized by ill-treatment sanctioned by the patriotics, and resentful of the advantages given to patriotic Catholics yet denied to the underground.

Other bishops reacted in a more serene manner, and were satisfied with openly professing their faith. Such was the case with Bishop Xiao Liren of Xingtai, whose Christmas message invited the faithful to emerge from their clandestinity, and to bear witness at once to their loyalty to the pope and their love for their country.

> We bring our efforts to bear on the two following points:
> 1. We are firmly resolved, with the supreme leader of our Catholic church, the pope, and under his guidance, to foster and develop our religious life, gradually to improve our knowledge of doctrine, to develop the church, and to save souls for the glory of God.
> 2. As for our country, naturally we do not wish to be left behind. We are firmly resolved, under the correct guidance of the government, to build a prosperous and powerful country, to rally all our forces to the service of a happy life, in unity and mutual love, with all of the people of this land.[6]

Following this declaration, Bishop Xiao Liren was deprived of the exercise of his ministry. A more conciliatory bishop, Hou Jinde, was later named to the see of Xingtai and ordained in October 1989, in a ceremony attended by great crowds of people.

Underground Catholics generally avoid such open declarations, which can only draw fire. On the other hand, they testify massively in silent fashion at burials of loyal bishops or priests. For instance, the following account was given of the funeral of Bishop Li Xinsheng, who passed away February 4, 1989, in Hebei province.

> Bishop Li Xinsheng was called back to God, to the bosom of the Lord, on February 4th of this year. The burial took place on the 11th. But for three days—the 9th, the 10th, and the 11th—the village had already been surrounded by all the Catholics, to keep the police and the folk of the Religious Affairs Bureau from interfering with the burial. In all, more than 20,000 Catholics were in attendance. There were twenty musical groups, besides the groups to light the firecrackers. Before the bier had even left the village, the cortege stretched for several *lis*. [A *li* is 500 meters.] Catholics came from all directions. Even non-Catholics opened their homes to faithful coming from a

distance. The burial passed without incident, in peace, and gave glory to God. Constantly, whenever he offered the Holy Sacrifice, as well as on other occasions, Bishop Stephen uncompromisingly proclaimed the Lord's teaching, which aroused the hatred of the enemies of the church. He had already spent more than twenty years in Qinghai prison. After returning to his native village, near Baoding, he was arrested again in 1981 and imprisoned for four years. He was very ill from being beaten and tortured. Finally he died of his injuries. Truly here was a faithful servant of the Lord for whom he offered himself in sacrifice. Baoding has lost a loyal missionary. But other leaders remain, to continue in his footsteps.[7]

Thus, the underground church has the strength of a popular faith steeped in persecution. Hebei Catholics experienced the extortion of the Boxers in 1900, the violence of the invading Japanese in 1937, and then the brutalities of the Communists. At Donglucun in south Baoding, Catholics venerate an image of Our Lady of China as protector of the village in these critical periods. Crowds of pilgrims stream to the recently restored basilica.

Chinese Catholics who visit their families in loyal Catholic villages report a religious life of vigor and vitality, with accounts of miracles, visions, exorcisms, sudden conversions of ranking Communists who become effective catechists, sacrilegious hands stricken with paralysis, cures on the tomb of a confessor of the faith, passionate devotional prayers for souls in purgatory, apparitions of the Blessed Virgin, and so forth.

Certain remote villages without priests or sisters are sometimes thrown into confusion by self-appointed "messiahs," whose ritual practices and teachings are more or less orthodox. Patriotic Catholics then seize the occasion to denounce signs of heresy in the underground and it becomes an easy task for party officials to condemn these religious practices as superstitious.

Generally, though, the underground church—while composed for the most part of simple peasantry—manages to keep up with the universal church. Due to outside contact through relatives and friends, underground priests often celebrate mass in Chinese and try to obtain modern programs of theological and scriptural training for their seminarians and novices. In the official seminaries, on the other hand, books from abroad are often kept under lock and key.

The Iron Hand of the Government

Paradoxically, this Catholic fervor, which goes far beyond the ranks of the underground and manifests itself throughout China, creates an impression that the government's religious freedom policy is being enforced. Patriotic officials often take credit for religious developments that local Christians have actually had to wrest from visibly unenthusiastic authorities. When a church is restored — despite all obstacles — when some land and two or three buildings are returned to the church, when a novitiate is reopened, national or provincial Patriotic Association officials can be relied on to pay an ostentatious visit to the lucky community. A banquet is held for civil authorities and each guest thanks God and the party for this manifest proof of government benevolence.

On the other hand, the same officials are merciless with persons who refuse to play this game, or who show hostility to official organizations. Recalcitrants are isolated and punished, and those who cooperate are rewarded with the concession of new freedoms.

Prohibition on Foreigners Meeting with Underground Christians

In October 1987 the world was delighted with the friendly reception accorded Cardinal (Jaime) Sin of the Philippines by Zhao Ziyang. However, officials ignored a request of the cardinal to visit priests and faithful of Xianxian in Hebei province, the home diocese of many Chinese priests living in the Philippines. Disappointed by this refusal, Cardinal Sin then traveled to Fujian province, the homeland of his ancestors. Communist authorities let him bless a bank in the special economic zone of Xiamen.

Some Catholic leaders hesitate to visit China because of this discrimination. This is the case with Chinese bishops of Taiwan, in particular. It becomes impossible for them to go back to see their families if they are kept at a distance from loyal Catholics and must instead join the festivities at a patriotic reception or banquet. Visitors who do manage to visit underground Catholics must frankly consider the risks to which they expose not only themselves, but also those whom they go to see. In recent years a number of arrests have been made on the strength of indictments listing "foreign contacts" as the most serious charge.

Other actions to repress the underground church have included two series of arrests in Hebei province. In May 1986 a sizable detachment of police blocked the roads leading from the village of Qiaozhai. Some forty clandestine seminarians and about twenty novices were arrested and subjected to verbal and physical abuse. Books and equipment were confiscated. Two 75-year-old priests were taken into custody, along with two nuns, who were 78 and 88 years old. A patriotic priest, it seems, played the sad role of informer.[8]

In Youtong, a village sixteen kilometers southwest of Shijiazhuang, the capital of Hebei province, of the seventeen hundred Catholics, only two hundred had rallied to the Patriotic Association. The remainder had been demanding a church for years after the demolition of their church and the transformation of parish buildings into a school. On March 13, 1989, Palm Sunday, these Catholics erected a tent to celebrate Holy Week and Easter.

On April 18, five thousand armed police invaded the village and began demolishing the tent. Women who attempted to stop them were struck with billy sticks. A young nun was struck on the head and lost an eye. Catholics filled the rectory and blocked the entrance. Police clambered onto the roof, tore away the tiles, and threw them down at the crowd inside. Two young women accosted along the road insulted their attackers and were trampled to death. Thirty battered or wounded Catholics were then arrested by the police. An attempt was made to force them to confess that they had attacked the police. Some three hundred wounded Catholics were left behind and the local government forbade the hospitals of Shijiazhuang to care for them.[9]

Arrests of Leaders

Arrests of underground priests, bishops, and laity have been frequent in recent years. They can spend from several days to several years in prison. For example, Bishop Fan Xueyan of Baoding has been repeatedly arrested and released. He lives under surveillance in rooms behind his church.[10] The police frequently act on tips offered by persons eager to exculpate themselves or to earn pocket money. This is how Bishop Liu Shuhe of Yixian came to be arrested at the end of 1988.

In 1989 the number of arrests soared. Hong Kong news services reported more than thirty arrests, of which six were of bishops in the provinces of Hebei, Gansu, Shaanxi, and Inner Mongolia. The new wave of repression seems in part a response to *Document 3* issued by the party in February 1989. Under the current regime, local government authorities are perhaps showing zeal in demonstrating that the democratic movement has not impaired their effectiveness. Underground Catholics are obvious victims— they will take no revenge, nor will an indifferent population come to their aid. By rejecting the Patriotic Association, they have knowingly violated the law and they are likely to be viewed as under the influence of unhealthy elements abroad. To boot, they are a bit superstitious and superstition is one of the Six Vices to be uprooted.

More Freedom for "Good" Subjects

The repression of the underground affects only a minority of Catholics. The church as a whole, rallying in various degrees to governmental structures, benefits from favors that are profitably advertised by the patriotic press and news services. A score of seminaries gradually opened since 1982 have received seven or eight hundred candidates. Over a third of these have dropped out, but some two hundred have been ordained priests. On July 16, 1989, fourteen priests were ordained at Hohot in Inner Mongolia, despite pressures exerted on them by underground milieus.

Communities of sisters that have regrouped since 1983 have trained young postulants who have since completed their novitiates. Private ceremonies in which these religious make their vows have taken place throughout the country for two or three years. In July 1989, the profession of seven novices at Nantang Cathedral in Beijing received unusual publicity.

Special attention has been called to certain reopenings of churches, like that of Yercalo in Tibet, in an era when international opinion was uncomfortable with the repression taking place in this autonomous region of the People's Republic. Indeed, hundreds of churches have been restored or rebuilt all over China. Credit belongs to local Catholic communities that have managed to take advantage of the official policy of religious freedom. They have had to form a local Patriotic Association to obtain the required permissions and a certain amount of financial assistance from the Religious Affairs Bureau. The participation of bishops and priests in the Chinese People's Political Consultative Conference has likewise proved effective. Representatives of the different religions find that they can defend their interests in the framework of this United Front organization.

Certain more spectacular instances of a successful appeal to the policy of religious freedom tend to vindicate Catholics who cooperate with the government, and thereby diminish the influence of the underground. This is the case with some large pilgrimages that bring throngs of worshippers to well-known sanctuaries. A pilgrimage to the shrine of Our Lady of Joy in Liuzhongguan in northern Guiyang was officially authorized for the first time in September 1988 and two bishops participated. A celebrated grotto of Lourdes in Jilin province in Manchuria has been rebuilt, and now boasts a basilica, modeled after the one at Lourdes. The Catholics of Shanxi have rebuilt the Marian Basilica of Banshishan, fifty kilometers northeast of Taiyuan and, to facilitate access, they have built a ten kilometer road up the mountainside. Every May, the Catholic fisherfolk of the Shanghai region flock to the Hill of Mary, Help of Christians, and most crowd into the hilltop basilica rebuilt by the Patriotic Association.

The freedoms enjoyed by the church have their political counterpart, however. Ever since the events of June 1989, prayer meetings have repeatedly been organized throughout China in thanksgiving for the government's victory over the rebels of Tiananmen Square and the reestablishment of peace. Catholic communities have even subscribed to a campaign to send financial aid to the victims' families—not to the families of the students who were killed, but to those of the soldiers fallen on the field of honor. And in October a series of liturgical celebrations marked the fortieth anniversary of the People's Republic of China, with thanksgiving for the enlightened policies of the Communist party. These religious ceremonies are obviously orchestrated from above, and are celebrated by all religions. The faithful themselves see no great reason to object as the news they have received of events that occurred in June stresses the wisdom of government action on behalf of law and order.

Divisions in the Church

Clandestine or underground Christians do not criticize government policy in general; rather, most try to live as good citizens and yet wish to enjoy real religious freedom. By and large, the Catholics of China, who constitute only a tiny minority in an enormous population of 1.12 billion, are not obsessed with a need for a critical analysis of their political society. For them, the major problem is not that of a church-state conflict, but instead the chasm that exists between Catholic groups.

The cleft is a deep one. At certain points of especially acute antagonism, underground and patriotic Catholics ostracize each other, even refusing to speak to or greet each other.[11] Each besmirches the other at will, spreading the most outrageous rumors. The underground side says that patriotic priests marry,[12] and seek creature comforts; that they have chosen the pleasures of this world; that they place the Chinese constitution above the Bible; that they receive fat salaries from the Communists; that they are Judases who denounce loyal priests and laity and should be shunned like the plague; that the pope has excommunicated them.

From the patriotic side, complaints are just as bitter against the underground: they are fanatics and make abusive generalizations; they misunderstand the deeper intention of the underground church, which is to serve the church and dispense the sacraments; they falsely accuse others of disloyalty to the pope; they ordain youngsters to the priesthood who have only an elementary formation; they give themselves over to religious practices that encourage superstition and heresy; they destroy communities by excommunicating "patriotic" Catholics.

These spiteful commentaries seem quite inconsistent. One side brandishes the standard of loyalty to the pope, but forgets the even more profound truth of Christian charity and the commandment of mutual love. Non-Christian motivations, like "saving face," revenge, and respect for a cliquish solidarity, lurk anonymously under all the petty arguments for fidelity, integrity, and truth. Large Catholic families, Christian for more than a century now, participate in systematic mudslinging against other Catholic families. Catholic villages throw themselves into merciless vendettas against other Catholic villages.

Some say that these conflicts among Catholics are cunningly fueled by the Communists. This is not necessarily the case. Civil authorities sometimes try to make peace, or simply to separate the squabblers. On the patriotic, Communist side, it is also alleged that Rome—and foreign visitors—are responsible for the divisions in the Chinese church. But this is to forget the history of these divisions. The United Front era, with the government advocating the unity of all citizens, was preceded by two decades of class struggle and revolutionary activism. Christians who rallied to the

Three-Self Movement were systematically invited at that time to denounce their brothers and sisters in the faith. Current rifts are the poisoned fruit of this policy.

Arduous Mediation

In the face of the complexities of the situation in China, and taking into account Chinese mistrust of foreigners, there will be those who think that the most prudent solution would be to let the Chinese work these problems out for themselves. But in this contemporary world of ours, which is more and more a world of solidarity, it would be insane for a people of 1.12 billion to continue to sequester itself behind its great, ruined wall, especially when the people actually wish to enter modernity and open up to international exchanges. The church, for its part, is one and universal. It cannot be indifferent to a member of its own body, nor can it dispense with the cultural and moral contributions of the Chinese church.

Finally, centuries of common history—centuries charged with sacrifice and suffering of every kind—cannot be totally disavowed. Christians of many lands have understood that the fact that there are no more foreign missionaries in China by no means signifies the end of the church's mission in that land. Besides the Chinese priests, sisters, and laity who visit their families there, numerous foreigners, as members of official delegations or as private individuals, have struck up a relation with the Christians of China. Some one hundred priests and sisters toil in China as lay persons, typically as foreign-language instructors. They cannot assume pastoral duties, but they bear witness to a willingness on the part of the church to be involved in exchange and service. Religious exchanges are still very limited, in view of the position of strict independence so fiercely maintained by patriotic leaders. These exchanges do exist, however. One task for concerned Christians is to determine what psychological factors favor dialogue, who are its principal agents at the present moment, and how that task should be pursued so that it will bear fruit.

Many Chinese priests and sisters scattered throughout the world remember pre-1949 China, in which church life was dominated by foreign missionaries. They still have a bitter memory of the somewhat inferior status to which indigenous clergy were relegated. On the other hand, they have a great admiration for Father Vincent Lebbe and other non-Chinese priests who succeeded in promoting a Sinicization of the church. Many also harbor resentment toward the Vatican for having been so slow to install a Chinese leadership in the church, and they continue to blame the Vatican for its wavering policy in recent years.

For a decade now, these priests and sisters of the Chinese diaspora have been returning to China to visit family and friends. Cautious at first, they stayed close to their own families. Loath to celebrate mass in public, they held aloof from the priests officially responsible for the parishes. For that matter, authorities of the Patriotic Association forbade them, in principle, any exercise of ministry. On their second or third trips, however, some have begun to render pastoral services and offer financial assistance — and often with the accord of local authorities. These Chinese priests and religious naturally trust the relatives and friends of their hometowns and old dioceses in China. They listen to their stories, and sometimes inherit their prejudices. They return to their adoptive countries with divergent positions and even, at times, reproduce the rifts dividing Catholics in China: some vigorously take the part of the underground, while others — the majority — mount a defense of the partisans of compromise.

Roman authorities keep abreast of these various liaison activities, but are careful not to become directly involved. It is true that the task at Rome is not an easy one. On the one hand, patriotic and underground Catholics seek clear directives, each side in its own favor. On the other, the Chinese themselves are wary of interference from abroad in their internal affairs.

It has been difficult for the Sacred Congregation for Evangelization to remain unresponsive to the repeated requests it receives from the underground Catholics. The latter ask especially for clergy and for directives confirming their legitimate status. On October 3, 1988 directives in preparation for over two years were finally sent confidentially to all of the bishops and religious superiors of the world. The eight points of this communique called for clarity and charity in relations with the church of China. "Clarity" means that there can be no Catholic church without the pope, the successor of Saint Peter. "Charity" means that persons adopting erroneous positions are often victims of insurmountable pressures, and need understanding.

While firm in matters of doctrine, these directives take account for the first time of an intermediate group of loyal Catholics willing to accept a degree of collaboration with the Patriotic Association. The directives even authorize enrollment of candidates in officially registered seminaries if there is no other adequate way to prepare them for the priesthood. Chinese Patriotic Association officials have reacted unfavorably to these directives, declaring to visitors that Rome should annul them.

The Vatican Secretariat of State, for its part, has sought improved relations between the Holy See and the Chinese government for years. Now, with improvements that have come about in church life in China since implementation of the new religious freedom policy, it has felt obliged to reciprocate with some recognition of officially approved church structures. Vatican conditions for a dialogue with the Chinese Catholic church require that it resemble a church, with the bishops actually directing it. The bishops of China ought no longer to tolerate the presence of married bishops. Finally, they themselves ought to express and manifest their desire for relations with Rome.

The Chinese government responded in some measure to these conditions in the spring of 1989 when the Bishops' Conference was placed at the head of Catholic organizations. Next is the Church Administrative Commission, with its primarily pastoral role. The Patriotic Association is third (although it acts, it is true, somewhat as the rudder at the stern of the ship). Its role does appear to be primarily political, and its habit of manipulating religious matters gives some reason to fear that the bishops are mere figureheads. Nonetheless, Chinese bishops gathering at Beijing in March 1989 were able to assert their respect for papal primacy and to decide to remove married bishops from official responsibilities. Unfortunately, the meeting of the Church Administrative Commission that followed in April reasserted the principle of independence so forcefully that a sinister shadow is now cast over any real authority lodged with the bishops.[13]

The Chinese government has imposed its own conditions for dialogue on Rome and has frequently reiterated them over the past ten years: a breach of relations with Taiwan, and cessation of all interference in the internal affairs of the church of China. Rome has not neglected to make a response to these demands. In May 1989 a representative of the Holy See, Bishop Jean Paul Gobel, discreetly took up residence in Hong Kong to study the situation of the church in China in relation to Rome. The role of the *chargé d'affaires* in Taiwan has been reduced to the supervision of religious affairs on Taiwan alone, and no longer extends to the Republic of China, of which the Taipei government claims *de jure* control.

As for "interference in the internal affairs of the church in China," the principal bone of contention is the ordination of underground bishops. Beijing has not yet protested the discreet "normalization" of "official" bishops by the Vatican. Rome is likewise uneasy with the proliferation of underground bishops, some of whom have been ordained in advance of Vatican approval. The current tendency in Rome is to restrict the use of special faculties to ordain by stipulating the precise conditions in which they are to be used.

Small steps have been taken on both sides, then, with widely different motivations. Beijing sees mainly the political interest of the operation — isolate Taiwan and withdraw from the underground church its *raison d'être*, and recover a certain moral credit with international opinion. Rome's interest is primarily religious — ensure the peace and unity of the church in China, dismantle the obstacles to exchanges vital to the expansion of Christian life, and work for real religious freedom.

Outlook for the Future

Article 36 of the Chinese Constitution excludes all foreign control over religious life in China. Underground Catholics thereby find themselves outside the law, and it is on these grounds that they are harassed, and not for their religious beliefs. From their viewpoint, however, they are persecuted for their religious faith in the authority of the pope, the head of the universal church. This conflict raises the delicate question of religion and politics. The experience of church-state relations in Western history does not necessarily furnish solutions applicable in China. It would be well to delve deeper into the question of how a Christian minority can live and express itself in the Chinese cultural context.

A second great question bears on the life of the church itself, and the witness of charity and unity it is called to bear in the Chinese world. Can current rifts be healed?

Much of the semi-underground lives in hope of an accord between Rome and the Chinese government. A few pockets of intransigent underground Christians, it is true, may survive, even after an accord with Rome, but it is certainly not by force that they will be led to rejoin the larger church. The *aggiornamento* of the church in China can only occur on the basis of great charity, lived in mutual trust and openness. The spiritual resources needed in order to surmount current difficulties are already present in the Catholics of China—patriotic or underground—through their great devotion to Mary, Mother of the Church and Queen of China.

Notes

1. Declaration of a spokesperson of the Three-Self Movement and the Christian Council of China, as reported in the newsletter *China Talk*, vol. 14, nos. 5/6 (November 1989), published by the China Liaison Office of the United Methodist Church, 2 Man Wan Road, C-17, Kowloon, Hong Kong.

2. Ibid., p. 5.

3. See text in Chapter 7.—Eds.

4. See Chapter 8 for the text of the "Thirteen Points."

5. See Chapter 7 for the English translation: "My Vision of the Patriotic Association," that appeared in *Zhonglian* 17 (July 1989).

6. Text in English and Chinese in *Guide to the Catholic Church in China 1989*, published by China Catholic Communication, A Queen Street, Singapore 0718.

7. Private letter to a French religious brother stationed on Taiwan.

8. See *Zhonglian* 12 (December 1986).

9. Extract of a photocopied letter received in Singapore in October, shortly after the events themselves, and published in English as "The Blood of Martyrs in North China," *Zhonglian* 17 (July 1989).

10. The Union of Catholic Asian News (UCAN) reported on May 1, 1992 that Bishop Fan Xueyan of Baoding, Hebei, died in mid-April at the age of 85 but added that the exact date and place of his death were yet to be determined. Other reports suggest that he died much earlier and that the body was brought back in April 1992.—Eds.

11. The reader will get a taste of this distrust and "mudslinging" in Chapters 7 and 8.—Eds.

12. It is estimated that 20 percent of priests may have married over the last thirty years. There are also said to be seven married bishops. In the greater number of cases, these marriages have taken place in extremely unpleasant circumstances.

Many of these married clergy no longer cohabit with their spouses, and the majority of them do not celebrate the eucharist. Nevertheless they continue to assist in the work of the church. They are elderly and repentant, yet they continue to be rejected by large numbers of the faithful. The law of celibacy has been reinstated by the Patriotic Association for candidates for the priesthood.

13. See note 18 in Chapter 1 for the latest developments in September 1992.

5

The Formation of New Church Leaders

MARIA GORETTI LAU

In China, religion is deeply affected by politics. It is not surprising, therefore, that the religious policy of the country often changes with the political climate. It is a general belief that Chinese Communists are basically opposed to religion and particularly to Christianity in view of its foreign origin. Since 1949 when the government of Communist China was established in Beijing, the Catholic church[1] in China has suffered both from political pressures from the government and from inner divisions between the so called patriotic Catholics and loyalist Catholics. Although the root causes for the divisions within the Chinese church are very complicated and various factors have combined to bring about such divisions, political pressure from the Chinese government has been a key element.

During the 1950s, all foreign missionaries were expelled, and Chinese Catholics were forced to establish an independent Chinese church according to the Three-Self Principle, namely, a church that would be self-supporting, self-propagating, and self-governing. In spite of great pressure, some Catholics stood firm and refused to cooperate with the government, feeling that such cooperation implied a compromise of their Christian faith. Some chose to cooperate with the government in its policies, believing that this would serve the best pastoral interests of Chinese Catholics. As a result, since the 1950s, the Chinese church has been divided into two camps, neither group accepting the other.[2] Reconciliation has become one of the most urgent tasks as division continues to affect not only pastoral work but also the formation of new leaders for the Chinese church.

Formation of Young Seminarians

Today the Chinese church suffers from a severe shortage of bishops and priests. Before 1950 there were more than five thousand priests in China,

This chapter is a shortened version of a talk given by Sister Lau in December 1990.

nearly half of whom were Chinese. After 1950, however, foreign priests were expelled, many native priests died, and the seminaries were also closed down. By 1982, it was estimated that there were only thirteen hundred Chinese priests left in China. Some were married and were not involved in priestly ministry, others had retired due to poor health or for other reasons, and still others worked in schools or in factories. Most priests still actively engaged in priestly ministry were over sixty years of age, with only a few who were between fifty and sixty years old. This meant that the pastoral care of more than three million Catholics scattered throughout China was provided by a small number of elderly priests. Obviously, the training of new church leaders is a most urgent priority.

Since 1982 the Chinese church has concentrated its efforts on restoring seminaries to form new candidates for priesthood. At the present time in China, there are, generally speaking, two kinds of seminaries: those officially recognized by the Chinese government, and those called clandestine or "underground" seminaries, which do not have government approval.

Formation of Seminarians in the Officially Recognized Seminaries

According to recent reports (1990), there are now about twelve officially recognized seminaries in China. The situation of these seminaries varies from place to place. For instance, the Sheshan seminary in Shanghai is, perhaps, the best organized. It now has 136 students, who come from thirteen provinces and thirty-three dioceses, and at present it is the only seminary with permission to invite professors from abroad to teach. Professors from the United States, Canada, Europe, Hong Kong, and Taiwan have all given various courses in theology and philosophy. The seminary has an excellent library of titles in English and French. However, since most of the students are not proficient in English or French, the library's foreign language section remains inaccessible to them. Unfortunately, the Chinese language section is very poor with a great need for Chinese-language textbooks in theology and philosophy.

Usually the students attend six classes a day, with half a day's classes on Saturday. Most of the seminarians are in their early twenties. There are a few older men, however, the remnants from pre-liberation days, scattered among them.

Sheshan seminary is also the first seminary in China to initiate post-Vatican II liturgical reforms. According to our knowledge, all public liturgies in the Chinese Catholic church are conducted in Latin, following the traditional Tridentine ritual.[3] Last year, the director of the Liturgical Commission of the Hong Kong diocese, Father Thomas Law, was invited to teach a course on liturgy at Sheshan. He introduced the liturgical reforms of Vatican II to the seminary. When I was in Shanghai last Easter, I attended the solemn liturgies of Holy Week at Sheshan seminary, and found no differences between the liturgical practice there and that in Hong Kong.

The seminarians prayed openly for the pope and the universal church.

However, not every seminary in China is as fortunate as Sheshan. In Guiyang, Guizhou province, twenty-nine seminarians are housed in the church compound at Guiyang. Of these seminarians, twenty-five are from the diocese of Guiyang, with the rest from Guangxi and Yunnan provinces. Apart from these, four other seminarians from the region are being trained at Sheshan seminary in Shanghai. More students want to enroll, but there are no facilities available for them at present. The twenty-nine seminarians live and study in overcrowded quarters in the church office building and sleep eight to a room. They are junior middle school graduates, unlike the seminary at Sheshan, which only admits senior middle school graduates. Seminarians in Guiyang have no library and must share a limited number of Bibles. Bibles and religious books sent to them from outside China are confiscated by regional government authorities. This also happens at the Chengdu seminary in Sichuan.

Difficulties

One can see that the future of these young seminarians now studying for the priesthood in China will be no less difficult than that of their predecessors. After they finish their priestly formation, they will be sent to work in a society that has been formed by materialistic atheism and is hostile to religion, with people who are disillusioned by the present national situation. The present society gives little thought to spiritual values at all, let alone religious values. As priests, they will, for the most part, be economically poor and socially powerless.

Also, since they come from government-recognized seminaries, they will be, in many places, objects of suspicion and rejection among many of their own Catholics. Some seminarians have revealed the painful struggle taking place in their hearts. They consider themselves victims of a cold war between the patriotic Catholics and the underground Catholics.

A foreign missionary who had visited Tianshui diocese in Gansu recently told of a young priest who had just finished his theological formation in Beijing. He was sent to Tianshui diocese where a majority of the Catholics were simple farmers. They were very hostile toward the Patriotic Association. The young priest was full of missionary zeal, wanting very much to serve the Catholics there. But when they realized that he had been educated in the Beijing seminary, they violently rejected him. They did not allow him to administer the sacraments and treated him with great hostility. Since he could not function as a priest among these Catholics, he finally returned to Beijing, hurt and frustrated. Rejected by the Catholics in Tianshui, he also incurred the displeasure of the Chinese government in Beijing because he participated in the democratic demonstrations in Beijing during May and June of 1989. Feeling downcast and depressed, he sought to leave

China. He hoped that perhaps he could best fulfill his priestly vocation abroad.

This sad story reveals the very real and very difficult situation faced by seminarians now studying at the officially recognized seminaries. The internal divisions of the Chinese Catholic church are deeply affecting the formation of the younger generation. These young priests will have to be true apostles, living a life of faith in which the Lord will be their only recompense.

Clandestine Seminaries

Little is known about these underground seminaries and their formation programs. However, from the reports of visitors to China and letters from inside China, it is known that the number of underground seminarians is much larger than originally thought. A rough estimate would put the number of underground seminarians scattered over different provinces in China at over one thousand. According to a report from Hebei, the number of new underground priests in that province is increasing rapidly. Usually, these underground seminaries follow a "master-disciple" pattern in forming new candidates, in which formation, for the most part, is not institutionalized. When circumstances allow, seminarians gather in groups to study and to share their faith and life experience. Since such gatherings are considered illegal by the government, and seminarians, if discovered, are punished, they meet only sporadically.

These underground seminarians do not have a well-planned curriculum, nor do they have textbooks of theology and philosophy. The aging priests or bishops responsible for formation transmit their faith and knowledge to the new candidates, just as Catholic parents hand down their faith to the younger generation in a family. The period of formation is not fixed and ranges from one or two to seven years. It depends entirely on the background and progress of the individual candidate, and on the concrete situation in which they live.

Difficulties

The training of new priests in these circumstances is fraught with difficulties. Underground seminarians are also objects of suspicion and rejection. They are often seen as unqualified, without adequate theological and philosophical training. After ordination, their pastoral activities are by and large limited to rural areas where the majority are underground Catholics. They are closely watched by government officials, and are always in danger of being arrested on charges of subversion. They are suspect in the eyes of the Chinese government and are rejected by the Patriotic Association.

Formation of Young Sisters

Present Situation

According to a recent report by Father John Tong on the formation of sisters in China, in 1948, there were more than seven thousand religious sisters in China and two out of three sisters were Chinese. After the Communist takeover, the foreign sisters either left voluntarily or were expelled from the country. While some of the Chinese sisters also left the country to go to such places as Hong Kong, Macau, Taiwan, or overseas, more than half remained in China.[4]

During the 1950s and 1960s, the fate of religious sisters in China was no less terrible than that of the Chinese priests and seminarians: some were sent to prison or labor camps; others married, due to difficult circumstances or pressure; still a large number of religious sisters managed to continue to live out their religious vows in private.

In the 1980s, following the reopening of seminaries, several convents were also re-established. One estimate is that there are now about forty formal and informal convents operating in China. As would be expected, the living situation and formation of young Chinese sisters varies from place to place. For instance, in Xujiahui, Shanghai, thirty-six young novices and fifty elderly sisters are now living together in one convent building. The older sisters originally belonged to different religious congregations, but young and old now form one community under the care of the diocesan bishop of Shanghai. One sister from among the older sisters acts as formator and is responsible for training the young novices. An elderly priest who was formerly the spiritual director for the seminarians at Sheshan now serves as the spiritual director of the convent at Xujiahui.

The situation of the sisters living in Guangzhou in Guangdong province is similar to that of Xujiahui in Shanghai. This convent was opened in 1987 and its fourteen novices are under the supervision of a sister who is now in her early seventies. In Xianxian, Hebei province, eighty sisters, including forty novices and thirty junior sisters, live together. Ten of the sisters are studying medicine to prepare themselves for an active role in society.

In the diocese of Guiyang, Guizhou province, two novices have been sent to the novitiate in Shanghai for training.[5] The other novices are at present training in the church compound at Guiyang. It is reported that at least thirty to forty more young women have applied to enter, but there is no room for them. At present, the community's sixteen novices are lodged in different parts of the church compound. A new novitiate is to be completed by the end of 1991, and it is hoped that more candidates will be admitted in the future. The education of these young women has not advanced beyond junior middle school and some have attended only primary school. Four novices assist at a small nursery school, directed by an older sister who is a retired teacher. While these novices earn a little toward their keep, the nursery itself is run primarily as a non-profit neighborhood service.

Vocations to the religious life are flourishing in China. The minimum requirements for admission into convent life are: first, the candidate must be an unmarried female Catholic of at least eighteen years of age; second, she must have her parents' permission and her parish priest's recommendation; and third, she must be of good character and in good health.[6]

It should be noted that, just like seminaries, there are also underground sisters' convents in China. However, little information about these is available. One can conjecture that they follow the same pattern of formation as do the underground seminaries.

Difficulties

The new convents are not without their difficulties. Many of these convents are not physically well-equipped, nor do they have well-planned programs. Almost none of them has a complete constitution and rule for religious life. In Shanghai, all the young sisters take the three traditional vows of poverty, chastity, and obedience. Traditionally, the vow of obedience is to God and their superior general, but since they have no superior general, they make their vow to the diocesan bishop. The bishop hopes that in the near future a complete constitution will be established for the local and diocesan congregation of sisters in Shanghai.

The present resources available for use in the formation of sisters are more inadequate than those for seminarians. In Suzhou, the young novices seem eager to learn, but their official director of formation is an elderly bishop who is very occupied with his own pastoral work. Classes are given to the novices only when the bishop is free. In the parish of Kunshan, a young sister tells of their desperate need for reading materials and their longing for spiritual books to nourish their religious life.

Formation of Lay Leaders

Unlike the formation of seminarians and young sisters, there seems to be no formal program initiated by the officially recognized Chinese church for training lay leaders. Some local churches might send a certain number of laypersons abroad for theological studies or for learning languages. For instance, one young woman completed three years of theological studies at Notre Dame University and is now teaching theology at the Sheshan seminary. A second woman studied language in Germany and is now teaching in Shanghai. Quite a number of lay Catholics serve in organizations of the officially opened churches, especially in the Chinese Catholic Church

Administrative Commission. The Administrative Commission and the Chinese Bishops' Conference are considered the "two hands" of the officially recognized Catholic church. Obviously, some lay leaders serving in these ecclesiastical structures are very active and are sometimes entrusted with responsibilities for important ecclesiastical affairs. However, they have not been trained in any well-planned program of spiritual renewal or pastoral studies, nor have they been given any real instruction in church administration. Their service to the church is either stimulated by personal enthusiasm or by a deep sense of commitment. It is also possible that some lay leaders are "encouraged" or even "recruited" by the Religious Affairs Bureau to work for the church in China through ecclesiastical structures.

Little information is available about the formation of lay leaders in the Chinese underground church. Because of the severe shortage of priests in rural areas, many lay Catholics play important roles in assisting the local churches to grow, particularly in those churches situated in very poor and economically underdeveloped areas. Catholic parents teach catechism to their children at home. Some lay leaders, both men and women, take initiatives to organize catechetical classes for children and adults in some Catholic villages. These lay leaders also help to conduct regular prayer meetings, visit the sick, fulfill other pastoral duties, and assist in the rebuilding of churches. In some Catholic villages in rural south China, lay Catholic leaders play a great role in the growth of the church and the spreading of the gospel, especially in places where priests are not available. In a word, both in the government-recognized and the underground churches, there are no well-developed programs for training lay Catholic leaders. The lay leadership is for the most part spontaneous, coming from a deep sense of commitment to the faith.

Theological Reflection

The present difficulties in forming new church leaders in China are a challenge to the larger question of the universal mission of the church and the role each local church must play in this mission.

As the *Dogmatic Constitution on the Church* of Vatican II indicates, the universal church is a sibling communion of local churches, with every local church in the world sharing in the missionary responsibility of the whole church. In the case of the Chinese church, missionaries are no longer allowed to preach the gospel as in former times. The work of evangelization relies now completely upon local church leaders. In the particular context of the existing political system of China, the Chinese church must present itself to the government as an autonomous local church that runs its own ecclesiastical affairs without any "foreign interference." The present constitution of China lays down two conditions for establishing relations with foreign churches: "mutual respect" and "equality."

Since 1979 the Chinese church has put much stress on the condition of "equality" in regard to its relations with foreign churches. By "equality," the Chinese church means that all churches are of equal status. The desire of the Chinese Catholic church for equal footing with foreign Catholic churches is prompted by two factors. First, politically, because China considers that it has regained its national sovereignty and independence in the international community, the Chinese government demands that all of its subordinate institutions, including religious bodies, must also lay claim to independence from any foreign control. Second, historically, the insistence on ecclesial equality can be seen as a reaction of the Chinese church against its past history of foreign missionary domination.

As for the second condition, the Chinese church views "mutual respect" as "ecclesial non-interference." In other words, if relations are to be established, foreign Catholics must respect the sovereignty of the Chinese church, and must not interfere in its "internal affairs."

Since the 1950s the Chinese government has insisted that the Catholic church in China never again become a colonial church dominated by foreign interests. With very limited resources and personnel, the Catholic church in China tries to carry out its mission of evangelization to the Chinese people. However, the internal conflicts and divisions of the Chinese church have not only weakened the strength of its witness to the gospel, but have also affected the formation of church leaders.

For nearly three decades now the Chinese church has been isolated from the universal Church. The Chinese church has not experienced recent changes in the theological understanding of the mission of the church. In the past, "mission" was a unilateral rather than a bilateral action. It was understood as a giving process, wherein the affluent and superior churches gave of their abundance to the poorer and inferior ones. Since Vatican II, the notion of mission has undergone a remarkable transformation. It has changed from a unilateral giving action to a process of mutual exchange. Now missionaries understand themselves as equal partners who serve local churches by invitation. They come not only to share their faith with the local people but also, at the same time, to learn from them, so that their experience of the faith may be enriched. It seems that the missionary enterprise which the Chinese church rejects is not the new but the old unilateral concept of mission. It seems less probable that the Chinese church would find objectionable the new bilateral concept of mission — a form of mission that respects the dignity and legitimate autonomy of the local church by treating it as an equal partner.

While the Chinese church has repeatedly declined help from outside in its determination to solve its own problems by itself, nevertheless, reconciliation with Rome and the restoration of relations with the universal Church would certainly benefit from the assistance of other local churches within the Catholic communion.

The problem of the relationship between the Chinese church and the

Holy See, though religious in nature, has from the beginning been so inter-woven with political elements that it is now very difficult to unravel the political from the religious dimension. Between 1949 and 1988, the relationship between the Chinese church and the Holy See has passed through four periods of change: the period from 1949 to 1978 was characterized by conflict; the second period, from 1979 to 1981, offered hope for dialogue and possible reconciliation; the third period, from 1981 to 1984, saw renewed confrontation when Rome appointed Bishop Dominic Tang (Deng Yiming) as archbishop of Guangdong; and the fourth period, extending from 1984 to 1988, saw some improvement in the relationship between the Chinese church and Rome.[7]

In 1985, Rome's relationship with the Chinese church, as well as with China, was improved through the assistance of other local churches that functioned as mediators and bridge-builders. Generally speaking, from 1985 to 1988, the Chinese church's attitude toward Rome softened, through the help of some foreign Catholics and Chinese Catholics outside China who worked as mediators between the two parties. They attempted to search for a possible and feasible way of promoting a face-to-face dialogue between the Chinese church and Rome in the future. A first and most important step toward this goal, in their opinion, was to foster friendly relations between the Chinese church and other local churches in the world. Hopefully, through the union with other sister churches that maintained communion with the Holy See, the Chinese church might ultimately be reunited with Rome.

Other local churches can play a very important role in the reconciliation of the Chinese church with the universal Church, and the reunion of the Catholics within the Chinese church as well. This is a mission of "bridge-building" that requires patience, understanding, and respect on the part of the bridge-builders. To become bridge-builders is a difficult task. It demands that the churches involved in this mission constantly transform themselves in conformity with the gospel ideal of reconciliation. Only those churches and Christians who are working hard for unity and reconciliation within themselves can be real and effective instruments for bridging the gap between these conflicting groups of Catholics in China. Therefore, the new mission of bridge-building can be seen as both a challenge and a call for a constant renewal of missionary churches in the gospel of peace and reconciliation.

Practical Suggestions

Practically speaking, what contribution can other local churches, particularly the Asian churches, make to the church in China? Three areas, in particular, seem appropriate.

First, overseas churches must try to keep themselves informed as much as possible about the complexity of the situation in China and what realistic options the Chinese church might take.

Second, it is important to refrain from any actions that might cause a deepening of the internal division within the Chinese church. This demands a rather sophisticated and informed understanding of the political situation as well as an understanding of to what degree freedom of religious practice is allowed and what are the limitations within which outsiders can help.

Third, material assistance as well as spiritual support is needed in the work of forming new church leaders in the Chinese church, with a particular need for written materials.

Finally, Christians around the world share the belief that God is the God of history, always present to all faithful and to the Chinese church. It is in this spirit that the Chinese church continues to face the future with faith and hope.

Notes

1. When I speak of "the Chinese church," I do not include those Catholics who have always remained loyal to the pope and are sometimes referred to as "loyalist" or members of the "underground" church. These Chinese Catholics have never severed their links with the Holy See, though they cannot express this openly in China. I use the term "Chinese church" in this paper to include Catholics who are affiliated with the Chinese Catholic Patriotic Association as well as those who are affiliated neither with the CCPA nor with the underground church.

2. For a more nuanced analysis see in particular Chapters 2 and 4. — Eds.

3. Mass in Chinese is now more and more prevalent. At its last national meeting held in Beijing in September 1992, the Chinese Catholic Bishops' Conference decided to introduce the Chinese language for liturgical use in all dioceses. — Eds.

4. A personal report by John Tong, director of the Holy Spirit Study Centre, Hong Kong.

5. A personal report of a European who visited China in 1990.

6. See John Tong's report on sisters' formation.

7. These periods have been reviewed in depth in Chapter 1. — Eds.

6

A Schismatic Church? —
A Canonical Evaluation

GEOFFREY KING

In May 1988, I had an opportunity to meet with officials of China's Bureau of Religious Affairs in Beijing. In the course of the meeting I raised the issue of the freedom of Chinese Catholics to communicate with the Holy See and to give expression to their acceptance of the Roman primacy. The officials responded by citing two major grievances against the "Vatican"[1] — that it continues to maintain diplomatic recognition of the Taiwan government, and that it has excommunicated patriotic Chinese Catholics. When Cardinal Sin was in China in November 1987, he mentioned in the course of a conversation with some bishops the word "communion." One of them immediately reacted — "I was excommunicated by Pius XII."

The presumption on the part of many outside China is that there has been a breach of communion between the Chinese Catholic church and the rest of the Catholic church. And inside China some members of the "underground" denounce the "patriotics" as excommunicated and refuse to share sacraments with them. At least until June 1988, when French Archbishop Lefebvre ordained bishops without approval from the Holy See, one could have been excused for thinking of Book VI *De Sanctionibus in Ecclesia* as one of the less pastorally relevant parts of the Code of Canon Law. In China, however, the issue of excommunication is a live one.

Illicit Ordination of Bishops

The bishop speaking to Cardinal Sin was probably thinking of the 1958 encyclical of Pius XII *Ad Apostolorum Principis*[2] and perhaps of a statement

This essay, which appeared in *The Jurist* 49 (1989): 69-94, is reprinted with permission.

of the Congregation of the Propagation of the Faith published in *L'Osservatore Romano* on April 26 of the same year.[3] The content of these documents is worth careful examination.

In his encyclical Pius XII states categorically that no one can lawfully confer episcopal consecration unless he has received the mandate of the Apostolic See. He goes on:

> Consequently, if consecration of this kind is being done contrary to all right and law, and by this crime the unity of the Church is being seriously attacked, an excommunication reserved *specialissimo modo* to the Apostolic See has been established which is automatically incurred by the consecrator and by anyone who has received consecration irresponsibly conferred.[4]

The pope makes reference to a decree of the Holy Office of April 9, 1951, which states,

> A bishop of any rite or dignity whatever who confers episcopal consecration on a cleric who has not been nominated by the Holy See, or expressly confirmed by the same, and also the person who received such consecration, even if impelled by grave fear, are subject *ipso facto* to excommunication reserved *specialissimo modo* to the Holy See.[5]

It will be noticed that the pope does not declare that any individual has incurred this excommunication. A similar restraint is exercised in the Propaganda Fide statement of April 26. The statement mentions two bishops, Dong and Yuan, who were ordained in Hankou cathedral on April 13, 1958, and goes on to recall that the right to appoint bishops in the Roman church, according to canon law, is reserved to the Roman pontiff. It notes that a telegram was received in Rome on March 24 informing the Holy See that at a meeting of clergy on March 18 Father Bernardine Dong Guangqing had been elected bishop of Hankou. A second telegram two days later announced the election of Father Mark Yuan Wenhua as bishop of Wuchang. The statement goes on to say that Propaganda Fide sent replies by telegram to the effect that the elections were void because bishops must be freely appointed by the Roman pontiff. The telegram called to the attention of the two priests the decree of the Holy Office of 1951, and urged them not to consent to ordination.

Thus, neither the pope nor the congregation declared any individual to have incurred excommunication, nor has any subsequent pope done so. The only explicit decree of excommunication issued to a Chinese prelate was addressed to Li Weiguang. He was ordained as a bishop without Roman approval, but this was *after* his excommunication. He had been excommunicated in February 1952, because of his support for the expulsion of the papal internuncio, Antonio Riberi, and this order was made public in 1955.[6]

What led to these illicit ordinations? By the mid-1950s many Chinese dioceses were without a bishop. Almost all foreign bishops and other foreign ordinaries had been expelled from the country. From 1950 to 1955, Rome appointed twenty-two Chinese bishops. But from about 1955 many Chinese ordinaries were imprisoned. Many dioceses elected vicars capitular or diocesan administrators, but by early 1958, 120 out of 145 dioceses (or prefectures apostolic) had no functioning diocesan bishop (or prefect apostolic).

During 1957 more than 200 "branches" of the Catholic Patriotic Association were set up in various parts of China. A general assembly of the association took place in Beijing from July 15 to August 2, 1957. It was attended by 241 "representatives," including 10 bishops and 200 priests. In the course of the assembly it was proposed that the church in China select and ordain bishops on its own initiative. The proposal was rejected. Moreover, some bishops, who gathered in a special session to discuss the matter, expressed their unwillingness to ordain if asked to do so. The assembly resolved to organize a pilgrimage group to Rome in order to inform the Holy See about the situation in China. However this was "discouraged" by the government and so was doomed to failure. Later, however, a compromise proposal was accepted: the Chinese hierarchy would elect bishops and present the names to Rome for approval. There was some confidence that the names would be acceptable to both Rome and the Chinese government.[7]

An exchange of telegrams with Propaganda Fide followed. Some evidence, at least, suggests that the Roman reaction took most Chinese Catholics by surprise.[8]

The Roman stance is easy enough to understand. It is, and was, clear that the Chinese government was trying to exercise a large measure of control over the church. Catholics had suffered imprisonment for resisting this control. Hence, Pius XII saw the independent selection of bishops by the Chinese as an attempt to put the church under the control of men who would simply carry out government policy. He added that because he was prevented from communicating with the church in China, he was unable to obtain sufficient information about candidates for him to make proper episcopal appointments.[9] The pope also could very reasonably point out that the shortage of bishops was due in large part to the fact that legitimate and capable bishops had been imprisoned or expelled.[10] Moreover, the telegrams asking for confirmation of those elected could easily be seen as presenting Rome with a *fait accompli*.[11]

Such a reading of the situation by the Roman authorities was rendered almost inevitable by the prevailing atmosphere of cold war and anti-communism, and by the highly centralized model of church authority taken for granted in Rome at the time. In his encyclical, for instance, Pius XII stated that those ordained without authorization "enjoy no powers of teaching or of jurisdiction since jurisdiction passes to bishops only through the Roman pontiff,"[12] a theory of the source of episcopal jurisdiction that was to be rejected by Vatican II.[13]

The Vatican attitude is understandable, but the published documents are utterly intransigent. There is no hint of conciliation, no opening for compromise, no sympathy for Chinese Catholics or the dilemma which they faced. The idea that there could be conflict between being Catholic and being patriotic was dismissed—a position which was theoretically unassailable but which took little account of the confused reality of China.[14]

The distinction that some Chinese Catholics had attempted to make between obedience to the pope in matters of faith and morals, on the one hand, and breaking off political and economic relations with the Vatican, on the other, is seen as an attempt to confine the teaching authority of the church within a narrow scope, implying that Catholics may ignore the directives and teachings of the Holy See on social and economic matters.[15] Again the papal position makes perfect sense *sub specie aeternitatis*—the gospel cannot be "privatized"; it has something to say about social relationships and social justice. No doubt, too, some Chinese Catholics under government pressure tended to stretch the meaning of the "political and economic relations with the Vatican." But all this is to focus on the weaknesses of the Chinese position rather than to attempt a sympathetic understanding of a distinction that the Catholics were trying to make, precisely in an attempt to remain both Chinese and Catholic.

Although the Vatican attitude may be understandable, so is that of the Chinese Catholics who supported the independent ordinations. With the great majority of dioceses vacant (for whatever reason) there was an urgent need to ordain new bishops. In a very difficult situation they did try to find ways of holding on to obedience to the pope in matters of faith and morals and to acceptance of the pope's right to appoint bishops. The distinctions drawn and the telegrams sent are evidence of this. The motives of Chinese Catholics may have been mixed and their methods may have lacked diplomatic finesse, but that does not mean that they were engaging in mere window-dressing. When these (admittedly imperfect) attempts were rejected, it is not surprising that some Chinese Catholics felt that Rome had no understanding of their situation. The language of a statement such as the following may be too self-righteous and too much influenced by Communist jargon, but the judgment it makes is far from groundless:

> . . . we see clearly that the society in which the Holy See is situated and our society are not the same, and that Rome evidently has no means of comprehending our way of thinking and our feelings, and that it is not possible for them to understand our just course of action. The fact is that we cannot fail to recognize that the Holy See has differences with us in its political stance, that is, it takes a reactionary position in its treatment of the Church of the new China. . . . The Holy See does not understand Chinese society; its political position

limits its understanding; and the natural result is its opposition to our legitimate action. . . .[16]

This attempt at a preliminary evaluation of the position taken up in 1958 will, I hope, facilitate an analysis of the present state of affairs. Important new elements have been introduced into that state of affairs by the Code of Canon Law of 1983. In the first place, the code makes a crucial distinction between *latae sententiae* censures which have been *declared* and those which have not. Canon 1335 provides as follows: if a *latae sententiae* censure has not been declared, the prohibition of the celebration of sacraments and sacramentals and of the exercise of the power of governance is suspended whenever one of the faithful requests a sacrament or sacramental or an act of the power of governance. Moreover, for any just reason it is lawful to make such a request. For practical purposes, then, an undeclared *latae sententiae* censure has minimal public effect. And we have seen that no Chinese bishop has been declared excommunicated on the grounds of illicit ordination. Where the only bishop who can publicly exercise the episcopal office in a given diocese is one who has been ordained without Roman authorization, there is clearly a "just reason" for Catholics to approach him for the sacraments and for acts of governance.

In a limited sense, this solves the practical problems. But the more fundamental question, "Has the alleged excommunication been incurred?" remains important. It is important to the individual concerned; it is important for "underground" Catholics, few of whom understand the nuances of declared and undeclared censures, and it is important for the relations between China and the Holy See.

A second change introduced by the 1983 code is a modification of the terms of the Holy Office decree of 1951. The decree had taken the unusual step of declaring that the presence of grave fear (*metus gravis*) did not excuse from the penalty.[17] This clause is omitted by canon 1382 of the code.[18] Thus, in accord with the ordinary discipline embodied in canons 1323 and 1324, the presence of grave fear is now sufficient to excuse from the censure of canon 1382. Where does this leave those bishops who were illicitly ordained before November 27, 1983, the date on which the revised code took effect? It would seem that the new, less stringent, discipline applies also to them, since canon 1313 provides that if after the commission of a delict the law is changed, the more favorable law is to be applied. The 1917 code excluded censures from this provision, an exclusion omitted by the revised code.

Mention of "excises" reminds us that a *latae sententiae* censure is "automatic" only in a qualified sense. The present code, like its predecessor, lays down the principle that no one can be punished for the commission of an external violation of a law or precept unless it is gravely imputable by reason of malice or of culpability (c. 1321). Where there has been an external violation, imputability is presumed. But presumptions can be overcome by contrary evidence.

The kind of evidence needed to overcome the presumption of imputability was discussed in two recent articles in *Studia Canonica*. Elizabeth McDonough pointed out a change introduced in the 1983 code. The earlier code required *proof* to the contrary. The new text is *nisi aliud appareat*.[19] She suggests that one can judge the magnitude of this change by imagining the effect that a similar change in canon 1060 (on the *favor iuris* with respect to marriage) would have on tribunal practice. But a question remains. *Nisi aliud appareat* demands less than proof, but how much less? There is a difference in English translation, after all, between "unless there is an appearance of its being otherwise" and "unless its being otherwise is apparent."

In his more extensive treatment of this question, Michael Hughes argues that if a defendant raises the possibility that his or her external violation of the law is not imputable (and produces some reason to back the claim), then the onus is on the prosecutor or judge to rebut the possibility. Thus, argues Hughes, canon 1321 is compatible with the common law presumption of innocence.[20]

This is a more liberal view than that espoused by Velasio de Paolis, who demands that the case for non-imputability be probable.[21] I find Hughes' argument persuasive, but the case which I will present on behalf of the Chinese bishops seems to me to meet even the more stringent requirements of de Paolis.

The canons following 1321 indicate various ways in which imputability can be diminished or even removed entirely. Particularly relevant is canon 1324, which in §1 lists, in effect, a number of causes which excuse from *latae sententiae* penalties.

A number of these "excusing causes" appear to be applicable to the Chinese situation. The most apparently relevant are those in 1324, §1, 5°: constraint by grave fear (even relatively grave) or necessity or *grave incommodum*. These now apply even where the offense is intrinsically evil or tends to cause harm to souls. Less directly applicable, but still relevant by a kind of analogy (a point to which I will return), are factors listed in 2° and 3°: lack of use of reason because of drunkenness or similar mental disturbance, and grave heat of passion (even if it does not totally impede mental deliberation and voluntary consent).

Grave fear. It is probably simplistic to think of the ordinations in the late 1950s taking place under some immediate and direct threat from government authorities. Indeed, some of those involved in the ordinations showed themselves over the years able to resist threats of violence. But it does seem to be the case that at least many of the ordinations took place in situations of fear and great pressure. In part the pressure was "internal" — that which came from wishing to remain loyal both to China and to the Catholic church. There was also great external pressure to "declare" one's loyalty to one's country. And all this was in a context of fear, of accusation, and sometimes of humiliation and imprisonment. Many confreres of these priests had been expelled or imprisoned. It was, moreover, the time of the Anti-Rightist campaign, a fierce reversal of the comparatively "liberal" policies of the brief Hundred Flowers period.

Necessity and grave incommodum. Even more to the point are the categories of necessity and *grave incommodum.* We have seen that by 1958 there was a drastic shortage of active bishops in China. There was real and justified concern for the survival of the church. After attempts at compromise had failed, some in China could reasonably judge that the only way to obtain bishops was to go ahead and ordain them without permission.

To understand this judgment it is necessary to put it in broader context. The broadest context is that of the self-understanding of the Chinese people. For over a century a nation which was the oldest continuing civilization on earth, which traditionally had seen itself as *Zhongguo,* the Central Kingdom, had been humiliated by the imperialist powers, had been conscious of its economic "underdevelopment," had suffered from political anarchy and from invasion by Japan. Vast numbers of Chinese (including many who had serious doubts about communism) saw the revolution of 1949 as enabling China once again to "hold up its head" among the nations. Undoubtedly some Chinese Catholics shared these feelings, and they also saw the Holy See and foreign missionaries as being in some way connected with the imperialism that had humiliated China, and as acting unreasonably in their total opposition to an (admittedly far from perfect) Chinese Communist party.[22]

Some of these feelings may appear to the outsider as more "justified" than others, but all of them were capable of shaping attitudes. One cannot, for instance, deny the fact that Christian missionaries had been able to reenter China in the nineteenth century on the coattails of imperialism, through the unequal treaties imposed on China at the end of the Opium Wars.[23] The treaties had also exempted foreigners in China from ordinary Chinese jurisdiction and set up a separate judicial system for them. Missionaries often took advantage of this (often for good motives), even demanding for Chinese Christians the "protection" of foreign consuls and courts. Christian hospitals, orphanages, and other forms of social service made great contributions to China, but they remained part of a Christian sub-culture. Moreover, it is easy for even the best desire to help others to be tinged with paternalism, and it is even easier for it to be perceived as paternalistic. There was often tension and even enmity between the foreign missionaries and native Chinese priests (of course, there were also many deep friendships formed).[24] Indigenization, let alone inculturation, of the church had been slow. Even though the prohibition of the "Chinese rites" had been revoked in 1939, two centuries of prohibition still rankled. That such grievances were not simply the product of a Chinese chauvinism is clear from the fact that one of the most vocal, and most influential, critics of the slow pace of indigenization was the papal legate, Celso Costantini.[25] A Chinese hierarchy had been established only in 1946. The fact that the record in China was no worse than in most colonial and immediately-post-colonial societies did not necessarily make Chinese Catholics, especially some priests and intellectuals, any happier with their situation.

Some recent comments of a Chinese Jesuit living in Taiwan are not necessarily representative but they are not to be lightly dismissed. He writes that Chinese Catholics were for a long time treated as second-class believers, incapable of governing themselves. Consequently, even today many Jesuits remain, in the eyes of many Chinese intellectuals especially, descendants of those who humiliated their country.[26]

In another way, too, the Catholic church could easily be identified with an antipatriotic stance. Many Catholic leaders had supported the Kuomintang, the Nationalist party. Before 1949 this could be seen as a progressive and nationalist position. After 1949 it was the opposite.[27] And, of course, it was a time when anti-Communist feeling in the Catholic world at large was at its height and when anti-Communist pronouncements were frequent in church teaching. From the Chinese perspective, the Korean War reinforced the perception of Western countries as the enemy and of the Vatican as aligned with that enemy.

These feelings were further fuelled by the activities of the internuncio, Antonio Riberi, immediately after the Chinese revolution. His actions and motives have been the subject of much dispute, and much is likely to remain obscure until the relevant Vatican archives are opened to scholars.[28] But it is clear that he took an uncompromising stand against Catholics cooperating with the government. His opposition to the Three-Self Movement among Catholics was absolute. He referred to it as a "schismatic" movement.[29] He threatened with excommunication any Catholic who supported his expulsion from China.[30]

What I have just presented is only one side of a complex picture. Only in passing have I mentioned the benefits that the church brought to China, the foreigners who worked for the building of a genuinely Chinese church, and the strong, even passionate, attachment of Chinese Catholics to the universal church and to the person of the pope. No doubt some of the negative feelings I have listed were the result of misunderstanding or partial understanding. But I am trying here to understand the mentality of significant numbers of Chinese Catholics in the 1950s, not to present a full and "objective" picture of the role of Rome and the missionaries.

From all this it seems to me very likely that many Chinese Catholics had conflicting thoughts and feelings about relations with the Holy See. In the event, some remained uncompromisingly loyal to Rome and suffered greatly as a result. Others adopted various degrees of compromise. But it would be surprising if the former never had any doubts or hesitations, and it is wrong, surely, to see the latter merely as cravenly capitulating to government pressure. One suspects that sometimes only a razor's edge separated the one choice from the other. Why the choice went the way it did depended no doubt on all sorts of personal factors. Probably many of us, when reflecting on our own experience, realize that we can give good reasons for important choices that we make, but that there are often good reasons on the other side, that a variety of semiconscious biases and instincts are involved, and that ultimately the reason for the choice remains partly mysterious. Perhaps we will understand the Chinese situation better if we focus on the complexity of factors that people had to weigh rather than simply on the different conclusions at which they finally arrived.

Those who concluded that Rome did not understand their situation seem to have taken a variety of attitudes to the requirement of a *mandatum apostolicum* for the ordination of a bishop. Some (at most a tiny minority) saw it as reason for a complete break with Rome. Others, while not advocating a complete break, concluded that the requirement of the mandate was wrong; they became, as it were, conscientious objectors to the law.[31] Others, however, in effect exercised the virtue of *epikeia*. They did not challenge the general justice or reasonableness of the law, but saw it as inapplicable in their special circumstances.[32]

Each group saw it as necessary to go against the letter of the law. The first group arguably chose to excommunicate itself. But the second and third groups are surely "excused" from excommunication by their perception that their action was necessary (or at the very least a way of avoiding grave difficulties, *gravia incommoda*). To be excused from a *latae sententiae* penalty it is, moreover, enough that one thinks that there is present necessity or *grave incommodum*, even if one is in error (even in culpable error!) in so thinking (c. 1324, §1, 8°). It should be added that there is evidence that the decision to ordain or to be ordained was for many a decision made with misgiving and regret, but one that was seen as a painful necessity.[33]

So much for the "necessity" of the 1950s. What of more recent ordinations, especially those that have taken place since the revival of church life after 1978? The need to "replenish" the hierarchy continues to be a pressing one, especially given the age and state of health of most Chinese bishops. Obtaining Roman approval remains, if not absolutely impossible, certainly difficult in the extreme. So it can reasonably be argued that independent ordination, even if not an absolute necessity, is at least the only way of avoiding *grave incommodum*. Moreover, it is clear that some priests have consented to be ordained bishop in order to avoid having someone less suitable (and sometimes someone less loyal to Rome) ordained.[34]

There is a further aspect of the Chinese context to be considered. Catholics there (like their compatriots) have been subjected to years of propaganda, of stringent control of news and information, and in varying degrees, especially before 1978, to processes of "thought reform."[35] The combined power of these forces cannot easily be underestimated. Studies of those subjected to "thought reform," for instance, have made it clear that many who began as strongly critical of the regime or of communism emerged at least ambivalent or confused and sometimes "apparently converted."[36]

This manipulation of people's perceptions makes relevant, I believe, the categories of canon 1324, §1, 2° and 3°. 2° mentions lack of use of reason because of drunkenness or some similar mental disturbance. The influence of drugs would seem an obvious example of the latter. But "thought reform" can disturb one's judgment with equal effectiveness. It would, of course, be extremely difficult to argue that in the case of episcopal ordinations the influence was such as to deprive participants of all use of reason. A much stronger case, however, can be made for their diminished imputability because of the pressures and influences to which they were subjected. Turning to 3°, "grave heat of passion" may not in a literal sense have been present, but the circumstances may well have been such as to "impede deliberation of mind and consent of will."

The argument of the preceding paragraph may be restated as follows. Canon 1321 contains a basic principle — no penalty without grave imputability. Canon 1324 (and other canons) then lists typical ways in which imputability may be diminished or removed. But the categories of canon 1324 cannot be taken as exhaustive, or at least cannot be expected to cover such extreme situations as that of China since 1949. Imputability can be diminished in ways analogous to those listed in canon 1324. The possibilities for diminished imputability in a society as controlled as that of China are numerous indeed.

What I have tried to present is a case for the non-imputability of the external violation of the law on the part of the Chinese bishops. We cannot, of course, know the deepest motives of those involved, a point very sensitively recognized by Pope John Paul II:

The course of history, shaped by human decisions, has been such that for many years we have not been able to have contact with each other. Very little was known about you, your joys, your hopes and also your sufferings. Recently, however, from various parts of your immense land, information about you has reached me. But in those long years you have undoubtedly lived through other experiences which are still unknown, and at times you will have wondered in your consciences what was the right thing for you to do. For those who have never had such experiences it is difficult to appreciate fully such situations.[37]

Even so, the Chinese context and the statements of some of the Chinese bishops seem to me to provide not merely a possible but even a probable case for non-imputability. Hence, the burden of proof falls on anyone who would assert that the action of any particular Chinese bishop is imputable.

It is difficult to go further and state categorically that the bishops have not incurred excommunication. But that is not because of anything peculiar to China, but because of the anomalous state of the law. It mixes public and private matters: we cannot know the deepest motives of those involved, but the law makes the public status of these persons dependent precisely on their motives. The presumption of imputability is intended as a way around this difficulty, but in the Chinese case it proves inadequate. I will return to this point later.

The argument that I have put forward does not necessarily condone the actions of the bishops involved in the illicit ordinations. At most I have argued that their motives were understandable and not unreasonable. It may well be that those who resisted government pressure, who still live in a precarious "underground" situation, have chosen the better part. One may disagree with the choice made by those who agreed to ordain or be ordained with government approval. But disagreeing with someone is very different from claiming that he or she has been excommunicated.

The Allegation of Schism

Thus far I have considered the question of excommunication only in terms of the illicit ordination of bishops. But an argument might also be put for the applicability of canon 1364's excommunication of the *schismaticus*. Antonio Riberi, after all, referred to a schismatic movement, and it has been common for people outside China to speak of a "patriotic church," on the one hand, and on the other, "faithful" or "underground" church.

Schism is defined in canon 751: the refusal of submission to the Roman pontiff or of communion with the members of the church subject to him. It should be noted immediately that since we are dealing with a law imposing a penalty, these terms must be interpreted strictly, that is, narrowly (c. 18). Schism is complete withdrawal of allegiance or submission, not simply some criticism of authority.

There has been no formal declaration from the Holy See to the effect that the Chinese church is in schism. John XXIII did refer once to the illicit ordinations as having "paved the way for a deplorable schism"[38] and later said, "We have already told the world that a very painful schism is being prepared in China."[39] Both references appear to be to a potential schism rather than an actual one. Moreover, during the first session of Vatican II, a group of bishops who had lived in China presented advice to the pope on the Chinese situation. It is reported that he told them that he would not use the word "schism" again when speaking of the church in China.[40]

There are at least three grounds on which it might be alleged that schism has occurred in China—1) the establishment of the Catholic Patriotic Association is alleged to be the establishment of a national church separated from Rome; 2) Chinese bishops and others have declared that their church is "autonomous" and have denounced Roman "interference"; 3) a promise made by bishops at their ordinations is alleged to involve a rejection of papal authority.

Documents from the Catholic Patriotic Association and statements of its officials reiterate that the association is not a church, but a "bridge" between church and state. For example, in June 1957, Dong Wenlung, the administrator of the diocese of Tsinan, referred to the association as "parallel to the Catholic church . . . a separate organization . . . a political organization rather than a religious one."[41] At the July–August assembly in 1957, one speaker stated, "The Patriotic Association is not an organization of the Catholic church. It is an organization of the Catholic masses who love their country and love their religion."[42] More recently (in 1981) Shen Baozhi, chancellor of the Shanghai diocese, commented,

> The Patriotic Association is not the church. It is just an organization of Catholics banded together to show love of country. Its audience is the whole Catholic church, all the Catholics. Our aim is to encourage love of country and support of the government among all the Catholics. We also want to explain to the Catholics the government's policy on freedom of religion.[43]

Since the reorganization of church government in 1980, Chinese officials have been at pains to emphasize that doctrinal and liturgical matters are the province of the Bishops' Conference, not of the Patriotic Association.[44]

The reality is certainly more confused than these statements might lead one to believe. In some places officials of the association exercise a great deal of control over church life, but in other places the existence of the association is little more than a formality that makes possible the public celebration of the sacraments. No doubt there are some officials and even a few Catholics who would be happy to have nothing to do with Rome. But, at worst, this means that there are some schismatic individuals and a church whose freedom is severely restricted by the government, not that there is a separate church.

Again, it is alleged that statements about the "autonomy" or "independence" of the Chinese church are evidence of the "refusal of submission" (*detrectatio*) of canon 751. But clearly there is a proper sense in which a local church is autonomous. Moreover, a Chinese bishop (Jin Luxian of Shanghai) who has made some of the most widely publicized calls for autonomy has stated that he uses the term "autonomy" in the sense in which it was used at Vatican II.[45] He says, too, that he wants the church of Shanghai to be in communion with the universal church, and that, of course, he sees this as including communion with the bishop of Rome.[46] In this statement, Bishop Jin does not expressly acknowledge a Roman primacy, but he certainly does not deny it. There is no evidence here of a *detrectatio subiectionis*.

Other statements object to "Vatican interference" in the affairs of the Chinese church. Such statements are open to a variety of interpretations:

1. They may be objecting to the recent practice of "secret" ordinations of bishops and priests. There can be disagreement with this practice on

pragmatic grounds (e.g., serious lack of theological formation in those being ordained, fear of provoking a backlash from the government), which disagreement is entirely compatible with loyalty to the Holy See.

2. They may be disagreeing with current church discipline on the selection of bishops (as expressed in c. 377). Given the different ways in which bishops have been and are (legitimately) selected, such a disagreement with the discipline does not necessarily involve any rejection of church teaching on the primacy. I will discuss these different ways below.

3. The disagreement may go further and touch on part of church teaching. For example, it may stress the first part of *Lumen gentium* (27) on the ordinary and immediate authority of bishops while neglecting the second part of the same paragraph on the regulation of the exercise of this power by the supreme authority of the church. Or, the disagreement may appear to involve a rejection of primacy of jurisdiction on the part of the pope. Even in this case one needs to look carefully at what is being rejected. It may be a certain way in which jurisdiction has been exercised, or a certain sense in which jurisdiction has been understood. Scholars whose communion with Rome has never been seriously questioned have debated the latter point, asking, for instance, whether Vatican I's disjunction of "primacy of jurisdiction" and "primacy of honor" is an adequate one.[47] Moreover, in the Chinese context, one needs to allow for confusion in the mind of the author between the Holy See as a "spiritual" authority and the Vatican as an entity in the world of international diplomacy.

4. Even if a statement cannot be given one of these "benign" interpretations (and it is difficult to find statements which clearly cannot), it needs to be remembered that the author may have been acting under extreme pressure, and that there has been in China what appears to an outsider as a continuing policy of encouraging and even demanding a kind of "ritualistic criticism."

A final piece of evidence for schism comes from the ritual of episcopal ordination, in particular from one of the promises that the bishop-elect is asked to make. We do not know exactly what formula has been used in each ordination, but one commonly used text contains the following question: "Are you willing to be detached from all control of the Roman Curia, and to insist on the ecclesial principles of Independence, Autonomy, and Self-Government?"[48]

"Independence, Autonomy, and Self-Government" have already been discussed. What, however, is to be made of "detachment from all control of the Roman Curia," which looks rather like *subietionis Summo Pontifici . . . detrectatio*?

Not all the "illegitimate" bishops have taken this promise. When Jin Luxian was ordained as auxiliary bishop in Shanghai he apparently insisted that the question be omitted. There are reports of similar omissions at ordination in more remote areas.[49] Another bishop omitted the word "all" when putting the question. But even the wording quoted above is open to "non-schismatic" interpretation. The detachment that is promised is not from the pope or from the Holy See, but from the Roman Curia. This can be interpreted as an assertion of freedom from the bureaucracy of the church or from its political dimension, not from the universal church as such. It is easy enough to imagine, for instance, an American Catholic saying, "I'm perfectly loyal to the pope, but I object to the control and interference of curial officials." No one would accuse him or her of schism. (It is reported that in some ordinations the term "Vatican"—an even clearer reference to the political dimension—has been substituted for "Roman Curia.") Some bishops have even declared under oath that they gave the promise an "exclusively political" meaning. Second, it is "control" that is rejected. This can be read as rejection of ways in which authority is exercised rather than of authority as such. The points made above about the different meanings of "interference" are again relevant here. Finally, it seems that the verb "to be detached" (*baitou*) has strong political connotations.[50]

For the sake of completeness, it should be added that another, more "damaging" form of the promise has been reported: "to break off all relationships with imperialism and any control by the pope of Rome." Even in this case, it is "control" that is rejected, not authority. More importantly, this sentence appears only in a handwritten version, and even the editor who published it has reservations about its authenticity.[51]

There are undoubtedly some deep divisions within the Chinese Catholic church, but there does not appear to be any conclusive evidence of schism in the proper sense of canon 751. Hence, there is no conclusive evidence that the excommunication of canon 1364 has been incurred in China.

Given that there is some popular perception that a schism has occurred in China, there is something to be said for a public acknowledgment by the Holy See that no schism exists. This might also help avoid further deepening of divisions within China, because at present ill-founded accusations of schism are sometimes thrown around by some "underground" Catholics. On the other hand, it would be very difficult for the Holy See to declare that the alleged excommunication on the grounds of illicit ordination has not been incurred. For in this case there has been an "external violation." How can a public authority state that excommunication has been "excused from" by subjective factors? But the problem here is not with the Chinese Catholics but with the law, which mixes in problematic ways the internal and external fora.

The Adequacy of the Law on Excommunication

Thus, the Chinese situation raises not only questions of pressing pastoral urgency, but questions concerning canonical theory and the adequacy of the present law. In particular, does not the Chinese example call into question the whole notion of the penalty *latae sententiae*? What is the sense of an "automatic" penalty, if its being "automatically" incurred is dependent on subjective factors, especially given the complexity of human motivation and decision-making? During the consultation process that led to the promulgation of the present code, many persons made this or similar points. Some cited the principles endorsed by the 1967 Synod of Bishops governing the revision of the code. Thus, these commentators wanted to retain only *ferendae sententiae* penalties.[52] The text that emerged is a compromise. It retains the *latae sententiae*, but leaves them publicly ineffective until they have been "declared." An undeclared *latae sententiae* penalty remains for practical purposes in the forum of conscience. For instance, it is understood to affect the conscience of an excommunicated cleric but still allows him to celebrate the sacraments publicly and to exercise the power of governance. Given the legislation requiring imputability as a condition for incurring the penalty, this forum seems a proper place: a confessor may well be the right person to help sort out motivation and imputability. In some cases, this—the code's "compromise solution"—may work well enough. But it encounters major difficulty when the person allegedly excommunicated is a public figure, especially one holding an important ecclesiastical office. This is the case *a fortiori* when we are dealing with a significant portion of a country's hierarchy. Does it make sense to leave the issue of their communion with the rest of the church dependent on factors that are able to be judged at most by themselves and a confessor and perhaps, indeed, only by God?

The penalty *latae sententiae*, when it is declared, becomes effectively *ferendae sententiae*. Would it not be better, then, to have only the one category, that of *ferendae sententiae*? The "undeclared *latae sententiae*" could be left as what it effectively already is, a matter of conscience. Why complicate matters by calling it an excommunication?

Perhaps, however, the problem goes deeper still and touches on the very meaning of excommunication. It is possible, for instance, to "resolve" our earlier difficulty by arguing that excommunication is not primarily concerned with the question of one's being in full communion with the church. De Paolis has recently proposed a distinction between excommunication as a primarily juridical category, on the one hand, and not-being-in-full-communion (a theological category) on the other.[53] Such a distinction is consistent with a view of communion as admitting of degrees rather than as an "all-or-nothing" category.

In a somewhat similar vein, Libero Gerosa has pointed to an ambivalence in the code.[54] The code's *de facto* treatment of *latae sententiae* penalties as the norm[55] suggests a view of excommunication as declaring the fact of a breach of communion. Such a view seems to have been endorsed by the present pope in his first address to the Rota in 1979.[56] On the other hand, many of the code's detailed provisions imply a view of excommunication as punishment. The first view reflects a theology of communion, the second the notion of the church as a perfect society with its *ius publicum ecclesiasticum*. Hence, the church's whole penal discipline rests on uncertain foundations.

Toward Reconciliation

Thus far my arguments have been apparently negative, arguing against the alleged excommunication of parts of the church in China, questioning the adequacy of the discipline of excommunication. Removal of the allegation of excommunication would, however, be an immensely positive step on the road to reconciliation. For there has been some breach of communion between China and the universal church and breaches of communion among groups of Chinese Catholics. It is not a total breach, not a schism, but divisions need to be healed. What further steps need to be taken on the road to that reconciliation?

It is not possible here to deal with all of the steps. In particular, the question of diplomatic relations requires quite separate treatment. Central, however, to any reconciliation is agreement on a model of communion and of the Roman primacy within that communion. A more specifically canonical issue involved in such a model is the method of selection of bishops.

With regard to the understanding of communion and of the Roman primacy, John Paul II made an important overture in a 1982 letter calling for prayers for China.[57] (It is a sign of the difficulty of achieving reconciliation that this positive step was given an unjustifiably negative interpretation by some in China.) The pope speaks of "the tie with Peter's See and with its apostolic ministry" as "the indispensable condition for participating in the union of the large Catholic family." Extremely significant, however, is the way in which he describes that union and his own place within it. It is a union of catholicity that is characterized as a receiving of the "abilities, resources and customs" of different peoples. "In virtue of this catholicity each part contributes its own gifts to other parts and to the whole Church, so that the whole and each of the parts are strengthened by the common sharing of all things. . . ." Difference can mean not division but enriched unity. As to the primacy, the pope makes no reference to papal primacy but each time to that of the "Chair of Peter" or the "Church of Rome."[58] Nor is the primacy expressed in terms of jurisdiction. Its task is (in the famous, if notoriously unclear, phrase of Ignatius of Antioch) that of "presiding in charity," or again "to unite brothers in truth and love," or of protecting "legitimate variety while at the same time taking care that these differences do not hinder unity, but rather contribute to it."

Such language is in a different ecclesiological world from that of Pius XII's three encyclicals on China, which refer to the primacy as one of jurisdiction, and to the jurisdiction of bishops as "flowing" to them not directly but "through the Successor of St. Peter."[59] The picture of the primacy presented by John Paul II is very similar to that which has found favor in dialogues between the Roman Catholic church and the Orthodox, Lutheran and Anglican churches. Of course, many details need to be filled in, and some Roman practice is not easily reconciled with the picture. Even so, the pope has offered a way forward.

One of the details needing further refinement concerns the method of selection of bishops. The code's norm of free nomination by the Roman pontiff (c. 377) is an ideal that will not be realized in China in any foreseeable future.

It is well-known, of course, that the code's norm is of recent vintage.[60] In the early centuries of the church, election by clergy and the people of the diocese was the usual practice. Intervention by the pope did not become common until the fourteenth century and did not become the legal norm until the code of 1917. Thus, there is abundance of precedent for selection of bishops by the local church. One must, however, distinguish local selection from state interference in selection. The "Gregorian" reformers of the eleventh century pressed for election by clergy and people in order to counter the predominant influence of emperors and princes. In modern Europe the move from local to papal nomination was in part inspired by desire to escape from the control of secular rulers.

In China such secular control is precisely the problem. Local selection of bishops means in fact selection influenced (in varying degrees) by government officials. But the church has a long history of accommodating its ideals in this matter to inescapable political realities. Even today, many secular governments are accorded (through a variety of concordats and *modi vivendi*) some say in episcopal selection.[61] The prince of Monaco proposes three names to Rome; the French president nominates the bishops of Strasbourg and Metz (although this is a mere formality). Much less of a formality is the system of "pre-notification" in effect in at least twelve countries. Rome consults the governments of these countries before making an appointment. Only in the case of Venezuela does the government have a power of veto, but in the other cases any objection raised by the government is taken very seriously in Rome.

There is no doubt that any such *modus vivendi* that the Chinese government would find acceptable would leave the Holy See much less freedom than it would consider desirable. But it need not lead to the appointment of bishops who would be mere puppets of the government. At present, many of the Chinese bishops are acceptable to both the Holy See and the government. Would not some compromise (not capitulation) be a fair price to pay for greater freedom for Chinese Catholics who are, at present, part of the underground, and for removing one obstacle to the healing of divisions among Chinese Catholics?

It may well be that this "internal" reconciliation will be the most difficult to achieve. Within the Chinese church there are deep divisions, often involving emotions born of years of suffering. Some evidence suggests that the divisions have become more bitter in recent years. Any process of healing of wounds and divisions can be undertaken only by the Chinese people themselves. But some "external" reconciliation between Rome and China is probably a precondition for such healing.[62] That there are obstacles to such a reconciliation is all too obvious, but my argument here is that they are obstacles in the area of human relations rather than obstacles of theological or canonical principle.

Notes

1. It is not without significance that, whereas I was careful to talk about union with the pope or the Holy See, the officials consistently referred to the Vatican. The perception of the Vatican as a state and the pope as its head appears very frequently to influence the judgments of Chinese officials on matters of ecclesiology.

2. *Ad Apostolorum Principis*, June 29, 1958: *AAS* 50 (1958) 601-614. English translation in *Papal Documents Related to the New China, 1937–1984*, ed. Elmer Wurth (Hong Kong: Holy Spirit Study Centre, 1985), pp. 51–60.

3. A summary is given by Wurth, p. 48.

4. Ibid., p. 58.

5. *AAS* 43 (1951) 217–218.

6. *AAS* 47 (1955) 147; *Canon Law Digest* 4:425–426; Kim-Kwong Chan, *Towards a Contextual Ecclesiology—The Catholic Church in the People's Republic of China (1979–1983): Its Life and Theological Implications* (Hong Kong: Phototech, 1987), p. 253.

7. Francis Belfiori, "The Chinese Catholic Patriotic Association" (unpublished transcript of a lecture, kindly made available to me by the author); Mark Fang Chéyong, "The Catholic Church in China: The Present Situations and Future Prospects," in *Re-Thinking the Church's Mission*, ed. Karl Rahner, *Concilium* 13 (New York: Paulist Press, 1966), p. 65.

8. George Dunne, "The Prisoners of Shanghai," *China Update* 6 (Winter 1983), 52–53.

9. Wurth, p. 59.

10. Ibid.

11. This view is taken by Laszlo Ladany, *Behold, the Catholic Church in China* (Hong Kong, 1984), p. 10, and *The Catholic Church in China* (New York: Freedom House, 1987), pp. 23–26.

12. Wurth, p. 57.

13. *Lumen gentium*, 27.

14. Wurth, p. 54.

15. Ibid., pp. 55–56.

16. Quoted in Chan, p. 241, and Louis Wei Tsing-sing, *Le Saint–Siège et la Chine, de Pie XI à nos jours* (Paris: Editions Allais, 1968), p. 273. I have translated Wei's French text.

17. The usual understanding, expressed in cc. 2205 and 2209, was that grave fear completely removed the offense in the case of merely ecclesiastical laws, unless the act was intrinsically evil or tended to bring into contempt the faith or ecclesiastical authority, or was such as to do (public) harm to souls. In these latter instances, grave fear diminished imputability but did not take it away. Thus, in these latter

instances, grave fear excused from a *latae sententiae* penalty only if the law contained the words *ausas fuerit*, etc. The Holy Office decree does not contain these words. In effect, therefore, the exclusion of grave fear as an "excuse" implies that the Holy Office considered the illegal ordination of bishops to involve contempt of the faith or of ecclesiastical authority, or was such as to bring harm to souls.

18. For commentary on c. 1382 see Alphonse Borras, *L'excommunication dans le nouveau Code de Droit Canonique: Essai de définition* (Paris: Desclée, 1987), pp. 57–63.

19. Elizabeth McDonough, "A Gloss on Canon 1321," *Studia Canonica* 21 (1987) 381–390.

20. Michael Hughes, "The Presumption of Imputability in Canon 1321, §3," *Studia Canonica* 21 (1987) 19–36.

21. Velasio de Paolis, "L'imputabilità dell'atto delittuoso nel libro V del CIC," *Apollinaris* 52 (1979) 166–174.

22. See comments made by Chinese Catholics in, for example: *Guangming Ribao* (Beijing) March 17, 1951, reported in *Survey of China Mainland Press* (Hong Kong) 85 (March 18/19, 1951) 7–10; *Kirin Ribao*, June 5, 1959, reported in *Current Background* (Hong Kong) 610 (January 15, 1960) 4–6; *Heilungjiang Ribao*, July 25, 1959 reported in *Current Background* 610 (January 15, 1960) 8–9. On pride in the new China see Pi Shushi, "Life of Catholics in China" (1960) in *Religious Policy and Practice in Communist China: A Documentary History*, ed. Donald E. MacInnis (New York: Macmillan, 1972), pp. 248–251. The intemperance of some of these comments does not necessarily mean that they are totally insincere.

23. For the nineteenth century see Paul A. Cohen, *China and Christianity: The Missionary Movement and the Growth of Chinese Antiforeignism, 1860–1870* (Cambridge, MA: Harvard University Press, 1963). A somewhat hostile, but documented, example from the twentieth century is given by William Hinton, *Fanshen: A Documentary of Revolution in a Chinese Village* (New York & London: Monthly Review Press, 1966), pp. 58–62.

24. Thomas A. Breslin, *China, American Catholicism and the Missionary* (University Park, PA: Pennsylvania State University Press, 1980), pp. 31–32.

25. Wei, pp. 114–117, 283–284, and see Index under "Costantini, Celso card."

26. Quoted by Michel Masson in an article "Réflexions sur les Jésuites et la Chine aujourd'hui," to be published in *Autrement*.

27. Eric O. Hanson, *Catholic Politics in China and Korea* (Maryknoll, NY: Orbis, 1980), p. 23.

28. A very negative reading of his activities is given by Wei, *Le Saint–Siège et la Chine*. Riberi is defended in Laszlo Ladany, *The Catholic Church in China*, p. 26.

29. Léon Trivière, "Le Saint–Siège et la Chine," *Informations catholiques internationales* 380 (March 15, 1971) 20. The stated program of the Three-Self Movement can be read as a perfectly orthodox statement of the autonomy of the local church. But it would be naive, of course, to think that the movement was not politically motivated. Moreover, the ecclesiological climate of the time made it unlikely, to say the least, that Riberi would be sympathetic to emphasis being placed on the local church. Even so, his talk of a "schismatic movement" was unnecessarily intransigent and excluded any possibility of dialogue.

30. Wei, p. 220. Jean Lefeuvre, *Shanghai—les enfants dans la ville: vie chrétienne à Shanghai et perspectives sur l'église de Chine 1948–1961* (Paris: Casterman, 6th ed., 1962), p. 54.

31. The writer quoted by Chan and Wei (see note 16 above) appears to be an example of this stance.

32. This appears to be the view of Louis Morel, former metropolitan of Inner Mongolia: ". . . étant donné la grave situation en Chine, il n'y a plus la moindre possibilité d'observer strictement l'ordre établi par l'Eglise, car la loi humaine ne peut pas imposer à l'homme de faire des choses qui dépassent sa possibilité positive. Or, dans cette circonstance absolument impossible, la loi établie par l'homme, évidemment perd sa vigeur. . . ." Quoted by Wei, p. 266.

33. One Chinese bishop, whose loyalty to the Holy See is unquestioned, has said, "In the past I had to ordain two bishops without the pope's permission—it was very painful." The same bishop has written about future prospects: "I desire to conse-crate a bishop as my successor. But the election of a bishop at present does not belong to our priests only, but also and specially to the government. Then I'll consecrate as my successor any one chosen, so long as the hierarchy of the Roman church would be continued. All my priests are good, and so, I would be willing to ordain any of them as bishop; my first choice is Father N." Unfortunately, the testimony of some Chinese Catholics quoted in this article must remain anonymous, in order to safeguard them from possible reprisals.

34. In addition to some testimony which must remain anonymous, we have the published comment of Jin Luxian to this effect: interview with Giancarlo Politi (Hong Kong, June 14, 1988), *ASIA–Informazioni* 37 (June 20, 1988) 15. See, too, the somewhat different testimony of the bishop quoted in footnote 33.

35. Robert J. Lifton, *Thought Reform and the Psychology of Totalism* (London: Pelican, 1960); James R. Townsend, *Political Participation in Communist China* (Berkeley and Los Angeles: University of California Press, 1967), pp. 175–181. J. W. Lewis, *Leadership in Communist China* (Ithaca: Cornell University Press, 1963), pp. 157–160.

36. For discussion of ambivalent attitudes see Lifton, p. 63. Note, too, his com-ment on "apparent resisters" (p. 133): ". . . their inner resistance was not nearly so complete as this external expression suggested."

37. "Address to the Chinese Catholic Communities of Asia," *L'Osservatore Romano* (February 25, 1981). Text reprinted in Chan, "Appendix V" (quotation is on p. 460) and Wurth (quotation is on p. 140).

38. Wurth, p. 75.

39. Ibid., p. 95.

40. René Laurentin, *Chine et Christianisme—après les occasions manquées* (Paris: 1977), pp. 186–187.

41. Peter Barry, "The Formation of the Chinese Catholic Patriotic Association," *Ching Feng* 24 (1981) 120. For further discussion of the nature of the Patriotic Association see "Catholiques chinois: Une Eglise, ou deux?" *Etudes* 366 (May 1987) 663–674; Pierfilippo Guglielminetti, "The Catholic Church in China: One Church, Two Testimonies," *Tripod* 37 (February 1987) 76–88; Jerome Heyndrickx, "Emer-gence of a Local Catholic Church in China?" *Tripod* 37 (February 1987) 51–75.

42. Barry, p. 122.

43. Ibid., p. 135.

44. A point made several times by Liu Bainian, spokesman for the Patriotic Association, and by Bishop Tu Shihua, rector of Beijing's national seminary, when I met them in Beijing in May 1988. Both men reacted very strongly when the interpreter made the (Freudian?) slip of translating *Aiguohui* as "Patriotic Church":

they rapidly corrected it to "Patriotic Association." The word *hui* can be used to denote associations of many different kinds (political, religious, etc.), including, for instance, the Society of Jesus (Yesuhui) and the political party (Tongmenghui) led by Sun Yat-sen.

45. Politi interview, p. 19.

46. Ibid., pp. 15, 20, Jin states, "I am a Catholic, not a schismatic" in answer to the question, "Can it be said that you are in communion with the pope and that you fully accept him?" (p. 18).

47. See, for example, J. M. R. Tillard, *The Bishop of Rome* (Wilmington, DE: Michael Glazier, 1983), pp. 148–150, together with the references there to the work of Alberigo and Schmemann.

48. Text in Chan, p. 446.

49. Laszlo Ladany, "The Beijing-Rome Dialogue," *Religion in Communist Lands* 14 (Spring, 1986), 102.

50. Points very similar to those made in this paragraph are made by Chan, pp. 248–249.

51. See the discussion in Chan, pp. 246–247.

52. For a comprehensive review of the arguments for and against *latae sententiae* penalties see Velasio de Paolis, "De opportunitate poenarum latae sententiae," *Periodica* 62 (1973) 319–373. De Paolis has taken up some of these issues again subsequent to the promulgation of the revised code: "Coordinatio inter forum internum et externum in novo iure poenali canonico," *Periodica* 72 (1983) 401–433; "Aspectus theologici et iuridici in systemate poenali canonico," *Periodica* 75 (1986) 221–254. See also Peter Huizing, "De iudicio poenali in foro poenitentiali," *Periodica* 75 (1986) 255–272.

53. De Paolis, "Aspectus theologici et iuridici," especially pp. 247–253.

54. Libero Gerosa, "Penal Law and Ecclesial Reality: the Applicability of the Penal Sanctions Laid Down in the New Code," in *Canon Law – Church Reality*, ed. James Provost and Knut Walf, *Concilium* 185 (Edinburgh: T & T Clark, 1986) 54–63; idem. *La scomunica è una pena? Saggio per una fondazione teologica del diritto penale canonico* (Fribourg: Editions Universitaires, 1984). See also Borras, *L'excommunication* (note 18 above).

55. Contrary to its statement of principle in c. 1314.

56. *AAS* 71 (1979) 415: ". . . the penalty imposed by the ecclesiastical authorities (but which is really a recognition of a situation in which the subject has placed himself) is seen . . . as an instrument of communion."

57. A translation of the letter is printed in Chan, Appendix VI, pp. 461–463; and in Wurth, pp. 144–147.

58. For the significance of this usage see Tillard, *Bishop of Rome*, pp. 68–74.

59. *Ad Sinarum Gentem*, October 7, 1954, *AAS* 47 (1955) 5–14; translation in Wurth, p. 41.

60. For the history see, for example, William Bassett, ed., *The Choosing of Bishops* (Hartford, CT: CLSA, 1971); *Electing Our Own Bishops*, ed. Peter Huizing and Knut Walf, *Concilium* 137 (Edinburgh: T & T Clark, 1980), especially the articles by Stockmeier and Gaudemet; Jean Gaudemet, *Les élections dans l'Eglise latine des origines au XVIe siècle* (Paris: Editions F. Lanore, 1979); John E. Lynch, "Co-responsibility in the First Five Centuries: Presbyteral Colleges and the Election of Bishops," *The Jurist* 31 (1971) 14–53.

61. A subject studied especially by J.-L. Harouel, "The Methods of Selecting

Bishops Stipulated by Church-State Agreements in Force Today," in *Electing Our Own Bishops*, pp. 63–66, and *Les désignations épiscopales dans le droit contemporain* (Paris: Presses Universitaires de France, 1977).

62. For his comments on these issues I am indebted to my confrere Christian Cochini of the Foreign Languages Institute in Guangzhou.

Part II

Tower of Babel
or
New Pentecost?

7

Perspectives on the Government-approved Church

In China, Appearances Can Be Different

THOMAS GAHAN[1]

Rev. Li did not impress me, at least not at first. He was a rather ebullient, zesty figure, not at all my stereotype of a retiring Chinese cleric. Our first extended meeting was on a bus that broke down, leaving both of us stranded on a rather remote rural road in southern China. At first we were unconcerned, even though Father Li (a pseudonym) was scheduled to say mass in an hour's time in a town about fifteen miles down the road. Another bus would come along shortly and we would continue our journey. Well, buses came but passed us by, jammed to the roof with passengers, assorted animals, and luggage.

Then Father Li decided to take a more active role in the proceedings. He took his stand in the center of the road and flagged down the next bus. To my inexperienced eye, the vehicle seemed to be bulging at the seams; certainly there was no evident space for my considerable bulk. Father Li insisted that the vehicle was almost empty and proceeded to prove his point. To make a long story short, I finished up sitting on the floor in the middle of the bus, unaware to this day of the forces that got me to that position or how many fragile elderly Chinese ladies may have lain trampled in my wake.

Not content with just getting on board, my clerical companion then got into a heated argument with the conductress about our fares. The young lady in question was firmly of the opinion that the large foreigner should

Published in *America*, June 9, 1990, pp. 580-83, this essay is reprinted with permission.

pay more than the locals, a fact of life that I have come to accept in China. Father Li, on the grounds that he had introduced this foreign body into the bus, was also assessed a higher fare! He threatened to start World War III unless both of us were treated equally and according to accepted local Chinese standards. Again he won the day.

Eventually the bus took us to the town where Father Li was parish priest. As we alighted, the cross on top of the church was visible in the distance, beyond a patchwork of vegetable plots and rice paddies. As we drew closer, I became aware of an array of flags flying underneath the cross, the center one of which was the familiar red flag of Communist China with its five stars, a particularly jarring symbol on a church building in light of church-state relations in China since 1949.

Yet, I mused, the linking of the symbols, especially with the cross on top, was rather appropriate; it was a reminder of how pervasive the cross has been in China. Over the past century and a half it has reached beyond ideology, political convictions, and religious persuasion. Communist and Christian, peasant and nobleman have each felt its weight. If the cross is pervasive, so is its salvific power. Surely much good will come to China from the suffering of its people as a whole.

My apprehensions about the significance of the flag were heightened as I entered the front door of the church. A large notice stated that we were entering the headquarters of the Catholic Patriotic Association in the area. This is a government agency, established in the late 1950s to control the Catholic church. Other religions have similar organizations. Today their influence and power varies greatly from area to area. Despite some notable exceptions, the association generally has a baleful influence; its members are an intrusive, inquisitive, and somewhat threatening presence in all church gatherings.

Against this backdrop, I would not have been at all surprised to find a very formal and tense atmosphere in the church foyer. Instead there was a group of animated local Roman Catholics avidly reading a notice board. On it were articles on the rosary, the sacred heart, and similar topics of broad Catholic interest. Another article briefly described the history of the Catholic church in China, dating back to the seventeenth century and clearly establishing links with the universal church. A notice in one corner caught my eye; it dealt with the number of Roman Catholics worldwide, and the source quoted was the Vatican.

No More Latin

There was little time to absorb the implications of all I had seen. Mass was about to start. The church was three-quarters filled. I settled back, anticipating the familiar sing-song chants of a Chinese congregation saying the rosary and other prayers, as the priest held his personal communication with God in Latin. To my considerable surprise, Father Li started mass in Chinese, using modern texts prepared in Taiwan and Hong Kong. The congregation was very much involved, responding clearly and promptly. Current usage in the government-approved Roman Catholic churches in China is to use Latin. Father Li's decision to use Chinese was a risky, independent, personal statement, which strongly suggested a desire to follow current usage in the universal church.

After mass we went to the parish reception room where I met many members of the congregation. They uniformly welcomed me with transparent sincerity and warmth, since they were obviously thrilled and delighted to have one of their own brothers in the Christian family present to share their eucharistic table and hospitality. As soon as they learned that I was a priest, there was renewed interest in me and many asked for my blessing. I could not have felt more at home, and certainly could not have been more warmly welcomed in my native parish church. We obviously belonged to the one church, though I rather doubt that my commitment to Christ and his vicar has been as severely tested as theirs.

One of the parishioners provided some further details about Father Li. Operating without any outside help or support, without adequate books and with a very meager income to support himself, Father Li has managed to baptize five hundred persons in the past eight years. He conducts regular catechism classes, and one young man from his parish is preparing to study for the priesthood. Father Li is a dedicated priest, a man deeply committed to Christ and deeply respected by those he serves.

There is much to commend in what Father Li and his parishioners have accomplished, despite the obvious difficulties they face. However, a group of their fellow Chinese Catholics in the same town consider them traitors and possibly schismatics.

There is an underground Catholic church in the area, which rejects any form of cooperation with the present Beijing government. These Catholics have maintained this attitude staunchly since 1949; they have gone to prison rather than compromise in any way; they have seen their brothers and sisters die for their faith; they dismiss the possibility of ever being able to cooperate with or work under the Chinese Communist party or any of its agencies. Thus they reject the actions taken by Father Li and his flock and feel that at best they have been duped by the government.

The leaders and many of the members of the underground church are persons of immense, timeless faith; they have suffered heroically for their commitment to Christ. For the most part, they adhere to a theology that has changed significantly during the years of their isolation. They know little or nothing about new theological insights from the Second Vatican Council and the impact that this council has had on the universal church. Their convictions about the untrustworthiness of the present regime condemns them to a ghetto existence as they await the day when they can worship without state interference. But as they wait, they find the "official" church gaining increased recognition and stature. It is particularly galling for them to see bishops and priests, who had apparently compromised their faith, now gaining public stature in China and increasingly receiving international recognition. Humanly speaking, they must wonder if they have suffered and witnessed in vain.

Some recent developments may in part indicate the degree of their concern over this. Despite their "illegal," underground status, reliable sources in Hong Kong say that they have set up an underground Catholic bishops' conference. When this became known to the authorities, the key figures were arrested.[2]

The Causes of the Division

Various factors combined to bring about such a division within the church. The political climate since 1949, which has generally been hostile to all religion, has been a key factor. For complex reasons, the Catholic church came under special pressure. All foreign missionaries were expelled, and the government used every possible means to force Chinese Catholics, especially religious, to establish an independent Chinese Catholic church. Though there has been some easing of pressure in the past decade, the government at best tolerates limited freedom of religious belief; it closely monitors all religious practice. These government policies and actions were and are primarily responsible for the divisions in the Roman Catholic church in China. Some Catholics stood firm and refused to compromise; some broke under pressure; some, especially in the past decade, have decided to cooperate with current government policies, convinced that this is in the best pastoral interests of the Chinese Catholics.

The Chinese people as a whole have lived through propaganda campaign after propaganda campaign; they have endured endless hours of tediously boring indoctrination at the hands of the Communist party; they have often built facades behind which they conceal their real aspirations. This has been necessary for survival. Those who, at different times, found it necessary to speak out during the Hundred Flowers campaign or more recently in Tiananmen Square in June 1989 quickly found how costly it was to drop the facade. They paid the price in blood or long years in prison.

In various ways, too, the government plays the facade game. If there is no inescapable challenge to their authority, the powers-that-be often seem content. If the individual citizen is physically present at a propaganda campaign meeting, this satisfies the letter of the law, or the requirement of the Communist party, even if the individual does not show the slightest interest in the proceedings.

Catholics, at least as much as others in Chinese society, need facades in order to survive. Father Li and his parishioners will not tear down the Communist flag over their church, nor will they remove the Catholic Patriotic Association sign, even though they might very well wish to do so. Having made those minor concessions, they seem relatively free to follow their own religious convictions and practices, praying publicly, for example, for the pope during mass.

The moral choices presented to believers in China in the 1950s were generally quite stark and clear-cut. People were clearly asked to renounce their allegiance to the pope and set up an independent Chinese Catholic church. The record of those Chinese Catholics who faced death and long terms of imprisonment rather than compromise their faith is one of the glories of the Chinese church. Those who broke away merit our sympathetic understanding; those of us who have not been tested in the same crucible could scarcely boast that we would have done better.

In the somewhat improved political climate of the 1980s, on the other hand, the clergy in the official church are not required to make any renunciation of the papacy, though they are required to function within a church that is only nominally independent. As bishops and pastors, they can build Christian communities and meet the spiritual and sacramental needs of their flocks. It is obvious that they can and are achieving much good.

If Father Li and many like him in the official church were required to make a formal, public declaration on the question of the papal rights vis-à-vis the government-approved Chinese Catholic church, this would be tantamount to issuing a public challenge to the government. The least unpleasant consequence of such an action would be the removal of Father Li from his post, though one could not rule out the possibility of reprisals against members of his flock. Thus one of the existing and functioning Christian communities would be left without a leader and the sacraments they so evidently cherish.

As freedom of religious practice and belief grows in China, the leaders of the underground church are also faced with some difficult moral choices. Should they continue to shun the official church when there is now very little, if anything, on a doctrinal level that keeps them apart? In doing so they may perpetuate a division within the Chinese church, though, of course, they themselves were not the original cause of the division. Should they risk gathering devoted followers around themselves and thus create divided loyalties that may long outlive themselves? If they agree to join the functioning official church, or to combine with the latter in a new Catholic entity in China, will this simply encourage the government to adopt even more repressive measures? Obviously, the answers to the questions posed to all Chinese Catholics at the present time are far from simple.

Seeing in a Dark Manner

It is important for many of us outside China to appreciate the good that is being done by persons like Father Li and the continuing heroism and fidelity of many Catholics in both the official and underground churches. Caught up in the rapid pace of change in our own world and engrossed in our own national affairs, many know little about recent Catholic history in China, the current plight of the church there and the moral dilemma many of its members face. We are all the poorer for this. The Chinese Catholics are left to battle alone while we ourselves are deprived of many inspiring examples of Christian living and coping. We have far more to learn from the Chinese experience than we realize.

As we seek more understanding, it may be important to avoid presuppositions. It would be all too easy to project onto the Chinese problems, attitudes and values found in the non-Chinese church as a result of the Second Vatican Council. We must bear in mind that the current situation in China evolved through its own dynamics, quite divorced from what was taking place theologically in the rest of the church in the past twenty-five years.

Neither Father Li, with his flock, nor the underground church will fall because of our misunderstandings. Both groups, though in different ways and degrees, have struggled successfully for Christ in the face of tremendous odds; they are living witnesses of faith and the power of the cross. But while they may not be diminished by misunderstanding, we can be both enriched and strengthened by mutual sympathy, understanding and concern.

In evaluating this quite complex ecclesial situation, we should always be positive and remember that both Catholic groups are deeply committed to Christ. It might be wise to call a moratorium on all judgments concerning the church in China and refrain from taking decisive steps to solve specific doctrinal questions, especially those that are not central to the faith, until we have a much clearer understanding of the total Chinese reality. We must be especially careful not to extract such questions from their full political and historical environment.

A Time for Reconciliation, Not Vindication

Major political changes may not be far off in China.[3] It is very unlikely that the current Beijing leadership can long withstand domestic pressures, allied to the worldwide decline of communism. Sooner or later, the days of genuine, full freedom will dawn in China. Then the reintegration of all Chinese Catholics into the universal church must be accomplished, and, even more importantly, a solution must be found for their internal divisions.

In terms of dogma, there are scarcely any serious problems. The papacy certainly presents no difficulties as far as the members of the underground church are concerned. In my experience, the vast majority of the members of the government-approved church subscribe fully in private to the whole range of Catholic dogma, including that of the papacy. Given genuine repentance, the canonical problem of illicitly consecrated bishops can readily be solved.

There are practical considerations that will not be solved so readily. The new era will find official church personnel, as they are at present, occupying and administering the open, functioning churches in most areas. For a decade or more, the members of the underground church have shunned these churches. Will they now expect to take them over? Will they expect to oust the official church leaders? How will official church members, who feel that they have been the architects of the progress made over the past decade, react? There are also some unconfirmed reports that some official church leaders have been secretly reconciled with the Vatican. If this is true, their relationship with underground church leaders in the same geographic area will at best be touchy. The solution to these problems will place as great a strain on the Chinese Catholic community as did government pressure over the past three decades.

It is a matter of the utmost urgency to bring about reconciliation between these divided Catholic groups. The real basis of ecclesial division may lie, not in the realm of theology, but rather in the area of tactical response to the present regime and its policies. The two churches differ primarily in their assessment of the political changes that have taken place over the past decade and the most appropriate strategy to follow in responding to them.

Christian faith and love are active in China. Christ's presence is evident in the lives of many people and in their communities. They have carried the cross with Christ. They now have the opportunity of bringing the fruits of the cross, forgiveness and healing, to one another. Christ will need them both united in order to address the task of incarnating the kingdom in China.

Notes

1. Thomas Gahan is the pen name of an author writing from Hong Kong.

2. For more on the underground episcopal conference, see Chapter 2 by Edmond Tang. — Eds.

3. Note that this text was written in 1990.

The Role of the Patriotic Association

BISHOP ALOYSIUS JIN LUXIAN

Esteemed Participants and Dear Bishops, Priests, Sisters, Brothers, Believers,

As a representative of the diocese of Shanghai, I take this opportunity to thank you most warmly for making time to participate in this study marking the thirtieth anniversary of the self-election and self-consecration of bishops in the Catholic diocese of Shanghai and the founding of the Catholic Patriotic Association of the city of Shanghai.

In fact I'm not really the right person to address this anniversary of the Shanghai Catholic Patriotic Association—the reasons why not are known to all of you. But I want to ask God to grant his blessing on our church and to ask for the guidance of the Holy Spirit, this meeting having been called just eight days after Pentecost. I also call upon my predecessor, Bishop Zhang Jiashu, who would have been a good person to address this meeting, to come before the Lord in heaven to ask him to guide my speaking. Finally, all I am doing in my speech today is to "throw out bricks to find a pearl." I know that you have all brought good material for discussion, so that following my speech, even more pearls will be discovered. I can but share with you a few impressions and thoughts.

At Thirty I Took My Stand

Thirty years have passed in the twinkling of an eye. "At thirty I took my stand" (*The Analects of Confucius 2, 4*). "To take one's stand" is a good expression. It implies that a person, or indeed a group, has matured, attained something, rendered service, and brought something new into being. Looking back over the past thirty years, our path has been roundabout; we have reaped successes, but at a high price. We want to use this study meeting to investigate our work and discuss and examine it in a spirit of self-criticism. We need to affirm our successes, but at the same time to

The Chinese text of this speech pronounced on June 11, 1990 at the occasion of the anniversary of the founding of the CCPA in the city of Shanghai was published in *Shanghai Catholic Documentation (Tianzhujiao Yanjiu Ziliao Huibian)* 19 (1990/91). The English translation appeared in *China Study Journal* 6 (April 1991): 39-44.

see clearly our deficiencies, to find out where we have not lived up to expectations, and to examine how much has remained undone that ought to have been done. And to learn how many things may have been done, but not to everyone's satisfaction.

The past has already been taken out of our hands, and is laid before God's throne. The future lies in our hands. How are we to take hold of it? We have to learn from experience, affirm our successes, avoid old mistakes, and improve our work style; we must also build peace and totally bury old enmities. Some of our believers still find it impossible to forget what happened in the past; their hearts are full of resentment and they continually put the blame on others. I recommend that we all take the building of peace as our goal, forget the past, take hold of the present, and make plans for the future, so that our service of our holy and just cause is continually improved. This is one of the goals of our study meeting.

The Rectification of Names Has To Be Put First

I'm quoting a classical saying: "The rectification of names has to be put first" (*The Analects of Confucius 13, 3*). This rectification also has to be put first with regard to the Chinese Catholic Patriotic Association (CCPA). In the course of the many visits abroad that I and others have undertaken, the great majority of people have given us a friendly reception, but out of ignorance a few have described us as being of the "patriotic church." Every time that I was referred to as a "bishop of the patriotic church," I made a point of saying with great seriousness that ours is a Catholic church, and that we haven't founded a new church. We also have organizations within our church, such as the Chinese Catholic Administrative Commission. Just because we have an Administrative Commission does not mean that we can refer to an "administrative church." In the same way it is a fallacy to describe us as a "patriotic church" for the sole reason that we have a patriotic association!

The CCPA is a political mass organization and not a church. Its role is to help ensure that church work is well done, but it is not a church itself. "The rectification of names has to be put first." The aim of this rectification is to stress that the CCPA is an important organization within the Catholic church that helps church work to be done well. There are people within our own country as well who attack the CCPA. We must therefore give these people no grounds for their criticism. We must not say that the CCPA is above the church, neither should we give the impression that the CCPA is secretly controlling the church. We can try to discover and clear up this matter in our discussions at this gathering, such as how we should present ourselves and our work style so that people see for themselves that the CCPA is helping the church with all its heart, all its strength, and all its mind, and is not a group which has only its own interests at heart.

"The rectification of names has to be put first." We are the Patriotic Association of the Chinese Catholic church, and not the patriotic association of any other group. The CCPA demands of its members both love of the motherland and of the church. My advice to whoever has love only for the motherland and not for the church, or whoever has lost a feeling for the church is to take part in patriotic work in another context, for example, in the patriotic work of the democratic parties or in the neighborhood committees. For what is there in the CCPA for someone who does not love the church?

"The rectification of names has to be put first." The CCPA is the bridge between the government and the church. The CCPA must maintain a link with the people and must help church work to be carried out well. I returned to Shanghai in 1982. Before that I was in many different places: Henan, Zhengzhou, Hebei, Dongbei, Beijing, and so forth. After my return, I noticed how much progress had been made by the Shanghai CCPA in the meantime. In the past eight years, esteemed participants, you have also achieved a great deal for which I am deeply grateful. I hope that at this meeting we can become clearer about the existence, aims, and duties of the CCPA in order that it can be continually improved and made more complete.

The Definition of the Church

We often speak of the need for church work to be done well. However, as a precondition for this, we should know what the church is. Up to the present time, in my personal viewpoint, the Catholic church throughout the world has not produced a definitive definition of the church. Prior to Thomas Aquinas, theology did not include ecclesiology; there is no ecclesiology contained in Thomas' *Summa Theologiae*. It was not until the nineteenth century that ecclesiology became prominent. The ecclesiology of Vatican II differs in a number of respects from that of Vatican I. Vatican I defines the church in the following way: The church is a self-contained community, including a legislature, the administration of justice, and an executive. It is led by Christ as the invisible head and the pope as the visible head, and the believers are its members.

The first constitution of Vatican II, *Lumen Gentium*, says that the church is the new people of God on pilgrimage, going hand in hand towards the Kingdom of God—the new Jerusalem. The word "new" appears, because the old chosen people—the people of Israel who came forth from the twelve tribes—failed to fulfill God's mission. As they rejected and crucified Christ, God chose a new people who also come from twelve "tribes," namely the twelve apostles. As God's people in the Old Testament travelled through the desert to the Promised Land, so are we also on the way to the new "Promised Land," the Kingdom of God.

In addition, the church is a body—the body of Christ. Since we were received into the church through baptism, we are members of the body of Christ; we are its limbs, Christ is the head. In his letters, the apostle Paul calls the church, "the body of Christ," without inserting the word "mysterious." In early Christian writings the "mysterious body" carried as much significance as the "holy body." The head is already with God; we, the children of God, its members, shall follow him to the Kingdom of God. Now we should fulfill our duty as members by being at one in word and deed with Christ, our head.

Thirdly, the church is a sacrament, the greatest sacrament. A sacrament is a visible sign for an invisible divine secret. In the visible bread, for example, we glimpse the body of Christ; in baptism when water is poured over us, we know that our sins are washed away; and in the visible organization of the church we glimpse the mystery of divine grace and redemption.

We all know the four features of the church as one, holy, catholic (*gong*), and apostolic. The Catholic church is named after the catholic feature, but strictly speaking the word "catholic" is not a correct translation. The original Greek and Latin "*catholica*" implies that the church is of all humanity, inclusive of the whole world. One can only really speak of the church having been inclusive of the whole world over the last few centuries. Nevertheless this unity was already beginning in the early church. Directly after the Pentecost happening, the Catholic church was still Jewish; later St. Peter and St. Paul destroyed this national limitation and began to go out in mission to outsiders such as Greeks and Romans who did not believe in Judaism.

The church took on and made sacred the quintessence of Greek and Roman culture. At that time the countries around the Mediterranean all belonged to the Roman Empire. The Romans may have conquered Greece and other countries, but Greek culture nevertheless remained intact despite having been conquered. As a result of the church's integration with Greek and Roman culture, Catholicism spread quickly over the entire Mediterranean area. In terms of our contemporary understanding of geography, the area covered by the Mediterranean is only a very small part of the earth. At that time in many parts of the world Christ was still unknown. If the Catholic church is to become truly a catholic church, the cultures of China, India, Africa, and Latin America have to be incorporated. We Chinese believers have to help our Chinese culture to become a part of the world church and we have to organize our church work in accordance with the context in which we live. Chinese Catholics therefore carry a great responsibility.

"The rectification of names must be put first." Once we know what the church is, we can be clear in our discussion how church work can be done well, and can examine how to organize concerns of the Catholic church. The goal of the CCPA and the task of its members is to establish how the CCPA should contribute to the church.

The Just Cause of Church Self-Government

In the early church, whenever the apostles founded congregations on their mission journeys, elders were selected from among the local people to whom leadership of the new church was then handed over. The apostles themselves withdrew once the task was completed, turning their attention to other places where new ground was cultivated to receive Christ. In this way they travelled widely, fulfilling Christ's instruction to "go forth and teach all people." It is both right and natural that local churches should be led by local people. Jesus never spoke of churches needing to be governed by others, and in the history of the church there are no reports suggesting the same. Some of our lay people do not want us to lead the church ourselves; they even maintain that autonomy and self-government are erroneous. Look at the history of the Catholic church. Could it have spread throughout the world had it not been for self-government?

When the apostles started on their missionary journeys, they tried to take care of everything themselves; it was not very effective, however, and led to complaints. They learned a lesson from this experience in that they handed over administrative and management work to seven men whom they selected, and they themselves concentrated on prayer and the ministry of the word.

After reaching China, why did not the church develop? Why was the history of the church in China so full of vicissitudes? Leaving aside early history, let us look at Matteo Ricci in the sixteenth century. History had taught him that for the church to spread in a country with a long history and a developed culture it was necessary for the church to accommodate itself to the culture and customs of that country. He therefore showed respect for the traditional Chinese customs of honoring Confucius and making offerings to one's ancestors, and had great success in the spreading of the gospel. But this favorable situation did not last long. Differences of opinion within the church finally led to the guiding principles of Ricci's missionary activity being quashed. The Catholic church in China has never recovered from this decline. It is worth reflecting in depth on the painful lessons to be learned from this episode.

Vatican II stresses that the sole high priest is Jesus Christ. The bishops, priests, and all believers take part in varying degrees in Christ's priesthood. Each of us bears responsibility for the church; even in the sphere of church government we must involve lay people in management. At this study meeting we need to consider how lay people can participate in church management, and how we can perfect management. The CCPA has been blazing a new trail for the past thirty years. We have to sum up experiences learned during that time and thus formulate theories that can guide our work.

In the early days in the United States, Catholics were discriminated against. Far-sighted persons within the American Catholic church saw that if their church was to function well, it first needed to become inculturated in the United States and in American society. For the church in Europe at that time, this was an unfamiliar and incomprehensible matter that was called heresy; Rome even issued a circular that condemned Americanism.

The efforts of the Catholic church in the United States at that time are widely acknowledged. The 25,000 Catholics at the time of the War of Independence increased to 55 million over the next two hundred years—an increase of almost two thousand times! The reason for this lay in the fact that the American Catholic church did its utmost to become inculturated, to become united with the country, so that all believers were at one and the same time authentic American citizens and authentic Catholics.

Our Chinese Catholic church faces the same task: we must remain authentic Catholics and maintain our faith unscathed. At the same time we must put down roots in our country, so as to become accepted by its 1.1 billion inhabitants. We are authentic Chinese citizens, we share the same fate and breathe the same air as its 1.1 billion people. We need to struggle to illustrate this through our actions, proving it to be true through our deeds. If believers in all manner of positions are respectively good citizens, good workers, good teachers, good pupils, and so forth, Catholics in all social circles will no longer be discriminated against, but will instead be respected, and the image of the "western religion," the view that "Christians aren't Chinese" will gradually disappear. These achievements should be high on our agenda. We cannot separate ourselves from the 1.1 billion Chinese people, but we must at the same time hold firm to our faith because we are Catholics, Chinese Catholics. I therefore propose making the following demands both on myself and on my colleagues in the CCPA.

The Members of the CCPA Must Have an Exemplary Love of the Motherland

The members of the CCPA must have an exemplary love of the motherland and they must take a lead in respecting the laws of the country. In their faith life, Chinese Christians should be a model for others. In the eyes of the 1.1 billion Chinese, we must be good citizens who do nothing that could harm the concerns of our socialist motherland. At the same time we know that God has chosen us out of the 1.1 billion people for his church. We should both treasure and lovingly nurture this faith, keep the Ten Commandments of God and the four commandments of the church in all our doings; we have to show that the characteristic of Chinese Catholics is love, and we must let this love shine on all those around us.

Sadly, the church in our country is divided, in that there is a so-called "secret church." What is that supposed to mean? We are one church! The spreading of the gospel is an honorable and just cause that should be pursued openly; what need is there for secret agitation? In a normal situation, secret activity only goes to endanger the church, and moreover is contrary to Christ's sacred will. We should convince those believers who are not ready to be a part of the church that they are not allowed to act illegally, and that they should support the government with us, and thereby see church work carried out well. Secret evangelizing gives rise to confusion and causes untold damage. Our Chinese Catholic church should not become divided and should not have internal troubles. Apparently the *Thirteen Points*[1] of a certain bishop that are currently being circulated maintain that "Anyone entering an official church is committing a grave sin and is entering hell!" If we take a look at church history, our holy church has only canonized people as saints but has never declared people to have already gone to hell or to be heading for hell. Remaining truly loyal to the church entails fulfilling the spirit of the gospel. "God is love." We can but immerse ourselves in love and make love and not hate known.

In the same way, when someone attacks us, whatever form that may take, we should forgive that person because he or she is our brother or sister. We should strive to fill our hearts with love and not hate. The holy apostle Paul said: "If one member suffers, all suffer together; if one member is honored, all rejoice together" (1 Cor. 12:26). We are brothers of the same stem, members of one body.

Some are blinded; we need to let them see, patiently trying to convince them. Some are lacking in vision; we need to wait for them. "Facts speak louder than words." They will come round. We should not mistrust them the whole time, blaming them constantly of counter-revolutionary activities; we should win them over with love, unite them with us, and go forward together in love of the church and the motherland.

Contact with the Masses

At the moment in the diocese of Shanghai there are 120,000 Catholics; if you include the Catholics from the bishopric of Nantong inherited from Chongming county there are 140,000 Catholics. On feast days in 1982, 10,000 Catholics came to church. This figure has increased by twofold to fourfold over the last eight years. We have made great achievements. But we cannot sit back on our laurels. How many believers does the CCPA actually have contact with? Contact with the masses of the believers is a matter to which the CCPA should give attention; it is a sensitive and long-lived matter. All CCPAs should know about the believers' allocation, work, and family relationships, and so forth. They should undertake home visits and become active. Fellow workers in the CCPAs should cooperate in their work and take note at regular intervals of the workloads of the bishop, the acting bishop, and the members of the standing committee. They should help those believers who are in genuine difficulty, so that all believers may unite together as model Christians and patriots.

Helping the Government To Realize Its Policies

Members of the CCPA should be even better acquainted with policy than ordinary believers, and should lead the way in enacting those things specified in political guidelines. In particular they should study the relevant documents thoroughly and support the government in putting them into practice. I still remember clearly the rigorous determination with which government documents in the 1950s were enacted. What about now? Has the CCPA studied documents thoroughly or not? Has it absorbed them? Are they properly understood and supported? The motivation for the CCPA to be exemplary in the way it puts government policies into practice should be that we have genuine support for the government and that, among Catholics, we are those with a particularly developed love of the motherland. At least in the present phase we should help the government to put all documents into practice as quickly as possible.

The Whole Nation Desires Social Stability with One Mind

Stability comes before all other tasks. The state cannot progress without stability, neither can the Four Modernizations be realized, or church work be properly carried out. In the ten years of chaos (that is, the Cultural Revolution from 1966-1976) the religions were the first to suffer—that is still fresh in our memories.

We need to concentrate the energies of the CCPA and the masses of believers on contributing towards the stabilizing of the situation in general. On the one hand we want to support the socialist system, and on the other hand we want to avoid divisions within the church. We must examine our consciences and think whether our words and actions contribute toward stability or whether they exacerbate contradictions. Let us all work to overcome the split and internal troubles, for it is only in this way that the church can exist and develop.

My speech is only intended to be a casting out of bricks to find pearls. I sincerely urge you to criticize those things which are incorrect.

Notes

1. See Chapter 8.—Eds.

My Statement

BISHOP MA JI

People still have living remembrance of the experience of religious affairs in society after Liberation, something not easily forgotten. At that time the Catholic church suffered great tribulations and was in danger of being wiped out during the Cultural Revolution. After the Third Plenum of the Eleventh Congress of the Chinese Communist Party (December 1978),[1] it is still struggling in the midst of great tribulations. External pressures have ended but the division within becomes more serious and more apparent every day. This causes very knotty problems for the government's religious policy, problems which seem impossible to solve. The division within the Catholic church in Gansu province is very great and well-known: it becomes more extensive and serious. The power of the "underground" believers is now well-known and has won trust and support from most of the Catholics. But the power of the so-called Chinese Catholic Bishops' Conference, Chinese Catholic Church Administrative Commission, and the "Patriotic Association" (we shall simply call them the Three Organizations) in each place is becoming weaker and more fragmented every day. These bodies are increasingly isolated and paralyzed. They have lost their attraction and have become very unwelcome, for the following reasons:

First, some of the most important leaders of the Three Organizations have abandoned the most essential and basic teachings of the Catholic church. The chief characteristic of the universal Catholic church is that its leaders, bishops, and priests have to be seriously and carefully considered and tested before they accept their office. Then they have to make a solemn promise to God that they will persevere in keeping chastity throughout their whole life, that they renounce marriage to live in chastity and willingly serve the church until death. But now some of these church leaders have publicly abandoned these rulings. They have given up their vows and trampled them underfoot. They have married and have children. But they still go up to the altar to celebrate mass, to pray, and to give absolution to others. They are so proud and arrogant, putting on the appearance of

This document, dated August 14, 1988, appeared in several publications. The present translation follows closely the text that appeared in *Sunday Examiner*, Hong Kong, February 12, 1989. Bishop Ma Ji is from the Pingliang diocese in Gansu province.

righteous people. This situation began to evolve during the 1950s, when an extreme leftist policy was being carried out. But now, at the end of the 1980s, this situation is still in existence and not corrected. At that time, because of the threat of the extreme leftist policy, the faithful dared not say anything, although they were angry about this development. But now, it is the time of reform, of socialism's greater development, so the situation of religion in society has radically changed. Believers can organize activities publicly, they can speak more freely, they dare to express different opinions and to put an end to disordered behavior and wrong situations. Therefore, seeing the wrong-doing of some of these leading members of the Three Organizations of the Chinese Catholic church in abandoning the church's precepts, the whole country has expressed its silent denunciation and public disapproval. We agree that this is perfectly correct and necessary: There is no alternative. No, we also unite in asking these leading members of the Three Organizations—the married bishops and priests—to take the initiative to resign, to give up all their titles and offices. They must be forbidden to wear religious vestments in carrying out the public liturgy in all the churches. We appeal to the Three Organizations to eliminate completely this element that no longer has any religious significance.

Second, the most powerful elements of the Three Organizations arrogantly and freely deny that St. Peter is the leader of the twelve apostles chosen by Jesus. They deny that St. Peter is the Rock of the church and that Jesus has built his church on St. Peter, the Rock. Thus, it follows that they deny the primacy and authority of the pope, bishop, Rome, and the successor of St. Peter. They deny that the pope is infallible when he proclaims a dogma that all Catholics must believe. They give up entirely the principles of the Catholic church and weaken its precepts and doctrines. They have lifted up the schismatic banner of the Chinese Catholic church: "To get rid of the control of the Vatican," and "to resist the penetration of foreign religious powers." They openly declare to the whole world that they deny that the pope's office as successor of St. Peter gives the right to govern the Catholic church throughout the world. This rebellious attitude of the leading members of the Three Organizations of the Chinese Catholic church makes all the faithful Catholics readily stand up to protect the inviolable integrity of the church's teaching. They are obliged to oppose and have nothing to do with this kind of major rupture and betrayal. The Catholic church of China has consequently diverged into this present situation of division, which is becoming more extensive and more serious as time goes on and causing countless complicated problems for the apostolate.

The basic reason for this split is that the leading members of the Three Organizations of the Chinese Catholic church adulterate and betray the teaching of the Catholic church. If these problems are not solved very soon, it will certainly have very harmful consequences on the apostolate, making the leadership half-hearted and indifferent. The bad name of the married bishops and priests, the leading members of the Three Organizations of the so-called Chinese Catholic church, is well-known inside by the people and outside by the world. Those who belong to that group and have relationships with them also feel embarrassed, and find it hard to speak in their defense.

Third, the unfaithful behavior of the leading members of the Three Organizations greatly affects the Patriotic Association's claim to be a bridge. People make propaganda that the Patriotic Association is a political organization of the people, that it serves as a bridge between the government and the church. But during these thirty years, what believers can see the function of a bridge in the appearance and behavior of these married bishops and priests? They keep a tight grip on the Patriotic Association of the whole country and of every province, city, and village. They are "holding the chalice with their right hands while their left hands are embracing their wives." What bridge functions can they carry out? Believers only need a little common sense and discernment to see through their aims and intentions.

How should believers react to them? They can only keep a distance from them and fear their influence (as they would the devils or ghosts). How could believers possibly listen to their propaganda about loving the country and loving the church? During these thirty years, they have caused a counter-reaction to the appeal of loving the country and loving the church, a reaction that is much stronger than any response to it. If they were not so strongly upheld by the government, they would have long ago been spurned by the people and would no longer be in existence. As long as they exist, the Catholic church in China cannot be united. The religious policy of the government will become more and more complicated and impossible to implement. The prestige and good standing of the Communist party and of the government among believers, both inside China and all over the world, will be lessened. For these reasons, we consider that this is the time to solve the problem of this organization: The solution should not be put off.

Fourth, the movements of anti-imperialism and patriotism, and the emergence of the Three-Self organizations inside the Catholic church were all part of the massive campaign of class struggle, anti-imperialism, anti-colonialism, and anti-feudalism at the beginning of the 1950s. It was a movement against foreign imperialism and colonialism in our country's religious and cultural life. Since the Opium Wars, the foreign powers used Western culture and religion to impose their will on China and to incur great guilt in their treatment of the Chinese people. At that time, the movement of anti-imperialism and patriotism inside the Catholic church took on an extremely leftist character. All foreign missionaries were treated as imperialist elements. All Chinese priests were treated as struggle instruments and running dogs of the imperialists. Everywhere, local patriotic associations were the instruments of this struggle-campaign. Consequently, the activities of these patriotic associations were very well-known by eve-ryone. Their activities had a very great effect on everyone; the people cannot forget this and the very mention of the "Patriotic Association" makes them turn pale.

Now, in the 1980s, the situation of China in the world has greatly changed. Everything has taken on a more human tone. The number one enemies of people all over the world, American imperialism and Japanese imperialism, have both disappeared. All the old ideas, which were supposed to be inviolable in the 1950s, have been put into the museum. The Thir-teenth Congress of the Communist Party (in October 1987) and the Seventh National Peoples' Congress (in February 1988) appealed for "reform, to put reform in every sphere of life." The economic, political, cultural, edu-cational, and every other system is being subjected to spectacular and dynamic reform. The party and government are now separated; likewise politics and business. The first stage of socialism proposes to establish a socialism with Chinese characteristics, and so forth. The forbidden zone of "theory" has been opened up. There only remains the "signboard" of the Catholic "Patriotic Association," still hanging high above the heads of all the Catholics. It seems too sacred to touch. Only the Catholics who are under this heavy signboard of the "Patriotic Association" cannot yet see the light of reform and the new openness, cannot hear the good news of reform and openness, cannot smell the breath of reform and openness. What we hear is still the extreme leftist slogans of the 1950s. What we see is still only the same old faces standing in the front line of the struggle movement. The leading members of the Three Organizations of the Chi-nese Catholic church relentlessly impose their infidelities on the heads of the Catholics. Under the party's slogan, "To reform, to put reform in charge of everything," our heads and minds become clear and we dare to express our views. We will never accept such behavior.

Finally, at the beginning when local "Patriotic Associations" were estab-lished, the cadres of the Religious Affairs Bureau made propaganda and many promises to believers and priests with honeyed and sweet words, putting forward their arguments time and again with ostensibly good inten-tions, saying "how important it is to establish Patriotic Associations," "how beneficial this will be in practice," and so forth.

As a result, in the provinces, cities, and villages, Patriotic Associations were successfully established. Most Catholics and priests loyally obey the government and follow its directives. But, until the end of the 1980s, prac-tical policy in dealing with the landed property of the Catholic church was very poor. The "Number 188 Document"[2] of the party's Central Committee was just like a stone dropped into the sea that disappeared and was never heard of again. In fact, the party and the State Council have clearly pointed out that the practical policy regarding the landed property of religious communities should be dealt with in a special way:

On principle, in dealing with the landed property of a foreign church, it is not for the government to take it back, but according to the development of the Patriotic religious organizations, it should gradually become the possession of the Church in China. According to the present situation, the time has come for the transfer of the landed property of the foreign churches. It is clear that they belong to the Church in China. If the rent-income of religious communities is substituted by the government giving money to religious ministers for their living expenses, it will seem as if we have confiscated the landed property of the Church, and will have a bad influence on the government-dominated church. It will also seriously hinder the firm policy of self-support. It will be very unhelpful both politically and in our relationship with the outside world. Therefore, dealing with the rent and properties of religious communities is not a simple economic matter but a political matter, and part of a very important overall policy. It should be seen from the viewpoint of politics, dealing with it as special case. Give back entirely to religious communities their house-properties. If there is no possibility of giving them back, they should pay them back in currency.

This policy of the party and the State Council has not been given enough attention by the people. People do not hear anything more about it. We Catholics believe the party and believe the policy of the Central Committee with sincere hearts, but what we experience is completely contrary to what we expect. The people in general do not take this policy as guiding principles. To them, self-interest comes first. They only use their rights to oppress others. They use as an excuse the fact that the country is poor. They use the government's financial deficits as their reason. They exercise their power over the helpless Catholics. The lands and house properties of the Catholic church become worthless. Not one cent is paid for houses that have been confiscated and used for twenty or thirty years. Very little money is given for houses that have to be pulled down. A house, whether it is good or bad, is worth only 200 to 300 yuan,[3] even though the government says: "Pay back entirely the house property of the original church of the Catholic church." The supervisory unit puts the seal on the matter and that is the end of it. They are very satisfied. If any chapels still exist, only the right of property is recognized but the chapels may not be used. They are so kind as to point out a solution for us: Pull the chapels down, or rent or sell them. They also change the appearance of the original buildings of the Catholic church, embellish them a little, and then sell them as units for approximately 180,000 yuan—exorbitantly high prices! But they will only pay the Catholics about 300 yuan for one house as compensation. It is not possible to give all the examples one could. What principles are being followed in this unjust treatment? What reason for this "special treatment" for the lands and buildings of the Catholic church? The government does not want to be known for confiscating church properties, but in fact they have confiscated them. They really put us in the situation of having nowhere to go and no people to ask for help. The Patriotic Association, the Catholic Church Administrative Commission, and the Bishops' Conference do nothing to help. Not having them would be better than having them. There are many examples of such situations. Those provinces that do not have these organizations can carry out a very successful religious policy. I wish that those who are in charge of implementing the religious policy of the government would go out and walk around and see these things for themselves.

To sum up all the above mentioned arguments, we request to be treated from now on in the same way as everyone else. As citizens of the country and as belonging to a Catholic diocese, we fulfill all our lawful obligations and should enjoy all the lawful rights that belong to us. We support the four basic political principles and the policy of reform and openness. As regards all the titles and offices of the present local Patriotic Association and the national Patriotic Association, we respectfully dismiss them. We wish to administer our church ourselves. We can carry out our religious ceremonies in caves or huts.

The land and house properties of the church have been taken over by the government and transformed into official buildings with a bronze plate sealed on the gates. They cannot, therefore, be given back. This is a problem that has not yet been solved. It seems that it will still exist in the year 2000. The land and house properties of the church belong to the church, they cannot be surrendered. The civil law of the People's Republic of China, Chapter 5, Clause 77, clearly affirms: "The lawful properties of social organizations, including religious communities, are protected by the law." Therefore, I send this letter to the Three Organizations of the Chinese Catholic church and all those departments that deal with religious affairs, making public my stand on this matter. If there is anything in this contrary to the law, I myself take all the responsibility.

Notes

1. This congress endorsed the modernization movement of Deng Xiaoping. The ensuing politics of economic reforms and openness led to some liberalization of religious policies. — Eds.

2. Document 188 deals with church properties.

3. In 1988, the official rate was 4 yuan = U.S. $1.

My Vision of the Patriotic Association

AN UNDERGROUND BISHOP[1]

The Chinese Catholic Patriotic Association (CCPA) was first nurtured by the government of the People's Republic of China with the name of "The Three Autonomies Reform Movement Commission." However, since the majority of Catholic Chinese and priests refused reform, it assumed the name of "Patriotic Association." Lately, as the majority of Christians and priests kept away from it, they used the new name "Church Administrative Commission (CAC)." Whatever its name, the reality is always the same. This has been admitted also by the civil authority.

Therefore, how do we define the substance of the Three Autonomies? In its gist, it requires for the church of China a form of self-government that excludes every directive from the Vatican, a kind of self-support that excludes any financial support from abroad, and self-propagation that reserves the evangelizing responsibility to Chinese Christians themselves.

Today, among the faithful, there are many who think that due to the changes of name the present CCPA or CAC is not the same as the former Three-Self Movement. Deceiving themselves, they become members of the CCPA and feel at peace, thus reasoning: "The government has its own objectives, the Catholics their own plan. The two ways of thinking are not identical and the difference of conception allows us to comply with the CCPA, while following our own principles." Such a way of acting is considered by these Christians very smart but, unfortunately, they do not realize that, by their external pretense, they actually confuse black with white, sow confusion in the hearts of those who observe and listen to them, and set bad examples.

In reality, they have become truly double-faced. At times, a feeling of "no real inner peace" disturbs their self-satisfaction and their conviction that there is no better way. However, they forget that evangelization has been entrusted by God under the direct guidance of the Holy Spirit and that individuals are only instruments in the hands of God. Exaggerating their function, they believe that evangelization is possible only in the name of CCPA. Otherwise, they think the church of Christ would be completely

This essay was published in English in *Zhonglian* 17 (July 1989):16-24, and is reprinted with permission of China Catholic Communication in Singapore.

destroyed. This way of deceiving themselves and others suits exactly the aim of the government.

The government is interested that Christians join the CCPA, whether apparently or fully convinced. The important idea is that there should be an adhesion to the CCPA, for this means to have already adhered to the reform of the three autonomies. From this starting point meetings will incessantly be held with the object of provoking a change of intention. In the end, they will ask the people concerned to sign a declaration that will be an open rejection of the pope. All the bishops and priests belonging to the CCPA are bound to do so, no matter what remorse or regret may follow. During their consecrating rite the "self-elected" and "self-consecrated bishops" are even obliged to kneel in front of the presiding bishop and, with their hands on the Bible, promise separation from the pope and obedience to the Communist party. Only through this open renunciation of the pope can you be allowed to exercise a religious ministry. This is the "method of evangelization" chosen as the most appropriate by these men "who have their conscience at peace" in doing so. Some of them think that thanks to them the church on the continent has been able to escape destruction: is not that true? Weren't many churches re-opened? Many holy pictures, Bibles, and books printed? New religious objects and so forth produced, so as to allow Christian faith to be deepened and spread out? If it weren't for these, the church would not be existing on this piece of land which is China! The church, therefore, seems founded on these men, not on the rock of Peter.

I ask myself: Is there any bishop or priest of the CCPA who has not exteriorly manifested his own separation from the pope? No, not one of them.[2] They even admit that some insulting expressions toward the pope do not signify anything. One just has afterwards to pray for the pope, and repeat to himself that he has been forced to insult and repudiate him during the meeting. This is the true face of these men "who have their conscience at peace." This is the true face of the majority of those who are members of the CCPA. To be true, among them there are a few who have totally betrayed the church. Others, on the other hand, have not been able to escape from the double pressure of the government and the temptations of the world. But even if the bishops and priests of the CCPA think in this way, the majority of the bishops and priests firmly refuses to accept it.

All know the article "I believe in one holy catholic and apostolic church" is an essential characteristic of the universal church, one of the twelve articles of the Creed.

Now a church that has been separated from the pope, what kind of church is it? A church that is independent, self-determining, self-propagating, does it not become a second church for this simple reason? Why should that kind of church still use its name "Catholic"? How could it still be called "one and apostolic"?

This is the reason why we oppose such an attitude of division and we do not accept what the bishops and priests of the CCPA are doing. By accepting the reform of "three autonomies" in one way or another, we contribute to the project of putting under control and dividing religion, in view of their ultimate goal, which is clearly that of destroying every religion.

This is the reason why we do not want them to spread the CCPA among our Christians, and we do not allow our faithful to support them. To support them amounts in fact to betray our faith and help the tyrant in his cruelty. Moreover, they, too, do not allow our bishops and priests to administer the sacraments in the territories under their jurisdiction or in the churches occupied by them. Rather, they even borrow the government's power to have our bishops and priests arrested. In the field of apostolic work, for a long time now we have been suffering oppressive action from the part of the CCPA. They treat us as enemies, with the only hope of catching us into their net. The confinement in his residence and the control to which Bishop Fan Xueyan has been subjected proves it enough.[3]

How can we abandon our principles and speak of unity and rapport with these people who decisively militate in the ranks of CCPA? The so-called "movement for unity" does not signify to bargain like in a "shareholding society." If we were to arrive at some compromises and were to be part of the CCPA, we would induce them to abandon the church even more and sink them deeper in an abyss of mud. The reasons why we cannot unite ourselves with them or make any concessions, are as follows:

1. Publicly they deny the primacy of the pope, such is the case among bishops, of Zong Huaide, chairman of the CCPA, and Yang Gaojian, who have written articles in which they deny the pope in the name of independence.

2. During the episcopal and priestly consecration, the candidates must first swear, with their hands on the Bible, to separate themselves from the pope and give assent to the leadership of the Communist party.

3. In the books used for teaching, in the missal and in all other sacred books published by the CCPA, the name and doctrine of the pope are systematically deleted.

4. In churches, the faithful are not allowed to pray for the pope and many traditional prayers are forbidden.

5. The liturgical year in use is that of pre-Vatican II.[4]

6. In many places, young people under eighteen years of age are not allowed to enter the church and no other persons are to teach them catechism or prayers.

7. In Inner Mongolia, the patriotic bishop, Wang Xueming, not only got married himself, but he encouraged his priests to get married too.[5] The priests who did not get married were discriminated against. In this region, priests coming from other places are not allowed to meet the faithful, and if they do, they are put in prison. Some priests have been married more than once.

8. Priests who are not members of the CCPA may be put in prison

anytime, while none of the priests of this association has ever been arrested. Before the Cultural Revolution, all those who supported the pope were put into jail, while those who opposed him enjoyed freedom.

9. When Father Pan Deshi of the diocese of Baoding was asked by the government officials what his reaction would be in case the government political project opposed the church teaching, he answered: "I would take the Bible in one hand and the constitutions of our country in the other. Whenever the Bible disagreed with our constitutions, I would put the Bible aside." These are his own words. Early this year (1988), with the permission of the government, he said to the Christians that such a way of speaking was not correct; however, concretely it is the same thing: it is only one more trick. People similar to this priest are many.

10. The Mass they celebrate daily has not been changed: it is still the old Latin Mass.

11. The open seminaries belong to the CCPA. Not only are seminarians selected and admitted to the priesthood through the authorization of the CCPA and the government, but also the pedagogical materials used in the seminary must be according to the indications and aims of the CCPA itself.

For example, there are courses of political education in the seminaries. The Chengdu seminarians are allowed to wear fancy trousers and go to ballrooms and publicly ask their professors why the priests cannot get married.

What is more surprising today is that not a few priests, coming from abroad on a visit to their families, believe that these seminaries are well run; consequently, they make propaganda and help them to expand; this is something that even atheists dare not do!

In fact, these priests coming from abroad, do they personally study well the situation? Have they examined the situation in death? Have they really come into contact with Christians and priests of the "suffering church"? From the moment you have entered the country, a private car and a room in the hotel are put at your disposal; you are invited to a banquet where you are offered many signs of welcome. What you hear is only one side of the story and you believe what you are told.

Let me ask you: How could a country whose party in power is atheist, educate for you a new batch of propagandists for God? Under the direction of the CCPA, the trained seminarians, once ordained priests, become part of the CCPA. Then gradually, these priests will become simply "professionals" and enjoy life. Do you think this correct? No wonder that they do not allow us to train men for the priesthood!

In reality, the object they are aiming at is to induce us to become members of the CCPA, cut ourselves from Rome, and become a "church with concrete Chinese characteristics." Naturally, after being separated from the pope, the "Creed" article, "I believe in one holy catholic and apostolic church," is in itself already eliminated. As for the other articles of the "Creed," we may step by step put them aside and the government will decide if a Christian can say that in God there are two or three persons, or downright if there is a God at all.

12. We have still to ask ourselves if there are many among those who belong to the CCPA who basically and clearly know what this Patriotic Association is about. However, at a glance, we can see what is going on among the priests: their love for this world is too strong, which is the reason why they do not take the trouble to leave this muddy pit. They betray themselves and others when they "innocently" say that in front of God they are at peace in their heart.

If we ask them if they feel truly at peace, they are capable of quoting the teaching of Jesus "not to judge," in order to close our mouths. Evidently, in front of God we are all sinners and cannot judge others. But why then do they avoid referring also to the teaching of Christ who proclaims: "I am the vine"? A branch that is separated from Jesus Christ, from the root of the vine, what kind of branch will it be in future? What kind of fruit will it bear? Why don't they think about these problems?

According to the way of thinking of these people, it is not necessary to have canon law, because, after all, this is only an instrument for judging people.

13. I don't understand why the priests coming from abroad, especially those from the Philippines, could alter in this way the identity of the CCPA. Perhaps, because at their arrival in their respective villages, they come into contact with bishops and priests who can express themselves in public, that is, those who are members of the CCPA. For this reason, more or less, all suffer the contagious influence. Or, perhaps, because they listen only to one side of the reality.

They make propaganda for the seminaries of Shijiazhuang and Sheshan in Shanghai saying that they are well run. What is actually the goodness of these seminaries? According to them, the seminarians are all very young, all are gifted with a high intellectual level (or standard); they are kind and fervent. There are, one says, some sixty Jesuits in the Philippines. Among them there is a Yao Tianmin who does not spare his efforts in attacking our bishops and priests who reject the CCPA, saying that our bishops and priests are young, superficial, of a low level of learning without a philosophical and theological foundation; that we teach our people heresies, almost that we are illiterate. This is simply reversing white into black.[6]

14. The bishops and priests of the CCPA receive a salary and pension; each of them receives more than one hundred (RMB) (some US $30) monthly. They can participate in meetings abroad, have a private car, and go on pension and vacations at the government's expense. When they go for pilgrimages abroad, the public bank pays for them. Since they have received much from the government, they naturally must take their orders from the government.

There are also priests who keep themselves at a distance from the government; apparently they obey, but in their hearts they do not want to be separated from the pope. These are considered good enough by the Christians and many attend their eucharistic celebrations.

15. Today, in the midst of the CCPA, there are bishops and priests who know that if they were to express their separation from the pope publicly, they would meet with opposition from Christians who do not agree with them. So they keep their mouths shut. They dare not say whether they are in favor or oppose the separation. When Christians ask them directly, they find any excuse not to answer. People of this type cannot clearly explain the changing of their minds and prefer the "non-speaking policy" to be able to disguise their leading attitude. One needs to be on the alert.

In the diocese of Xianxian, for example, apparently no one speaks of the CCPA, no posters are seen about, but the bishop is a member of the CCPA Church Administrative Commission (CAC). Many priests of his diocese are also members of the CAC and members of the Chinese People's Political Consultative Conference (CPPCC), participating directly in politics.

Another example is the bishop of Shanghai, Jin Luxian. When this man attracts people to his seminary, he does not speak about the CCPA; he does not mention the problem of the separation or union with the pope. To be true, these men are more dangerous than those who join the CCPA openly. They are more deceitful. In their inner hearts, they are patriots who have separated from the pope!

16. There are also priests who reprimand the faithful, do not allow them to go to confession, and deny them the sacrament of matrimony, because these faithful have discovered that the priest is a member of the CCPA and do not attend his mass. And those priests who have not adhered to the CCPA are not allowed by them to administer the sacraments in their sphere of jurisdiction.

17. As for the way in which Bishop Fan is treated in prison, actually the Christians are not allowed to visit him. It is necessary to obtain permission of the person responsible for the visits to such a place and that of the Bureau of Religious Affairs in the city of Baoding. Actually Bishop Fan is under the supervision of three young priests who are members of the CCPA and of public security agents. Bishop Fan lives in a small house in the backyard of the church compound in Baoding. All his movements are being controlled.

18. In the diocese of Xianxian, the priests from abroad have declared that Liu Dinghan is a legitimate bishop appointed by the pope. For this, and also because Xianxian never speaks about the CCPA, numerous local Christians have no knowledge of the true aspect of the CCPA. The priests have formed a group which affirms that "one cannot participate in the CCPA, but can be part of the Church Administrative Commission." Now, it is a fact that this bishop is truly a permanent member of the CCPA (see *Catholic Church in China* 1 [1987]: 49). How to explain this? Is it necessary to believe that the priests of Xianxian who support their bishop are right?

Maybe they are afraid of being arrested, so they allowed themselves to act in this way? This way of acting in the diocese of Xianxian is very sly, but facts prevail on the heroic discussions and people of the region are not deceived with these lies.

19. According to the canon 844 of the Canon Law, all those who enter the churches opened by the CCPA are always in danger of setting bad examples, and of making those who see their behavior believe that they are members of the CCPA; such suspicion is so evident; they induce people to think that the CCPA churches and those which do not belong to the Association are the same. In this way, it is easy to confuse truth and falsehood, mixing up truth with error. In the actual situation one should not enter in any of the CCPA churches.

20. In Donglu of the Baoding diocese, there are many Christians who are still divided into two parties: one in favor of the CCPA and the other against it. On both fronts there are numerous faithful, though the CCPA group is smaller than the second group. Consequently, clashes are frequent.

Those Christians who do not belong to the CCPA have reserved certain rooms in their houses for the celebration of the mass; some members of CCPA have destroyed these rooms and taken away the spoils. Now they have to celebrate mass in the courtyard, but the number of participants is two to three thousand. It is said that in many places Christians do not attend the CCPA church celebrations. On Sundays and days of obligation, they go out into the countryside to attend mass celebrated by any priest of the clandestine church. A certain number of Christians cannot do otherwise but go to the CCPA churches. However, these are a minority.

21. Among the priests of the CCPA, some really set bad examples and cause many difficulties to the Christians in their faith. This is a reason why Christians do not accept them and refuse to receive the sacraments from them. This is the case for a Tianjin priest.

22. Must we not remember for what end the government created the Patriotic Association? No doubt it is an instrument meant finally to destroy completely the Catholic church. The followers of the Communist party intend to destroy all religions; this is their "great duty" to which they consecrate their entire life in view of a future realization of their dream.

Among us, there are priests who become members of these organizations to help atheists. What kind of help is this? These people with the excuse of helping the "church grow" think it convenient to use the methods of compromise for the general interest, "talking things over," and "exercising forbearance" in order to obtain the right to practice religion. In reality, the advantages they derive are decisively few. There are some who abandon their principles to save the situation. Why can't they see that it is only a temporary evasion, that in a constant way it leads to change little by little and it makes one pass from an initial position of faith to the end point at which faith is denied? Today, we consider it wrong to separate ourselves from the pope. Progressively our mistake will consist in the effort to avoid transgressing the article of faith and the commandments so as not to commit sin. Very soon, however, church and faith will be realities far away from our life.

In our country, fifty years ago, Wang Jingwei[7] devised a policy of "crooked tactics to save the nation." Today, there are persons who have devised "crooked tactics to save the church." Can we use these methods for the holy church? Can the shining light of the Christian faith rely on the strength of humans? Can the objectives consecrate the means?

We have learned that in problems of discernment of the Spirit there is one rule which says: "The good is in its nature perfect. Evil comes from some defect" (*Bonum ex integra causa, malum ex quocunque defectu*). This applies to what has been said above. We believe that belonging to the CCPA with the only objective of preserving the apostolic work is incorrect. In fact, to adhere to the CCPA is not the only possible way to act, but there are many others.

In conclusion, we cannot make use of this method of adhesion to the CCPA because it is fundamentally wicked to do so; it divides the church, goes against the doctrine of the faith, and it is sinful. There are people who with the excuse of the "apostolate" betray themselves and others; they are caught in a trap. He who does not know how to save himself, can he pretend to save others? Consequently, many are led in the wrong direction. This is the reason for which we should know how to discern clearly and not to be more or less satisfied. Again, we cannot be satisfied with a short-sighted calculation of profit and loss, advantage and disadvantage. This is often a matter of different points of view, consequently, different ways in which things are seen.

Can people of different conceptions come together? According to the manner of observing what is going on in the CCPA, a vast number of holy martyrs have been foolish. Would it not be sufficient for them to say only one word and save their lives, thus securing their happiness and power? Why then didn't they say this word or sentence?

The members of the CCPA think that, in case the government wants to kill the priests, they would have their lives saved and would not suffer any harm. But they forget the teaching that Jesus himself left: "He who wants to save his life will lose it." They forget that our lives are in God's hands, and that to lose our lives for the sake of faith is a glorious deed!

Finally, I can't help but repeat a sentence: "We cannot belong to the CCPA. We cannot be united with them."

I believe the church is one, holy, catholic, and apostolic. This is the doctrine of faith. The contents of our faith, the necessity of not being separated from the pope—of being united with him—is of essential value. We cannot discuss these values. We cannot make concessions. I hope that by verifying these facts the other priests will be able to form a clear and correct opinion.

Notes

1. This English translation appeared in *Zhonglian* 17 (July 1989). It follows a Chinese text received from Hong Kong. Another slightly different Chinese text was used in Hong Kong for translations into Italian and French. The bishop's document is from the first months of 1988. It has been widely circulated in Catholic circles in China. The bishop—we know for sure—has suffered a lot on account of this, on the part of civil authorities and of the CCPA. The accusing leaders made grievous accusations against him, accusations which had nothing to do with the "crime" of having freely expressed his opinion.

The author is a bishop consecrated secretly some years ago. As such he is not recognized either by the civil authority or by the CCPA.

2. The author does not seem to know the courageous stand taken by Bishop Duan Yinming, bishop of Wanxian in 1986. In a written document prepared to be read during the national meeting of bishops held in Beijing, Bishop Duan expressed his adhesion to the pope. But it seems that Bishop Duan was not allowed to read his own declaration to the assembly. The bishop of Wanxian was consecrated in 1949 and is currently a member of the CCPA.

3. Joseph Fan Xueyan is the bishop of Baoding (Hebei). He was appointed bishop by Pius XII and consecrated in 1951. After a long period in prison, Bishop Fan appeared again in Baoding at the end of 1979 or the beginning of 1980. In 1982, he was re-arrested and condemned to ten years in prison. Set free in 1988, but always kept under strict watch by the authorities, Bishop Fan is a very well known and venerated figure, and undoubtedly considered the "guide" of Catholics, at least in the north of the country. (The Union of Catholic Asian News (UCAN) reported on May 1, 1992 that Bishop Fan Xueyan of Baoding, Hebei, died in mid-April at the age of 85 but added that the exact date and place of his death were yet to be determined. Other reports suggest that he died much earlier and that the body was brought back in April 1992.—Eds.)

4. We have translated the sense, omitting a long list of feasts which belong to the old liturgical calendar, no more celebrated in the universal church, but still observed in Chinese churches.

5. Bishop Wang Xueming explains that he and his priests had to face such pressure that he had to take this decision. In some circumstances, the bishop has to "judge." No outsider should condemn them, he says.

6. We omit the end of this paragraph which is a bitter criticism of the stand taken by Father Yao Tianmin of the Philippines. Other documents written in Hebei province also attacked the comments made by this priest on the "Thirteen Points" signed by the bishop of Baoding, Bishop Fan Xueyan. These articles warned the faithful against any participation in the church activities sponsored by the CCPA. Father Yao Tianmin advocates a more tolerant attitude (see Chapter 8).

7. Wang Jingwei (1883-1944) supported the left wing of the Nationalist party in Wuhan during the end of the 1920s. In 1927, for fear that the government would fall under the control of the Communists, Wang became friendly with General Chiang Kaishek.

8

Perspectives on the Underground Church

Who Is Not Loyal to the Church?

FATHER JOSEPH YAO TIANMIN

When I returned to China in June of this year, all of the underground priests and faithful with whom I had contact reflected the same views on the revolutionized Patriotic Associations and the Catholic Church Administrative Commission as expressed by an anonymous Catholic bishop. Their views are riddled with errors. They cannot differentiate between those who are members of the Chinese Catholic Patriotic Association (CCPA) and those who are not. They automatically brand anyone who is evangelizing publicly and anyone who is in contact with the government as members of the CCPA.

It is wrong for the CCPA to have self-administered churches and to sever communion with the pope. However, there are many bishops and priests who evangelize publicly and are in communion with the pope. Is it fair to brand them as CCPA members?

The underground bishops and priests are not well-informed. Their knowledge of theology is limited and they arbitrarily decide that those who evangelize publicly and participate in meetings of the Church Administrative Commission are members of the CCPA. They also say that the Three-Self Movement commission, the Patriotic Associations, the Church Administrative Commission—whatever its name, the reality is always the same. What an absurd thing to say.

The government does not require those who participate in meetings of

These comments written in late 1989 offer an alternative opinion to the views expressed by the underground bishop in the preceding essay. This article appeared in *Zhonglian* 18 (January 1990), pp. 8-12, and is reprinted with permission of China Catholic Communication in Singapore. Father Joseph Yao Tianmin is a Chinese priest from the Philippines.

the Church Administrative Commission to raise their hands, state their stand, or sign declarations to sever their relationship with the pope. However, it seeks to explain national policies to such members: it advises them how to go about building churches and how to evangelize; it explains the way in which the government safeguards regular activities of the church.

Seminaries, convents, and classes for seminarians that have the approval of the Church Administrative Commission are protected by law. Only bishops and priests who are approved by the Church Administrative Commission are allowed to evangelize. If the policies of the government do not oppose Catholic articles of faith, is there any harm in complying with government policies?

Bishop Fan of the Baoding diocese has repeatedly requested that underground bishops and priests evangelize openly and comply with legitimate orders. Why don't they comply?

The anonymous bishop says that we should not unite or compromise . with the CCPA for the following reasons.

1. "The patriotic clergy publicly deny the primacy of the pope; for example, Yang Gaojian, Chairman of the CCPA, Zong Huaide, and others."

We must realize that only a small number of bishops and priests belong to the CCPA. They do not represent the Catholic church in China. It does not mean that all bishops and priests who are evangelizing openly in China belong to the CCPA or that they deny the primacy of the pope. From May 24 to May 29, 1989, a national conference of the Catholic church was held in Beijing. Sixty-one bishops attended the conference as well as the ringleaders of the CCPA. Leaders of the Communist party's Central Committee, heads of the United Front, chiefs of the Religious Affairs Bureau and other national leaders addressed the conference. These leaders further explained the religious policy of separating politics from religion and acknowledged that the pope is the leader of the Catholic church, in other words, the primacy of the pope.

2. "At the ordination ceremonies of bishops and priests, the candidates must take an oath to renounce the pope."

This requirement has been abolished. On May 22, 1989 at Shijiazhuang in Hebei province, Bishop Zong Huaide consecrated three bishops. They did not take an oath to renounce the pope. Several batches of new priests have been consecrated at Xianxian, Xingtai, Handan, and other dioceses. During the consecration ceremony, the new priests took an oath to acknowledge the primacy of the pope and to accept his authority.[1]

3. "In the books used for teaching, for example, the missal and other sacred books, all references to the pope in these books have been deleted."

Only a small number of CCPA members are thus involved. The majority of bishops and priests who are evangelizing openly in Xianxian, Xingtai, Shijiazhuang, Handan, and other places are using missals and other pedagogical materials approved by the church.

4. "In churches, the faithful are not allowed to pray for the pope and many traditional prayers are forbidden."

I know for a fact that in places like Xianxian, Shijiazhuang, Xingtai, and Handan, prayers are said for the church. All prayers are recited.

5. "The liturgical year in use is that of pre-Vatican II."

In Xianxian, Xingtai, Handan, and other places, they use the new liturgical year.

6. "In many places, young people below eighteen years of age are not permitted inside the church. They cannot be taught catechism."

Young people are permitted to enter most of the churches that are open to the public. They also learn the catechism.

7. "The patriotic Bishop Wang Xueming of Inner Mongolia not only got married himself, he even encourages his priests to get married too."

The bishops and priests in Xianxian, Shijiazhuang, Xingtai, and Handan are not married. New priests are not allowed to be married.

8. "Bishops and priests who are not members of the CCPA may be put in prison anytime, but not even a single CCPA priest has been arrested. In accordance with government policy, only bishops and priests who have government approval are allowed to evangelize freely."

Obtaining government approval does not mean that a person has become a member of the CCPA. It merely certifies the professional status of the bishop or priest. What they have obtained is a certificate of identification.

9. "When Father Pan Deshi of the CCPA in Baoding diocese was asked by government officials what his reaction would be if government policy conflicts with church doctrine, he replied thus: In one hand, I hold the Bible, in the other hand I hold the constitution. Where the Bible does not agree with the constitution, I will put the Bible aside."

Father Pan Deshi does not represent all the priests in the CCPA. He certainly does not represent all bishops and priests who evangelize openly.

10. "The mass they celebrate daily has not been changed. It is still the old Latin mass."

It may be that where the Chinese missal is not available, the old Latin mass is used. However, the mass is still valid. Even the pope himself occasionally says the mass in Latin. All the priests in Guangjing, Xianxian, Xingtai, Handan, and other places say the mass in Chinese.

11. "The open seminaries belong to the CCPA. Not only are seminarians selected and admitted to the priesthood through the authorization of the CCPA and the government, but also the pedagogical materials used in the seminary must be according to the indications and aims of the CCPA itself. The Chengdu seminarians are allowed to wear fancy trousers and go disco-dancing.[2] Quite a number of priests from abroad visiting relatives believe that these seminaries are well run. Consequently they make propaganda for them."

The criticisms levelled by the underground church against the seminaries are not correct. Have members of the underground church ever visited these seminaries? They believe any rubbish that they hear. Take the case of the Shijiazhuang seminary. The leaders here have a harmonious relationship with the pope. They do not belong to the CCPA. The selection of seminaries and admission to the priesthood are decided by the bishop of the diocese. The pedagogical materials are based on church teachings. The aims and objectives of their teaching are to glorify God and to save souls. But the underground church maintains that the Shijiazhuang seminary is a school of the Communist party; it is a brothel; it is hell. They insult the Shijiazhuang seminary the same way they insulted the Chengdu seminary. The underground church also asks: How can one expect an atheist government to educate a new batch of propagandists for God? It is sheer nonsense to brand such seminarians as CCPA priests or professional priests. In fact the priests of Xianxian, Xingtai, Shijiazhuang, Handan, and other dioceses are loyal to the Catholic church, the pope, and their faith.

12. This underground bishop says that many CCPA priests deceive themselves and other people when they claim that they are at peace in their heart. If we ask them if they truly feel at peace, they reply: "Don't judge."

They further conclude that if a priest is separated from the pope and the church, what kind of a priest is he? This bishop arbitrarily classifies all bishops and priests who evangelize openly as members of the CCPA. In effect, how many bishops and priests have separated themselves from the pope? How many have left the church? What is the CCPA?

13. This underground bishop says that the priests who are from abroad, especially those from the Philippines, take pleasure in painting a good image of the CCPA. They make propaganda for the seminaries in Shijiazhuang and Shanghai, saying that they are well run. Among them is a Yao Tianmin who does not spare his efforts in attacking our bishops and priests who oppose the CCPA. They even reverse white into black and say that the confusion in Baoding diocese is of our making—that we have disrupted the unity of the church and the dissemination of the gospel and that we teach our people heresies. They say that Yao Tianmin has become a propaganda officer of the CCPA and done for the CCPA what it could not do for itself. He is even more CCPA than the CCPA itself. In effect, Yao Tianmin and others like him do not fully understand the situation of the church in China or the whole situation in China.

I consider the points recorded above as rubbish and fantasy. This confirms that this bishop does not understand what the CCPA is about. The bishops and priests of Xianxian, Xingtai, Handan, and other dioceses are all loyal to God, to their faith, to the pope, and to their missionary work. Why lie about them and insist that they are members of the CCPA? A good shepherd should go out from the CCPA to pull people in and save them. He should not force people in and trap the good people. This is what the underground church is doing. Those who hoist high the flag of anti-reform and shout slogans like "Besiege Sun Wenyuan, attack Bishop Liu Dinghan, isolate Bishop Chen Bailu" are in fact the henchmen of Satan.

These are the people who are responsible for the great confusion in the Baoding diocese. They have disrupted the unity of the church, the dissemination of the Holy Gospel and have preached heresies. Ninety-nine percent of the faithful are willing to testify against this group of people. Yao Tianmin does not say that the CCPA can replace the church. He has not painted a good image for the CCPA and most certainly he has not become the propaganda officer for the CCPA. What he has done is to speak the truth and defend the good name of those bishops and priests who are faithful to God and to the pope. Yao Tianmin does not attack those bishops and priests who are resolutely opposed to the CCPA. He attacks those who claim themselves to be traditional, loyal, and genuine. He attacks those who label the bishops and priests of Xianxian and Handan as schismatics, renegades, and rebellious. We question the intention of people who are so proud and haughty and who like to sing the praises of themselves and run down others. Remember what Jesus said: "Those who exalt themselves will be humbled. Those who humble themselves will be exalted."

14. "Bishops and priests of CCPA receive salaries and allowances from the government. Each person receives RMB 100 per month. They go on leave and summer holidays at government expense."

It may be true in the case of bishops and priests of CCPA, but not so in Xianxian and Handan.

15. "Some bishops and priests of CCPA, realizing that the faithful would oppose them if they declare publicly that they have separated from the pope, choose to keep their mouths shut. They will not say whether they are in favor or oppose the separation. On the face of it, Xianxian diocese has no sign of being CCPA-controlled. However, the bishop is a member of the CCPA. Many priests of his diocese are not only members of the Church Administrative Commission but are also members of the Chinese People's Political Consultative Conference (CPPCC) participating directly in politics."

What is stated above runs counter to the truth. In their homilies the bishops and priests of Xianxian have always declared that they are in a harmonious relationship with the pope and that they will not break away from the pope. Priests from abroad will testify that bishops and priests of Xianxian are not commission members. Neither are they members of the CPPCC.

16. "There are also priests who reprimand the faithful, do not allow them to go for confession, and deny them the sacrament of holy matrimony because the faithful have discovered that these priests are members of the CCPA and do not attend their masses. Those priests who have not adhered to the CCPA are not allowed by them to administer the sacraments in their sphere of jurisdiction."

What is stated above is again contrary to the truth. Ninety-nine percent of the faithful in Handan diocese attend the mass celebrated by the priests in the open churches. It is not true that they have ceased to administer the sacraments. They do not allow the underground priests to say mass because they teach heresies.

17. "They have tightened their control over the movement of Bishop Fan Xueyan. They do not allow the faithful to see. ... "

I have no comments to make on this point as I am not conversant with this case.

18. "Priests from abroad declared that Bishop Liu Dinghan[3] of Xianxian diocese is a legitimate bishop. However, it is a fact that Liu Dinghan is a permanent member of the CCPA [from *Catholic Church in China* 1987, Vol. 1, p. 49].[4] How does one explain this?"

It is a fact that Bishop Liu Dinghan's name is in the CCPA. But did he ask for it to be included? No, his name was added unilaterally by the CCPA without his consent. So how can it be counted? You do not believe the priests from abroad. Neither do you try to get at the truth. How absurd.

19. "According to Clause 844 of the Canon Law, all those who enter the churches controlled by the CCPA are setting bad examples; one should not enter."

Clause 844 does not state that all churches that are open to the public belong to the CCPA. One must be able to distinguish between CCPA churches and non-CCPA churches. Subsections (2), (3), (4) of the Canon Law 844 provide that where Catholic clergy is not available, clergy of non-Catholic denominations may listen to confession, distribute communion, and anoint the sick. These are considered legitimate acts in the church.

20. "The faithful in Donglu of Baoding diocese are divided into two camps. One belongs to the underground group. The other is in favor of the CCPA."

Father Su Ruowang, parish priest of Donglu, has a harmonious relationship with the pope. The faithful in his church also obey the pope. There is no CCPA in Donglu. It is wrong to include them as CCPA.

21. "CCPA priests, namely Sun Buxin, Pan Deshi, Wang Yuanpu, Xu Lizhi, and Wang Xueming, have given bad examples. Many priests avoid them. There are many more like them."

Why don't you list out all their names?

22. "The object of the CCPA is to destroy the Catholic church. The Communist party wants to destroy all religion. Yet among us are priests who become members of these organizations to help atheism."

How many joined the CCPA? You hold the wrong view about the CCPA. Did anyone ask you to unite with the CCPA? Did anyone ask you to join the CCPA? The government is not out to destroy all religion. It is necessary to have contacts with the government and to obey legitimate orders. Participation at meetings of the Church Administrative Commission is a means of seeking to understand national policies, not a case of compromising. Jesus said to his disciples: "When you are on a mission, be as prudent as the snake and as simple as the dove."

Can the lesson of the tragedy at Youtong be applied? Martyrs are not fools. The fools are those who are self-opinionated and think highly of themselves. The church in China today is different from the days of the Boxers and the days of the 10-year Cultural Revolution. The two periods cannot be placed on a par. The faithful are not forced to renounce their faith.

Notes

1. Father Yao's arguments refer to the experience of a few dioceses in Hebei province, south of Beijing. There are similar conflicts in south Zhejiang, north Fujian, and Gansu provinces. The situation is not so tense in other parts of China. (See also Chapter 6, pp. 91-96 for a canonical evaluation of the alleged rejection of papal authority. — Eds.)

2. There were, in fact, problems of discipline in the Chengdu seminary. The seminarians were sent back to their dioceses in 1989. A new start was made in September 1989 with the appointment of the newly consecrated Bishop Xu Zhixuan as superior.

3. For more information on this bishop see "The Present Chinese Church" on pp. 148-49 below. — Eds.

4. This Chinese-language periodical is published in Beijing by the CCPA under the title *Zhongguo Tianzhujiao*. — Eds.

Thirteen Points

ATTRIBUTED TO BISHOP FAN XUEYAN

Question 1: Rev. Bishop, the Patriotic Association points out the "independent self-administration and self-governance of our church," free from external interference. Is this kind of church still a holy church?

Bishop Fan answers: The holy church is established by our Lord Jesus Christ. The church is one, holy, Catholic, and apostolic. Humans cannot be independent from God. The churches cannot govern themselves separately. The self-organized Patriotic Association that separated and disobeyed the pope is no longer Catholic; it is not in communion with the church. The so-called self-governing church naturally is no longer a Catholic church.

Question 2: Is it all right to choose and ordain clergy by themselves?

Bishop Fan: There are two ways to explain this. First, in China before, we had no missionaries of our own. The missionaries were all sent by the pope from other places so we could not choose and ordain by ourselves. After a long period, we had our own missionaries, and our own bishops could then ordain our own priests and bishops. However, permission must be obtained from the pope in order to ordain a bishop. It is so everywhere in the world and there is no exception in any country. Second, the Patriotic Association cannot choose or ordain because it has broken away from the pope and does not submit to his leadership. If the Patriotic Associations, nevertheless, just go ahead and ordain bishops, then it is an act of rebellion against the pope and Jesus.

Question 3: Is a sacrament or a mass celebrated by the priests of the Patriotic Association valid? Do they have the power to forgive sins? If Catholics were allowed to attend these masses and they did attend, did they commit a sin?

Bishop Fan: Although the sacraments performed are valid, and the hosts are still the body of Christ, nevertheless Catholics cannot receive sacraments from them or attend their masses. If they do, they commit a sin. If they confess to these priests, not only can they not obtain forgiveness but they will have committed another sin.

The authenticity of the authorship of this document is disputed. See the following selection on pp. 146-52.

Question 4: If a priest commits mistakes, he himself is responsible, and this has nothing to do with other Catholics. If they all are worshipping God, is there anything wrong with it? It is much better than just playing cards or watching television. Is this correct?

Bishop Fan: It is not correct, because if they (priests of the Patriotic Association) are wrong, then you should not support them in making more mistakes. The wrongdoing of a priest is of two kinds—the first is private or personal and the second is public. We can make a distinction between personal sin and public sin. Personal sin will not affect Catholics in their worship of God. But we cannot say they have nothing to do with us if they have openly organized anti-papal organizations, rebelled against the holy church, and openly separated from the pope.

Question 5: Is extreme unction given by the priests of the Patriotic Association valid?

Bishop Fan: It is valid, but we Catholics are forbidden to receive it. I said before that it is forbidden to receive the sacraments from them; unto death we are not to receive sacraments from people who rebelled against the pope. By our faith, we are sure to have the forgiveness from God.

Question 6: Some aged priests, who neither joined the "reform" nor followed the line of the Patriotic Association, are not associated with any bishop. Do they act correctly?

Bishop Fan: Correctly, when ... the old bishop is no longer there and a new bishop cannot be found. Under such circumstances, their actions are in accordance with the church's regulations.

Question 7: Is it valid for the seminarians of the Patriotic Association seminary to be ordained by their bishops?

Bishop Fan: It is valid, but without faculty. Let me repeat again that our faithful must not participate in or receive any of their sacraments. It is a sin to participate or receive.

Question 8: Some faithful Catholics, though they understand the doctrines, prefer the proximity of these churches and hear patriotic masses. Is this allowed?

Bishop Fan: No. Since they understand the doctrines, they know that it is forbidden to hear these masses; if they still go there, it is doing so wittingly. Without knowing, one is blameless; to do it wittingly is a sin.

Question 9: When it is forbidden to go to nearby churches and it is not possible to get to distant churches, then the faithful do not go anywhere. Isn't this considered as an omission of Sunday obligations?

Bishop Fan: I said again and again that it is forbidden to receive and to participate in any of their sacraments. Whoever receives and participates commits sin. If there is no priest of the holy church nearby, one can pray at home on Sundays. This can be considered as a fulfillment of Sunday obligations.

Question 10: Some Catholics think that in the end the pope and the bishops did not suspend these priests. In this case, do they still have the faculty?

Bishop Fan: There is no need for suspension, for as soon as they leave the hierarchy, the faculty is naturally withdrawn. What faculty is there to suspend, since they no longer have it? As soon as anyone intends in his mind to secede from the pope, he immediately loses all the faculties bestowed by the holy church. This *ipso facto* excommunication is prescribed in canon law.

Question 11: Some reformed priests, in tears, told the faithful that they in fact submit to the authority of the pope and realize that there is no salvation if they secede from him. Some of the faithful were deceived. How do you analyze this problem?

Bishop Fan: This is their usual method of deception, playing a double game, in that they are a two-faced clique that deceives both sides. To the government they say: "We firmly uphold independence, self-government, and separation from the pope." To the faithful they say: "Never, never secede from the pope." Here I particularly point out that Bishop X is such a person. The faithful should not only listen to their words but watch their conduct.

Question 12: Some Catholics ask if those who follow the patriotic organization go to hell?

Bishop Fan: God is merciful, most merciful. God will not allow the Patriotic Association to last that long. God will not let the Catholic church remain for long in difficulty and suffering. Those who are under the shadow of the Patriotic Association must understand the question of truth and falsehood. "Whoever declares publicly that he belongs to me, the Son of Man will do the same for him before the angels of God." They must clarify their incorrect point of view, believing the whole body of religious beliefs, and not deceiving themselves. The Patriotic Association declares itself as the Catholic church but secedes from the pope. This self-contradiction leads to self-destruction. As I see it, Catholics today do have a clear recognition of their own church and all of them can clearly be witnesses of the faithful. Catholics everywhere have come to visit me and their faith is very firm and strong. They are quite clear about the nature of the Patriotic Association and the Church Administrative Commission.

Question 13: How do you feel about the intention of the government to return the property of the church. Catholics are all eager to have the property of the church returned. There are places where the government encourages us to build a church. Is it better for us to accept or not accept the property if the present parish priest is one of the Patriotic Association?

Bishop Fan: It is better to accept. As soon as we have the church we may be able to increase the glory of God. As has been said before, the government has declared several times its intention to return the church's property. If the church is built up and is being occupied by the Patriotic Association's priests, then we Catholics have to exert efforts to resist and to fight for our rights. If they take over the church, we just give up because we cannot receive the sacraments from them. When they have left, we shall use it. The above answer is my own opinion. Each place has its own circumstances; Catholics must talk it over together and obey the order of the local superior. In one word, as far as the property of the church is concerned, the church must not be the loser. Nobody can sell the church's property; if so, they will go down in history in infamy.

The Present Chinese Church

A PRIEST FROM NORTHERN CHINA

(The writer begins this section by identifying terms that, he feels, have created confusion. — Eds.)

The expression "Chinese Catholic church" is ambiguous. For some, it refers to a church in China that is separated from the Roman Catholic church and independent from the pope in Rome. Those who support this opinion are few, one in every thousand. The only correct meaning of the expression "Chinese Catholic church" is the local church of China within the universal church with the pope and under the pope.

There is not, and has never been, such a thing as a "patriotic church." What exists is the Chinese Catholic Patriotic Association whose members help the government. The "patriotic church" is a fiction created by people overseas. There have been some positive developments in the Patriotic Association in the past few years. One should not, however, pass judgment on the Patriotic Association throughout China on the basis of the Patriotic Association in Beijing. Not all members think in the same way. In recent years, the names of some very good bishops and priests have been placed on the list of the Patriotic Association against their will.

This organization was originally established by the Communist party to harm the holy Catholic church. In recent years, however, the Patriotic Association has been undergoing some important changes, and its control of the life of the church is not the same throughout the country.

The expression "loyal church" has also been created by people overseas. What we have in China are "underground" Catholics and "above-ground" Catholics. We live under the control of the Chinese Communist government, which requires that any person who wants to open a small store, a workshop, or a new house, or to establish an institution or organization, especially if it is of a purely religious nature, needs a permit. We requested and obtained the permission of the government to open the seminary and the sisters' convent. The "underground" Catholics, on the contrary, refused

This is an excerpt from a longer document sent to Father Ismael Zuloaga, S.J., in May 1989 by a seventy-year-old priest from northern China who spent many years in jail. Minor deletions and editorial changes have been made by the editors.

to ask for the required permit and continued to work in hiding. Furthermore, they led people to believe that because Catholics "above-ground" requested and obtained the government permit, they have betrayed the church! This is totally untrue!

The Underground Group

From 1978 to 1979, when the Chinese Communists relaxed their policy toward religion, and after suffering through common difficulties, the whole Catholic community in China was very happy with the new religious freedom. But soon afterward, the government had new thoughts about proceeding with plans made before the Cultural Revolution, that is, to establish an independent church separate from the pope. It refused to obtain the pope's approval and started to select and elect its own bishops. This is against the principles of the church.

At that time some Catholics under the pressure of the government elected and ordained some bishops. Some Catholics felt that, because of the special situation, this was acceptable. Others had no clear understanding of the problem and were without opinions. Still others objected strongly, saying that these self-ordained bishops were illegal and had been excommunicated by the church. They refused to recognize these bishops and called them schismatic. They said that Catholics—especially priests—who recognized these self-ordained bishops had gone astray. The priests ordained by these bishops were also considered illegal.

Catholics opposing these self-ordained bishops wrote the pope. According to my personal information, the Vatican gave permission to these people to ordain their own bishops secretly without the prior approval of the pope. Bishop Fan Xueyan of Baoding ordained several bishops, who ordained other bishops, who, in turn, ordained many priests. All these self-ordained bishops and priests have a faithful following, and this is how the underground group was formed. After many years, this underground group has become known as the underground church.

The ideas and the activities of the underground group are very complicated. Briefly, they are the following:

1. The underground group knows of the atheistic principle of the Communist party. This principle opposes theology. That is the reason Christians should not go near the Communist party or the government. Whoever approaches the Communist party will in time betray his or her beliefs. Believers must avoid the government. In the beginning underground priests preached openly and were recognized by the government. In order to unite the country, the government gathered all levels of people together. It also tried to unite the people of the holy church, inviting many bishops and priests as representatives of the people. Of those invited, some refused to join or attend the meeting and insisted on fighting the government.

2. These many years, the underground bishops, not recognizing the self-ordained bishops, have themselves ordained many bishops. These underground bishops can be found in many dioceses. In their opinion, self-ordained bishops are not real bishops; rather, those ordained by them (the underground bishops) are the real bishops. In one diocese there are four to five underground bishops who have ordained many underground priests.

3. My diocese has the papal-appointed legal Bishop Liu Dinghan John.[1] A bishop from another diocese then ordained Li Zhenrong, who refused to accept Father Liu as bishop. Li Zhenrong then ordained around ten priests.

Most of these priests are very young, around twenty years of age; thus they are called "little black priests." Some who are fervent and work hard can be called good priests. Some continued to work in the diocese after ordination, obeying Bishop Liu and refusing to be manipulated by Li Zhenrong.

With a few exceptions, most of these priests are poorly educated. Some do not even have an elementary-school education. A couple of them failed the entrance examination to the Xianxian seminary, or were even dismissed, and then went to the underground seminary directed by Li Zhenrong. In speaking of their formation, Bishop Li has said: "In those days, all the apostles were fishermen, without education. After receiving the Holy Spirit, they knew foreign languages and could preach."

These underground seminarians not only lack cultural knowledge, they also lack knowledge of the church. They studied a few months under Li and were ordained priests. When they studied canon law, they chose the chapter on excommunication and specialized in excommunication in order to preach about the excommunication of bishops and priests. They memorized all these points, but neglected to study the requirements and qualifications for priesthood.

An example is a twenty-year-old youth who was an official in the Communist party. He was suddenly baptized and, after baptism, he signified his desire to become a priest. After a few months, Li Zhenrong ordained him. He had no knowledge of the catechism and, after a couple of years, his lifestyle was such that it gave a bad name to the church. Li tried to stop him from exercising his priesthood, but failed.

Some of these "instant" priests remained to serve locally, and some were sent to other places—to the northeast or the northwest. The bishops who ordained all these "little black priests" do not require study of the catechism, but require instead that the new priests denounce the bishops and priests of the Patriotic Association, and that they tell the people not to attend their mass or to receive their sacraments.

The underground group stated that all the self-ordained bishops and the priests they ordained are illegitimate and illegal. Some in the underground group said that the sacraments performed by priests in the Patriotic Association are acceptable; others said that they are void and that every time they say mass they are committing a mortal sin, and that those who attend the mass assist them in committing sin and commit a grave sin themselves. They also said that all the priests in the Patriotic Association, including those that are simply listed on the government roster—even those who are not really in the association, but merely have a contact with the Patriotic Association—are all excommunicated. Summarily, all the priests at Xianxian, even those not with the Patriotic Association, are considered excommunicated. Because the bishop has joined the Patriotic Association, masses offered by these priests should not be attended. These priests should not even be asked to perform the sacrament of extreme unction. They said that at the hour of death, even having committed mortal sin, all one needs to do is to make a good act of contrition and one will be forgiven. There is no need for confession.

In one place, the underground group said that previous baptisms or marriages of the faithful were not proper and must be re-performed. Holy pictures, prayer books, rosaries, and holy medals provided by the Patriotic Association are not acceptable. Underground Catholics should not marry non-underground Catholics, unless the non-underground person follows the underground person.

The underground group preaches that this is still the time of persecution with no freedom of religion or belief. This group is against building churches, saying: "A church is a symbol of the freedom of religion. Building a church will lead people to think that there is freedom of belief and give face to the Communist party. . . . It is better to stay at the residence of people . . . to say the mass."

There are some underground bishops and priests who operate beyond their areas of assignment. They say: "Jesus told the apostles to go and preach the good news to the whole world. [He] did not draw area divisions for the apostles, so nobody can give us any area limit." For example, although Xianxian has an officially appointed bishop and each parish has its own priest, underground Bishop Li Zhenrong insists he is the bishop of Xianxian. He also goes to various provinces in the northeast, calling himself the bishop of Xianxian and meddling in their activities. Even the "little black priests" that he has ordained go to other counties and other dioceses for pastoral activities.

The underground group has objected to all seminaries not set up by the underground group and has spread rumors about seminaries established by the Patriotic Association. For example, the open bishops of Hebei province were discussing establishing a seminary at Shijiazhuang. The underground group started a rumor, and persuaded Catholics to oppose the seminary. Last year the seminary had some problems with its management. Xianxian Bishop Liu went to help as rector, but underground Bishop Jia Zhiguo tried to stop him, saying: "Shijiazhuang is in my diocese and I will not permit you to be active in it."

The underground group is against the use of the Latin mass. They say:

"The pope has ordered that mass be said in Chinese." They forbid the use of a Latin mass, even going as far as saying that the Latin mass has no effect. In the past the Chinese Catholics used to say their prayers in the classic way. At present, some prayers have been translated into a conversational style.[2] Some Catholics prefer to say their prayers in the new way, and others prefer the old way; the underground group is opposed to praying in the old classic way and it maintains that the pope ordered all prayers to be said in the new way and that those who do not listen to the order of the pope are being rebellious.

In order to build its own name, the underground group uses the authority of others. In the past, they relied on Bishop Fan Xueyan. When Bishop Fan was still in jail, they started rumors: "Bishop Fan is a cardinal; he is a special representative of the holy father, bishop of the whole nation, with authority over all China." Then they voiced their own opinions, attributing them to Bishop Fan. They even wrote a lot of statements using the name of Bishop Fan. Among these are the "Thirteen Points" known both inside and outside of China. But the points that they have stated are against the rules of the church, as is obvious to all who have some knowledge of theology. That is the reason people brought the Thirteen Points to Bishop Fan. Finally, Bishop Fan answered: "Of the thirteen points, at least three should be completely eliminated. ... " They had wrongly used the name of Bishop Fan to express erroneous statements, which were later denied by Bishop Fan. The underground group should not be allowed to use Bishop Fan to build up its own image.

Now they have found another force to rely on—Father Zhang Gangyi Antonius. Father Zhang is against the Patriotic Association. The underground group had spread a lot of propaganda about Father Zhang, saying that Zhang Gangyi spoke with the pope and fully understands the thoughts of the pope. Father Zhang says that the pope told him that he was most fervent among the priests of China and a hero of today who has performed many miracles. As a result, the underground group has called him a living saint. A lot of people from the northeastern and northwestern areas have gone to see Zhang Gangyi, and his biography has been written. Many pictures have been reprinted and disseminated showing Father Zhang being embraced by the pope. And this is all because Zhang is sympathetic toward the underground group. The underground group has used him and elevated him to the position of a living saint. They are using his name and influence, just as they made earlier use of the influence of Bishop Fan, to elevate their own position.

The underground group does not distinguish friend from foe, does no analysis, and forms its opinions obliquely, as seen by its narrow view on the Patriotic Association. The association has a lot of bad members who openly separated themselves from the pope; they are disliked by everybody. But not all people in the Patriotic Association are bad people; many of them are just listed on rosters. The underground group looks at them all in the same manner. Even priests who are not in the Patriotic Association are treated as members and looked on as enemies because they do not agree with the underground group.

The division of the underground church and the open church in recent years has greatly hindered the development of the Chinese Catholic church. All who are fervent Christians, whether clergy or faithful, sincerely hope that the priests of the entire nation will be united, and the division removed. For example, the bishop of Xianxian diocese and the priests all hope that underground Bishop Li Zhenrong will meet with them to talk. Li has made several trips to Xianxian, and the results of the talks were adequate. But later on Li went back to his old ways and insisted on his own point of view. Many priests, hoping for the unity of the church, visited him to talk with him, but he refused to see them.

The underground church also creates confusion. In places where the underground group has not gone, the church is peaceful. In the past years, the faithful of the three provinces of the northeastern areas were united in one mind in honoring the Lord, praying, and attending mass. But when the underground group arrived there, they said that the open priests were schismatic and had been excommunicated, and if the faithful followed them, they would go to hell. The result is that many faithful stopped attending the mass of the open church, and divisions were thereby created among them. There are several hundred parishioners in a village called Li Dong who are fervent Catholics, very united, and amiable. Last year, when the parish priest went to Tianjin for medical treatment, the underground priest went there, saying that the parish priest had been connected to the Patriotic Association and was excommunicated. He said that if Catholics followed him, they would go to hell. The result was that a lot of fervent parishioners joined the underground group and stopped going to the mass of the parish priest.

In conclusion, places that have no underground group are united, and peaceful. The arrival of the underground group has caused division. Even within a family opinions are divided — some are for the underground group, while others are for the open priests, to the extent that they refuse to talk to one another. The underground group has one mentality and accepts those whose opinions coincide with theirs; they attack those with different opinions.

On May 20, 1988, the pope made an unofficial statement to the bishops of the world about the problems of the Chinese church, giving guidelines. There was mention of the excommunication of the self-ordained priests in China. The underground group interpreted this guideline and widely spread the news that all self-ordained bishops had been excommunicated. Recently, Cardinal Jaime Sin of Manila wrote a letter about this matter, stating his own personal view on the Chinese church, saying that one cannot say that the self-ordained bishops of China are all excommunicated. Some of us transmitted this opinion of Cardinal Sin to the underground group.

One underground priest angrily replied: "A hundred cardinals cannot have the same power as a pope."

Notes

1. Bishop Liu Dinghan was elected to the episcopal seat of Cangzhou by the CCPA and ordained bishop in 1982. There has been no confirmation by the Vatican that Bishop Liu Dinghan's ordination was recognized by the pope.—Eds.

2. At its last national meeting held in Beijing in September 1992, the Chinese Catholic Bishops' Conference decided to introduce the Chinese language for liturgical use in all dioceses.—Eds.

9

A Church in Transition

EDWARD J. MALATESTA

During April 1990, I offered a seminar in the Institute for Religious Studies recently established in the philosophy department of Beijing University. The topic of the seminar was a book titled *Confucius, the Buddha, and Christ* (Ralph Covell, Orbis, 1986). During the last meeting of the seminar, the participants requested that we discuss an essay on "Catholicism and American Culture: The Uneasy Dialogue" by Avery Dulles (*America*, January 27, 1990). They also asked me to reflect on the present situation and possible future of the Catholic church in China, something, I told them, I would not have done unless they had asked — a reply that naturally evoked much laughter and applause.

It might seem contradictory at the present moment of history for an institute of religious studies to be inaugurated in the very university that has endured the most severe repression since the events that occurred in Beijing in 1989. And it might appear even more strange that an American Jesuit should be named visiting professor at the new institute, precisely when some foreign teachers were being reprimanded and also expelled for engaging in unauthorized religious activities. I leave it to detectives and diplomats to try to discover "whys" and "wherefores," but, as far as I know, I am just a friend, not a spy either of the Vatican or of the Chinese government, although I have been accused of being both. (I must confess it would be an interesting challenge to be one or the other, and even more interesting to be both at once!)

But contradictions, a part of human living everywhere, appear especially numerous in contemporary China in both the political and the economic spheres, as well as in cultural and religious matters. The country is still engaged in what Jonathan Spence has so wisely chosen as the title for his

Published in *America*, June 9, 1990, pp. 584-586, this essay is reprinted with permission.

latest book, *The Search for Modern China* (Norton, 1990). And Chinese Catholics, with varying degrees of awareness, understanding, and commitment are engaged in the painful quest for a modern Catholic Chinese church.

On Palm Sunday, Holy Thursday, Good Friday, and Easter Sunday I attended liturgies celebrated in the North Church (Bei Tang) of Beijing. On each occasion, the beautiful restored church was crowded with people of every age and condition who filled the aisles and every inch of available space. The liturgy is still celebrated there in Latin; from time to time, the older people chant from memory prayers in Chinese, which have a long history. Reverence and devotion were much in evidence, although there was no understanding of the Scriptures proclaimed in Latin, no homily, no commentary. After the liturgies, I visited the diocesan seminary relocated behind the church in quarters that, although still too small, are a definite improvement over the previous, miserable site in the country. The seminarians, like most of those in the other twelve publicly permitted seminaries, do their best to prepare themselves for their future ministry. The formation program, carried out in material poverty and under the restraints and intrusions imposed by the present régime, is a demanding one. Those who persevere to the end of their training period are led, in some parts of China, to wonder whether or not they should accept ordination when they have doubts about the bishop of their diocese. And all new priests who have been trained in the officially sponsored seminaries must face the fact that they and their ministry may be rejected by some of the faithful.

Many Chinese Catholics frequent the hundreds of government-approved churches, while others refuse to do so and will only attend mass celebrated in secret by "underground" priests, or in some chapels or churches where the clergy, while ministering publicly, are known not to accept affiliation with the Catholic Patriotic Association. The situation is further complicated by the fact that a dual hierarchy is functioning. The authoritative and very informative *Guide to the Catholic Church in China* of Jean Charbonnier lists sixty-two bishops recognized by the Chinese government in 1988; of these, it is known that at least fourteen bishops have been legitimized by expressing their communion with the pope. But there are many underground bishops. It is also reported that in one diocese there are two underground bishops who are opposed to each other as well as being hostile to the bishop approved by the government.

No one can tell when this distressing situation will be resolved. It would seem that the longer these divisions endure, the harder they will be to overcome. When the Vatican and the Beijing government finally do reestablish relationships, something to be hoped for, it should be possible for a process to be worked out concerning the nomination of bishops — the main point at issue — that will be acceptable to both sides; namely, a process that would recognize the ultimate authority of the pope to appoint bishops, while attending to the concerns of the government. Such arrangements, while not ideal, are not unprecedented and would, in the judgment of many, be far preferable to the present very muddled state of affairs.

The Catholic church in China desperately needs renewal, not only in its structures, liturgy, and ways of thinking, but also in its way of proclaiming the gospel to the millions who are seeking meaning and hope. But whatever efforts are made toward renewal—and there are some—must be carried out within the narrow limits allowed by the ruling powers. Freedom of religion is only partial, and every publicly authorized religious activity is carefully scrutinized. The government itself sometimes complains of the undue interference exercised by local officials who may be quite ignorant about allowed religious beliefs and practices. But even within these constraints, which many Catholics have learned to cope with, the gap created by almost forty years of separation from the church in other countries is beginning to be bridged. Chinese Catholics from Hong Kong, Macau, Singapore, Taiwan, and other places are visiting China in increasing numbers. They are ideal bearers and interpreters of the universal church's experience during and since the Second Vatican Council. Non-Chinese friends are often asked to offer various forms of assistance, and their presence and help, when adapted to the circumstances, are sincerely welcomed.

Regarding the relations between American Christians and China, it must be admitted that our Protestant brothers and sisters have been much more generous in reaching out to China. With the approval of the Chinese government and the Chinese Protestant church, they have established the Amity Foundation, which channels funds and teaching personnel to assist China. Apart from a few imprudent zealots, Protestant teachers arrive in China well prepared and well disposed for a ministry of service and witness, which is having very positive effects upon those to whom they are sent and upon the servants themselves. In February 1990, during the Chinese New Year holiday period, some one hundred and fifty Protestant teachers of English, sponsored by one North American group, gathered in Hong Kong from many different areas of China for several days of retreat to refresh themselves and renew their vision of Christian service. Another Protestant office, this one located in Berkeley, California, sends scores of committed Christian teachers in various fields to serve in China. They, too, have a preparatory training period and a mid-year retreat.

The program of Chinese-American academic exchanges at Loyola Marymount University in Los Angeles assists teachers and students of American Jesuit colleges and universities who wish to teach in China and facilitates the placement of Chinese scholars in these same schools. It is to be hoped that the United States Catholic China Bureau established at Seton Hall University will further help to inform American Catholics about developments in China and the church in China, so that more mutually beneficial friendships can be formed. A recently published book edited by Archie Crouch abundantly documents the long and rich tradition of American Christian relationships with China: *Christianity in China: A Scholar's Guide to Resources in the Libraries and Archives of the United States*, and identifies some 7,000 U.S. Catholics and Protestants who served in China. The missionary activity of past decades—and centuries—is over in China, but the time of a new style of cooperation is just dawning. This period promises to be even more fruitful since the Chinese will be the principal agents of their own evangelization, the creators of an authentically Chinese church, and the inspiration and guide to the foreign friends they invite to collaborate with them in supporting roles.

The present moment is, in a special sense, a transitional one for the Catholic church in China. The old is passing away and the new is just beginning to appear. The old provides the deep roots of fidelity, perseverance, and heroic suffering from which will spring the new flowers of a truly indigenized church within the climate of the changing social situation in China itself and in the worldwide family of nations and the universal church.

One of my greatest joys during the thirteen years that I studied and taught in Rome was to learn from the international body of professors, students, and visitors about the situation of the church in their respective countries. At the beginning of the 1966 academic year, the students who came from India spoke, thought, and acted very much like the English who had colonized them. Thirteen years later, the Indian students who arrived in Rome had spent years during their seminary training learning Indian native languages, reading Hindu sacred texts, learning to meditate and to celebrate the eucharist in a manner that reflected their Indian heritage. As a result, Indian contributions have begun to enrich the universal church and will continue to do so.

Similarly, I foresee the day—probably twenty to thirty years from now—when exegetes, theologians, spiritual writers, artists, and apostles in China will share with the universal church the results of their fusion of Christian faith and Chinese culture. They will build upon what other Chinese Catholics are beginning to create in places like Taiwan and Hong Kong. In this interim period, it is the grace of the rest of the church to be edified by the heroic example of Chinese Catholics in their present difficulties and to walk with them humbly and generously in the ways they suggest to us.

The first day of May is traditionally a day of pilgrimage to China's national shrine of Our Lady that crowns the Sheshan (Zose) hill near Shanghai. This year (1990), under sunny skies, thousands made their way up the slope. During the liturgy of the solemn pontifical mass celebrated in Latin, every available space in the basilica, from the entrance to the communion rail, was occupied by devout pilgrims. After the mass, various groups prayed the Rosary and carried out other devotions in the church and at the outdoor shrines to St. Joseph, Our Lady, and the Sacred Heart. Others made the outside Stations of the Cross on their knees.

Many pilgrims were fisherfolk from the surrounding areas who came on their houseboats; these were neatly lined up for a great distance in the canal, which flows near the entrance of the shrine at the base of the hill.

But there were other pilgrims who came from the provinces of Shandong, Jiangsu, Anhui, Zhejiang, Fujian, and from as far away as Guizhou. It was very moving to witness such an outpouring of faith and to meet the families and friends of some of the seminarians I had taught last fall. Especially impressive were the elderly nuns who had persevered through so many upheavals and who were obviously respected by the younger generation.

The country roads that lead most directly from Sheshan to the outskirts of Shanghai fascinate every visitor. While traveling this short distance of twenty miles through the rich, carefully cultivated fields, one sees an immense variety of means used to convey vegetables, animals, and other products to the promising city markets: bamboo poles borne on strong shoulders; carts pedaled by human legs, drawn by water buffaloes or mules, or by small, smoke-belching engines; bicycles, and vans and trucks of every size, age and description.

On the way to Sheshan in the early morning of May Day, I was contemplating this familiar but still intriguing scene when I caught sight of a small boy of six or seven years. With a stick in his hand, he was following a flock of geese alongside the road, his task for the day. The image remained with me. Some ten hours later, during the return journey, I passed the same little boy still tending the same geese and could see reflected in him the 800 million peasants who day after day, from dawn to dusk, draw their living from China's land.

I could not help but think that the liturgies in China's cathedrals, chapels, and homes will achieve their purpose, that the prayers and devotions of Sheshan will be answered, and that the greatest challenge to the church in China will be met when that little boy and the millions like him will understand what the tending of geese and the planting of rice has to do with the Risen Lord Jesus and the Kingdom of God.

10

The Local Church

HANS WALDENFELS

One of the most challenging results of Vatican II has been the rediscovery of the importance of local churches. This was due mainly to two factors: first, biblical and historical research, and second, an increased awareness of the need to respond to the rapidly changing world. Both factors have led to a rethinking of the self-understanding of the church and to a reexamination of the concrete relationship between the church and the world. The world we share is formed by a multiplicity of cultures and nations, political and economic systems, religions and philosophies, and language and thought patterns, all of which must be taken into consideration when we talk about the "world."

Biblical Research

The results of biblical research have proven that all those who follow the way of Christ form a community that is called the church. It also shows, however, that this church consists, in turn, of many local communities that are called churches. In fact, there are two basic conceptions by which the church is understood in the New Testament. On the one hand, the church is mentioned in a rather general and universal way, for example, "On this rock I shall build my Church" (Mt 16:18), or "He — Christ — is the head of his body. ... the body, however, is the Church" (Col 1:18; cf. Eph 1:22). On the other hand, the New Testament refers even more frequently to a specific Christian community or to several communities that are called equally "church" or "churches." This is seen, for example, when St. Paul and others are writing letters to "the church of Thessalonica" (1 and 2

This essay was published in *Tripod* 57, no. 3 (1990), pp. 27-32 and is reprinted with permission from the Holy Spirit Study Centre in Hong Kong.

Thess 1:1), or when greetings are sent "from the churches of the province of Asia" (1 Cor 16:19; cf. 2 Cor 8:1, 18; Gal 1:2, 22), or again, in the Apocalypse, where we read of letters sent to the angels of the seven "churches" (Rev 1:20, 22). All these churches are local communities, as we know today, perhaps differing somewhat in structure, but united in the same faith in the Lord Jesus Christ.

Undoubtedly, this situation changed as history unfolded. There were divisions, ways of dealing with dissensions, and the building up of common church structures. In the occidental church, there was a growing centralism, with its concentration on the local church of Rome and its bishop, the Roman pontiff, as the successor of St. Peter. Eventually, the Catholic church was defined in terms of this central local church as the Roman Catholic church; the concept of the Roman Catholic church and the universal church became one and the same. The process that led to this development in church history can be explained by a study of its theological and non-theological causes. We can also ask what essential elements define the unchangeable substance of the church, and what elements can legitimately undergo historical change. All these points, however, we shall leave undiscussed. Instead, I would like to call attention here to the basic idea of church and churches in Vatican II that stems from biblical and historical research.

The Local Church in Vatican II

The way in which, for the first time in centuries, the term "church" is now being used not only in the singular but also in the plural might be described as revolutionary. Since Vatican II, the terms "universal church and particular churches" and "world church and local churches" have been in constant use. In a way, these two modes of speaking are very close, even though the use of world church and local churches relates more explicitly to a locality—the world or a special place in the world. Nevertheless, their meaning starts with the concept of particularity, which implies the relationship of a part to the whole or to the totality, meaning the particular church to the universal church.

This, however, is not to be misunderstood in the sense that the church is realized only partially in a particular church and totally only in the universal church. On the contrary, the church in its full substance is essentially realized in every particular church. Therefore, Vatican II states in *Lumen Gentium* (23) that the universal church "exists in and by the particular Churches." Accordingly, the mystical Body of Christ is nothing but the *corpus ecclesiarum*.

Today, in our understanding of Vatican II's ecclesiology as an ecclesiology of *communion*, we prefer the term communion of churches (*communio ecclesiarum*). However, according to *Lumen Gentium* (26) we are

allowed to add: "The Church of Christ is truly present in all local communities of the faithful which in the New Testament—connected with their
pastors—are called themselves 'Churches.' " This is to say that one decisive
point in the concept of particularity is the locality of a church; it thus
becomes a question of defining what is meant by local: a city (the Roman
church), a country (the Chinese church), a region (the European church),
a continent (the Asian church), or something else.

Returning once again to *Lumen Gentium* (23), this text concerning the
particular churches adds that the "various Churches which were founded
at various places by the Apostles and their successors, during the course
of time, grew into a number of communities which were connected with
each other in an organic manner." Without prejudice to the universal
church, these particular churches enjoy their own discipline, their own liturgical rites, and their own theological and spiritual heritage. In the same
article, Vatican II points this out with special regard to the Eastern patri-
archal churches; it even calls these churches "mothers of faith giving life
to others as their daughters."

What is applicable to past history can be applied to the present and the
future as well. Moreover, the question arises whether the restoration of a
Bible-oriented concept of the church does not call for some necessary
amendments in the realization of the concrete church structure today.

Also, without any detriment to the dogmatic understanding of papal
jurisdiction and the unique position of the pope within the universal church,
the exercise of papal power and authority in the course of history—and
today—can and should be discussed. It should be done wherever the concrete exercise of papal authority has led to a confusion of spiritual and
political power. Actually, even a small sovereign state like Vatican City
gives the pope the appearance of a political ruler, at least outside the
church itself. Although it does seem ridiculous, apparently quite a few
people still worry about this. To give only one instance, in April 1990 I was
invited to participate in a conference held in East Berlin dealing with "East
Europe and China in Transition—Past, Present and Future." According to
the program, one of the afternoon sessions was to discuss the topic of
"Communism and the Churches—How Many Divisions Does the Pope Still
Have?"

China and the Catholic Church

It seems to be rather difficult for people outside the church, influenced
as many persons are by ideologies unfavorable to religion in general and
the Christian religion in particular, to make a fair judgment about the true
intentions of a supra-national religious institution like the Roman Catholic
church. Confusion in China today was echoed earlier in Germany. After
Vatican I's definition of the pope's jurisdiction, Prussian government leaders under Bismarck were strongly disturbed about the influence they

thought the pope could exercise over German Catholics. German Catholic leaders had the impression that German citizens were going to be forced into a dual political loyalty that could lead them to stand up in the name of the pope against their own people and the German government. Their own German bishops seemed to be officials appointed by a foreign government and acting in its name.

In order to diffuse the fear of the Prussian government, the German bishops worked out a formal paper in which they corrected the false impression originating from Vatican I's ecclesiology. In it, they emphasized that teaching bearing upon the pope's universal jurisdiction and infallibility was never understood in the political sense of a sovereign ruling over all Catholics in the world. On the contrary, the pope exercises a purely religious authority, which is completely different from the sovereignty of a worldly ruler: "the full sovereignty of the ruler in a State is nowhere contested by Catholics." According to this declaration of the German bishops, which was approved by Pope Pius IX on March 15, 1875, not even in spiritual matters does the Roman pontiff enjoy an authority that can be called "absolute."

This instance of modern German church history is instructive in two ways when speaking of the present context of China. First, the source of tension in the relationship between church and state in China—namely, the possible interpretation of the church's leadership in terms of political leadership—is neither a new problem, nor a problem limited to China. Second, the basic understanding of the "dual loyalty" allegiance to country (and government) and loyalty to God (and church) has relevance to Chinese Catholics who are also Catholic Chinese. As Pope John Paul II has repeatedly pointed out, there is no contradiction between true patriotism and true love of the church. We have to insist on this point—even if the experiences after the Chinese revolution of 1949, especially the frictions that prevail between the Patriotic Association and the church of Rome, seem to prove the contrary.

The Local Church of China

Applying the teaching of Vatican II to the Chinese situation, it is highly conceivable that a local church will develop that corresponds more explicitly to the thought patterns and the social and individual behavior of the Chinese people. Over thirty years ago Gottlieb Söhngen, a German Catholic professor of fundamental theology who taught at Munich University after World War II, dreamed of the exciting experience of developing a truly Chinese theology. When the time comes that the Chinese work out their own system of doing theology, he mused, the Europeans will "lose all sight and hearing," so stunning will it be. In any case, if the development of such an authentic Chinese theology can realistically be foreseen, certain changes in church structures are certainly imaginable, including the procedures for selecting and appointing bishops.

The gravest problem in building a Chinese local church, however, is the fact that the relationship of the Roman Catholic church with China does not begin with a blank slate. There is the experience of Chinese Christian history that has, for various reasons, repeatedly ended in disaster and become a burden for both the Chinese people and the universal Catholic church. The fact that the Catholic church in China is divided today and that there are Catholics who are trusted as Chinese citizens and other Catholics who are not cannot be overlooked, although peace and reconciliation are desired by the great majority of all the people involved.

Of course, it is not the right of foreigners to interfere; yet, since Christians throughout the world see themselves as sisters and brothers in one family, they cannot be insensitive toward the fellow Christians of a local church who must suffer, *either* because these Christians cannot live peacefully in a state that treats them unfavorably, *or* because they are cut off from the greater community of the followers of Jesus Christ that is the universal church, *or* because the faithful are divided among themselves and are "excommunicating" each other from the Christian community.

In such a situation, negotiations and deliberations between the various groups involved are urgently needed. As long as people are talking with each other, there is hope that they will resolve their problems and find peace, but a process of mutual understanding is required to restore confidence and partnership. This is first and foremost a matter for the Chinese themselves. Trust and friendship must be restored inside the Chinese nation, independently of the fact of whether the people are Christians or not.

The Chinese, as citizens of China, and Christians, as members of the church, must be aware of the fact that they belong to communities surpassing national local church boundaries. Concretely speaking, all Chinese people belong at the same time to the community of humans and all Christians as members of the Chinese local church belong at the same time to the universal church. The local church is only truly the church of Christ as far as it lives in communion with all other local churches forming the *communio ecclesiarum*.

In modern history, many nations who have isolated themselves from the greater human society, which we call "humankind," have had to learn the painful lesson that a nation can scarcely survive without granting freedom to its citizens and allowing the free exchange of thought and communication between peoples of different nations, cultures, religions, and political systems. China cannot stand outside of the family of nations. In this context, Christians will claim their rights as citizens and as human beings, although they are only a very small minority group inside an overwhelmingly vast population of other religions and ideologies.

On the other hand, what is requested in the field of politics must be equally granted by religious authorities. It is a fact that throughout history the church has again and again defended human rights whenever they were threatened by political authorities. However, history also shows that often enough the church has not been equally sensitive in situations when the same rights were requested inside the church.

The question I would like to raise is not so much the question of the individual rights of the faithful, but rather the question of the rights that the local church can demand within the *communio ecclesiarum*. More concretely speaking, whenever it can be done for the good of the people, Rome and the central authorities of the church should grant greater freedom in solving local questions on the local level, and restrict this freedom only where it is necessary for the good of the unity of the universal church. In fact, only when the relationship between China and the universal church is adequately restored will the process of true inculturation and the building up of a truly local Chinese church begin.

11

The Catholicity of the Chinese Church

MARIA GORETTI LAU

The catholicity of the Chinese church has always been challenged because of its antagonistic relationship with Rome. The whole controversy regarding the relationship between the Chinese church and Rome is surrounded by two issues: first, the diplomatic relations of the Vatican with Taiwan, and, second, recognition by Rome of the Chinese church's independence and self-governance, which includes the legitimizing of its independent bishops.

My concern here is with the theological aspect of the catholicity of the Chinese church in view of its insistence on independence and self-government. Has the catholicity of the Chinese church been completely undermined? Are the concepts of independence and self-governance totally incompatible with the notion of catholicity understood by Vatican II and modern theologians?

The Concept of Independence

Certainly, the Catholic church cannot accept a local church that proclaims total independence. A local church that intentionally severs ties of communion with the universal church and that overtly denies the primacy of the pope puts itself in a schismatic position. Is the Chinese church advocating such a concept of independence? According to my understanding, the idea of independence has been changing in the Chinese church during the past three or four decades. During the 1950s, the word independence had two meanings. Negatively, it meant a radical break of the

This essay, part of Maria Goretti Lau's dissertation, has been edited and abridged. Lau's dissertation entitled "Towards a Theology of the Local Church" was defended in 1989 at Leuven Catholic University in Belgium.

Chinese church with its semi-colonial missionary past. Positively, it referred to the establishment of an autonomous local church based on the principle of "Three-Self": a church that is self-supporting, self-governing, and self-propagating. In this regard, the word independence was closely linked with the concept of Three-Self.

In the 1950s the concept of Three Self had two different interpretations in the Chinese church. One interpretation was found in a document issued by the bishops in China in 1951 and entitled *The Church in China: Declaration of Principles*. The second interpretation was given by two groups of Chinese Catholics in manifestos issued in Sichuan and Chongqing and in a resolution adopted at a meeting in 1957, at which the Chinese Catholic Patriotic Association was formed. This difference in interpretation has been the main factor leading to the split of the Chinese church into two opposing camps.

According to the missionary bishops and the majority of Chinese church leaders and Catholics, the concept of Three-Self should be interpreted in light of the teaching of papal encyclical letters, and in harmony with the traditional Catholic position. In the 1951 document issued by China's Catholic bishops, who were mostly missionaries, self-supporting meant support of the local church by Catholics of any country: only subsidies with political implications, whether from abroad or from within China, could not be accepted. Self-propagating meant that foreign missionaries would propagate the faith in the interests of the Chinese church, not in the interests of foreigners. This document insisted on the right to continue using foreign missionaries until there was a sufficient number of native Chinese clergy. The document affirmed that a native Chinese hierarchy would gradually be established, not according to political principles or criteria, but according to ecclesiastical regulations and canon law.

A second interpretation was given by a group of Chinese Catholics in Sichuan, under the leadership of a Chinese priest named Wang Liangzuo, who issued a manifesto in 1950. Later a similar manifesto was issued by a group of Catholics in Chongqing. These Sichuan and Chongqing manifestos called for severing connections with Western imperialism, and they condemned the way in which Western imperialists used the church and the missionary enterprise as instruments of Western domination.

Issuing these manifestos to overthrow Western domination was a necessary step for Chinese Catholics toward establishing an indigenous Chinese church of Three Autonomies. Chinese clergy did not accept the Communist ideology of Marxism and Leninism, but they believed that the church in China could co-exist with the Communist government. According to some "progressive" or "patriotic" Catholics, the Chinese church, to a certain extent, could cooperate with the Communist government in reconstructing the country and in promoting the greater good of the Chinese people.

During the 1950s, the State Administrative Council of the Chinese government formulated the principle of Three-Self in unequivocal terms: The government should assist all religious bodies to become completely self-supporting; to those who experienced actual financial difficulties, the government might give appropriate financial help. No foreign subsidy was permitted without ratification from the government. Self-governing meant that all religious organizations were to be operated completely by Chinese people. No foreign missionaries were allowed to take charge of any cultural, educational, medical, or religious organization in China. As a consequence, the foreign missionary movement ceased to exist in China and the gospel was preached only by Chinese Christians.

In 1957 three preparatory meetings were held to form the Chinese Catholic Patriotic Association (CCPA). In the third meeting, the delegates adopted a resolution that conformed with the government's stand on the principle of Three-Self. The resolution stated clearly that the Vatican was anti-Communist and anti-socialist in nature and that, therefore, the church in China had to break financial and political relations with the Vatican in order not to contradict the position of the Chinese government.[1] The Chinese church would submit to the pope in matters of doctrine and ecclesiastical practices and retain only a religious link with the Vatican. Chinese Catholics would work for an autonomous church governed by Chinese clergy.[2]

Evidently, such an interpretation would not be accepted either by the Vatican or by the missionary bishops and the majority of Chinese Catholics who held the traditional Catholic position. Obviously, Pope Pius XII's understanding of catholicity reflected the ecclesiology of his time and was understood mainly in geographical and temporal terms. The notions of independence and Three-Self of the Chinese church were seen as radically opposed to the catholicity of the Roman Catholic church. A national church was seen as dangerous, and a likely source of separation and schism.

In the 1950s, particularly during the Anti-America/Aid-Korea movement and in the period of the exodus of foreign missionaries, the independent movement of the Chinese church focused on self-support and self-propagation. However, since 1980, the focus of that movement has shifted to "self-government, self-management, and self-rule." In many statements of the officially established Chinese church, the word independence always occurs with self-rule and self-government, with the concept of self-government highlighted.

The Concept of Self-Government

This shift of focus from self-support and self-propagation to self-government is not without important implications on the part of the Chinese church leaders. In 1980, two new ecclesial structures were established, the Chinese Catholic Bishops' Conference (CCBC) and the Catholic Church

Administrative Commission (CCAC). The CCBC is modelled on the episcopal conference in the universal church. The Administrative Commission is an unprecedented ecclesial organization for which there seems to be no counterpart. These two ecclesial organizations, especially the CCBC, have gradually taken over the leadership of the Chinese church and are responsible for guiding the religious life and for organizing the religious activity of that church.

Since 1980, the Patriotic Association (CCPA) has been functioning in a low-key manner while the CCBC is gradually emerging as a new ecclesial structure with ruling and teaching authority. It is interesting to see that although the present Chinese government still insists on the principle of Three-Self (Document 19), the Chinese church, now under the leadership of the CCBC as well as the CCAC, stresses self-government, self-rule, and self-management rather than self-support and self-propagation. In fact, as the Chinese church resumes its contacts with other churches in the world, unconditional assistance, both spiritual and material, is given to the Chinese church "in charity" by many other churches. Sometimes donations from abroad are so abundant that the Chinese church must learn to be discerning and cautious to ensure that the principle of self-reliance is not violated. Although the Chinese church officially states that no missionary activity is welcome in China, some foreign missionaries, when circumstances allow, have been invited to lecture at certain seminaries and to share their viewpoints with seminarians and Chinese Catholics.

As for self-government, it is a principle related to Rome rather than to other churches in the world. For the majority of the Chinese bishops in the CCBC, self-government does not necessarily imply a radical break of the relationship of the Chinese church with Rome, though a visible contact between Rome and the Chinese church is not possible because the Vatican has no diplomatic relations with China. China still regards the Vatican basically as an anti-Communist organization, and adopts a cold attitude toward it.

Except for a small number of Chinese clergy and Catholics, most Chinese bishops (whether illicit or legitimate), priests, and lay Catholics wish to re-establish normal relations with Rome. They hope that Rome will understand their concrete and real situation and will accept their request for self-government. For the Chinese church leaders in the CCBC, independence is synonymous with self-government and self-management. For them, self-government means not only the right to run the church in a Chinese way and to make their own decisions regarding the most expedient manner for the Chinese church to deal with social policy, but also the right to elect their own bishops.

According to Chinese church leaders, self-government is a possible way to solve this dilemma. In the concrete situation of the Chinese church, self-government means that the Chinese church is governed by a Chinese hierarchy with the right to make its own decision regarding the nomination of bishops and the way in which the local church is to deal with the Communist government. Theologically speaking, such a concept of independence, or self-government, does not necessarily include a break of relationship with the pope and the church of Rome.

The Catholicity of the Church

The catholicity of a church is composed of different elements: *extensive* catholicity describes its relationships with other churches; *temporal* catholicity describes its historical relationship with the universal church; and *vertical* or *spiritual* catholicity describes the indelible presence of the Holy Spirit within the church.

It must be admitted that the extensive catholicity of the Chinese church was defective during the 1950s. This aspect of catholicity refers not only to "all places" and "all members," but also to the "universal communion of all local churches." A portion of its members, for instance, the CCPA, did not acknowledge the role of the Holy See in the life of the Chinese church. Furthermore, having closely cooperated with Mao's government, the CCPA members endorsed the government's "closed-door" policy, at the risk of leading the Chinese church away from communion with the Holy See and the other churches in the world.

The temporal catholicity of the Chinese church was also defective since temporal catholicity means not only the church existing in "all ages" and in "all generations," but also the "continuity of the church in history" through its relationship to the church of the apostles. This defectiveness became noticeable as a portion of its members (CCPA) advocated severing ties with the church of Rome, which is presided over by the pope, the successor of Peter.

I do not question the good intentions of the members of the CCPA who attempted to reconcile the Catholic church in China with Mao's government, so as to enable the Chinese church to be accepted by the new Chinese society. However, their excessive union with the Communist government and their over-emphasis on the "Chineseness" of that local church did weaken its catholicity. The local character of the church was stressed so much that the universality and particularity of that local church were polarized.

As far as the particularity of the local church is concerned, an over-emphasis on particularity often creates a tension between the local church and the universal communion of churches, as well as among the local churches themselves. This tension can be destructive or it can be productive and salutary. It is destructive when it gives rise to narrowness and division. It is productive when an increasing consciousness of its own particularity enables the local church to recognize its limitations and inadequacies. This recognition, in turn, makes the local church aware of its need for a universal communion with the other churches in the world. Only in communion with other churches can the life of a local church be completed, the authenticity of its faith be protected, and the practices of its faith be corrected.[3]

The awareness of such a need, particularly the need for union with the church of Rome, was overtly expressed by a group of Chinese Catholics who have been called "loyalist" Catholics. They profess publicly their allegiance to the pope, and disapprove the close relationship between the CCPA and Mao's government. They risk their personal freedom, endure great hardships, and some have even suffered imprisonment. With their suffering and death, they witness to the truth that authentic local churches are and must remain in union with one another as members of the universal church.

In the 1950s another tendency in the Chinese church was to emphasize the universality of the local church at the expense of its particularity and its legitimate autonomy. For some Chinese Catholics, communion was almost equivalent to absorption, union with Rome implied absolute and unconditional obedience, and dissent meant disloyalty. This tendency does not represent the true catholicity of the local church. True catholicity, as Avery Dulles says, is "union of opposites."[4] In other words, it is the union of the two opposites of universality and particularity.

Since 1980 the Chinese church has made a significant move to actualize its catholicity. As the Chinese government relaxed its control of religion, churches continued to open in every major city, and many Chinese Catholics returned to officially opened churches to participate in worship and prayer meetings. The underground church gradually resurfaced. When opportunity allowed, some Chinese church leaders explicitly expressed their wish for reunion with Rome and with other churches in the world. In spite of the fact that misunderstandings still existed between Rome and the Chinese church, both parties attempted to search for a suitable way to initiate a mutual dialogue. Many foreign churches assisted by trying to serve as a "communication bridge" between Rome and the Chinese church.

From a theological point of view, the interpretation of independence and self-government by Chinese church leaders in the 1980s is not totally incompatible with Vatican II's understanding of catholicity. The meaning of the indigenous Chinese church has been explained by Chinese bishops in *Catholic Church in China*.[5] The explanation can be summarized as follows:

1. The Chinese church is independent and self-governing.

2. It represents the majority in service to the whole.

3. It participates actively in the construction of a socialistic society along with the whole nation.

4. The Chinese church is autonomous; namely, it is governed by local clergy.

5. It works to create a theology that will adapt itself to the country's

needs and special circumstances, and will be in harmony with the mentality of its people and the Chinese culture.

Independence is linked with self-government. From a practical point of view, autonomy means self-government, that is to say, the Chinese church is ruled by the local clergy; independence, self-government, and autonomy are synonymous. It is noteworthy that Rome is not mentioned in the Chinese church's interpretation of independence and self-government. This may imply that the Chinese bishops intentionally leave some room for a dialogue with Rome, and that the self-government and independence of the church do not necessarily mean the rejection of the spiritual leadership of the Roman pontiff.

In comparison with the CCPA's resolution in 1957, which explicitly stated that independence meant a break in financial and political relations with the Vatican, the interpretation in the 1980s, relatively speaking, was broader in scope and less political in tone. When asked about the meaning of independence during an interview in Hong Kong in August 1988, Bishop Jin Luxian explained that independence meant autonomy, in the sense used by the Second Vatican Council. Bishop Jin said:

I have said nothing against the Pope, nothing. You know it: I said that I want the "autonomy" of the Catholic church of Shanghai, but in Chinese, autonomy and independence are written with the same characters. When I say autonomy, the press puts independence, and consequently, people outside have the idea that I am a schismatic. The Western press places the emphasis on independence. I, instead, talk about autonomy, such as was spoken of in Vatican II.[6]

According to some authors, the main functions of the CCPA specified in its 1980 constitution "are not directly opposed to communion with the universal church."[7] In reality, a wide range of opinions and attitudes exists within the CCPA regarding the concrete realization of the Three-Self principle and the interpretation of the CCPA's main functions. For some members, "the spirit of patriotism seems to prevail over everything else, and this often is joined to a certain hostility towards the Vatican."[8] Other members conform only outwardly to the CCPA's directives, but privately adhere to a faith-communion with the pope as the successor of Peter. In such a circumstance, it is very difficult for us to discern to what extent and in what manner the Chinese church has actualized its catholicity.

The situation of the Chinese church in the 1980s seemed to be more complicated than it was in the 1950s. It has become more and more obvious that many followed a third option, that is, to violate the ecclesiastical regulations and accept illicit episcopal ordinations in order to help the Chinese church survive. Faced with such a complicated situation, I am inclined to state that, as outsiders, it is not in our competence to judge our brothers and sisters in the Chinese church regarding the actualization of the catholicity of their church. As Pope John XXIII said in 1961: "We had best refrain from launching criticism, but rather continue to pray."[9] Besides, as John Linnan has observed, it is important to note that one of the contributions of Vatican II is to enable us to see clearly that there is a hierarchy of values in ecclesial reality: "Thus participation in the life of the church as the mystery revealed in Christ takes priority over defects in catholicity no matter how important that may be."[10]

Catholicity is realized through all the constitutive elements of the local church, such as the teaching of the apostles, the breaking of bread and the other sacraments, prayer, fellowship, the presence of the Holy Spirit, and the bishops and clergy. These theological elements that constitute the assembly of the faithful as an *ecclesia* in a given place can by no means escape the influences of cultural, historical, social, and political factors.

In China today, the structures of the church are its most vulnerable aspects. Traditionally, these structures are considered necessary instruments for the actualization of catholicity, and they include both the sacramental and hierarchical structures of the church. The relationship between the local church and the Holy See is one aspect of these ecclesial structures. Suppression, distortion, or destruction of these structures weakens the actualization of catholicity in the Chinese church. Nevertheless, as a gift from above, the spiritual or vertical dimension of catholicity can never be defeated by human forces, which include all human limitations, weakness, and sins. The irrevocable self-communication of the triune God and the indelible presence of the Holy Spirit are the ultimate foundations of catholicity, as well as the ultimate sources of the holiness of the church. Although the extensive and temporal aspects of the catholicity of the Chinese church may be defective, the trinitarian aspect—the vertical dimension of catholicity—is always present in the hearts of Chinese Catholics.

During the past four decades, the agonizing struggle of the Chinese church for an authentic ecclesial selfhood within the context of an atheistic and Communist China has had its lights and shadows. For instance, the Chinese church now enjoys a full native Chinese leadership; on the other hand, the official leadership of the Chinese church does confront difficulties in making visible contacts with the universal church, especially with the church of Rome and its bishop, the pope.

From a theological point of view, although both "pro-government" and "pro-Roman" Catholics witnessed the need for the legitimate autonomy of the local church and the truth of the undivided unity of the church of Christ,[11] the bitter conflicts between the two groups of Chinese Catholics have obstructed the internal unity of that local church, and have left deep wounds in the hearts of many Chinese Catholics in both groups. The reconciliation of these two groups remains a difficult pastoral problem to be faced by the Chinese church leaders.

Challenges to the Universal Church

If Rome is to normalize its relationship with the Chinese church, there are several practical problems Rome must consider, including the role of the laity in the government of the local church, the power of the episcopal conference, and a new vision of the church's mission in the world.

The Role of the Laity in the Local Church

At present (1989), there are two main leadership bodies, namely, the Catholic Church Administrative Commission and the Catholic Bishops' Conference of China . According to Chinese church leaders, the Chinese Catholic Patriotic Association is a political organ with no real ecclesial status. The structure of the archdiocese has been abolished and the titles of archbishop and metropolitan practically do not exist. The CCAC is a new ecclesial structure for which there seems to be no parallel. The CCAC includes in its membership bishops, priests, and laity. Although the Chinese church stresses the supreme authority of the bishops by placing the CCBC in a top ecclesiastical position, it has also expanded the scope of collective leadership by calling upon not only bishops but also religious, priests, and laypersons to guide the Chinese church through membership in the CCAC. The CCBC is a part of the CCAC.[12] At the moment, two important administrative positions—the chairmanship of the CCAC and the presidency of the CCBC—are held by the same bishop. The CCAC is an ecclesial structure created according to the principle of "democratic administration." Its existence implies that the leadership of the church is no longer an exclusive episcopal privilege, but a responsibility shared by all the members of the local church, regardless of their ecclesiastical rank. It also indicates that the laity can now play an important and a decisive role in the government of the local church.

The involvement of the laity in decision-making has some practical implications for the structure of the universal church. At least in the CCAC, the involvement of the laity, clergy, and religious in decision-making may serve to counterbalance the national episcopal conference, which is regarded as the spiritual authority of the local church. Moreover, in China, a bishop is elected by the people in order to serve the people. A wider participation of the laity in the government of the local church may help the national or regional bishops' conferences to fulfill their role as "servant" among the people and to be more attentive to the peoples' real needs.

The idea of the democratic administration of the Chinese church may give rise to the idea that the voice of a minority might be suppressed by the opinion of the majority. Nevertheless, the new structure of the CCAC, which involves a wide participation of the laity, clergy, and religious decision-making, is seen as implementing Vatican II's teaching on the laity in the universal church (*Lumen Gentium*, IV). The faithful, who by baptism are incorporated into Christ, in their own way share the "priestly, prophetic, and kingly office of Christ" (*Lumen Gentium*, 31). They are called to the best of their ability to carry on "the mission of the whole Christian people in the Church and in the World" (31). The Council teaches that "by divine institution the holy Church is ordered and governed with a wonderful diversity" (32). The new structure of the Chinese church challenges the universal church to re-think these theological questions.

From a biblical point of view, the church is a communion of charisms. Leadership of the church is understood as one of the charisms conferred by the Holy Spirit for the building up of the Body of Christ. The question posed to the universal church by the new phenomenon of the Chinese church is: Is it possible, on the one hand, to preserve the episcopal college headed by the pope as a responsible leadership body of the whole church, and on the other hand, to integrate the laity in a real and concrete way into the process of decision-making so as to allow the laity to fulfill its "kingly" function in the church?

The Authority of the Episcopal Conference in the Local Church

As one of the main ecclesial structures, the CCBC exercises the powers of teaching and ruling. Since Rome does not have any visible contact with the Chinese church and cannot provide direct guidance for it, the CCBC, along with the CCAC, is *de facto* the superior authority of that local church.

In my view, the superior authority of the CCBC may have to be recognized and accepted by Rome if Rome is to reconcile itself with the Chinese church, because according to Chinese law no foreign power is allowed to interfere with religious affairs in the country, and all Chinese religious organizations are required to maintain their independence, which is considered to be a part of China's strategy to safeguard national independence.

Even if the pope is recognized as the supreme head of the Chinese church, and even if Sino-Vatican relations are normalized, it would seem that Rome might not be able to directly exercise its leadership and power over the Chinese church as it is exercising its leadership and authority over other local churches in the world. Rome may need an ecclesial mediation, an intermediate instance, which can serve as a "bridge" between the pope and the whole company of the Chinese faithful in China. This intermediate instance should exercise a superior power of teaching and governing, and have the right to discern the best way for the Chinese church to deal with social policy and to maintain its communion with the universal church. At the same time, it must be able to serve the entire Chinese nation. In my opinion, the CCBC can become such a real intermediate instance. Thus, to create a strong Chinese Bishops' Conference "endowed with some power under an intelligent president"[13] who is loyal to the teaching of the apostles and to the successor of Peter is of crucial importance for the reconciliation between Rome and the Chinese church.

To endow the CCBC with a "superior" or "sovereign" power that permits more autonomy and freedom will not hamper the communion of the Chinese church with Rome. On the contrary, it will expedite the procedure for rapprochement between Rome and the Chinese church. Through the real intermediate instance of the CCBC, the pope will be able to resume his Petrine function in the Chinese church in a way more acceptable to both the Chinese church and the Chinese government—a way that shows more clearly the catholicity of the Petrine office with regard to the local churches.

On the part of Rome, recognizing the CCBC as a real intermediate instance with a sovereign or superior power over the Chinese church implies an acceptance of the challenge to the positions of *Instrumentum Laboris* issued by Rome. If the teaching of the universal church expressed in this document is intended to be applicable to all local churches in the world, including the Chinese church (and perhaps other local churches in Communist countries in Asia), then the positions of the *Instrumentum Laboris* will have to be modified. The teaching and ruling powers of the episcopal conference in the local (whether regional, national, or supra-national) church must be theologically and juridically recognized. The recognition of the superior power of the episcopal conference implies a decentralization of ecclesiastical authority on the part of Rome. This decentralization will have a profound significance for the ecumenical dialogue of the "Roman" Catholic church with other Christian denominations, at least with the Orthodox and Anglican churches. It is interesting to note that acceptance of the theological and juridical status of the episcopal conference and recognition of the conference's sovereign power over the local church in its territory are particularly significant for dialogue with the Orthodox church, which is basically guided by a synodal government.

A New Mission: Bridge-Building

The Catholic church in China presents itself as an autonomous local church determined to run its own ecclesiastical affairs without any foreign influence. The two conditions for establishing relations with foreign churches, namely, mutual respect and equality, are repeatedly emphasized by Chinese church leaders who insist that the Chinese Catholic church should never again become a colonial church.[14] Because of humiliation in the past and political pressures from the present government's religious policy, it seems necessary for the Chinese church to declare openly that foreign interference in its ecclesiastical affairs is forbidden.

In any event, a careful analysis of the present situation of the Chinese church indicates that a new type of missionary work is emerging that benefits not only the Chinese church but also foreign churches. In the past some missionaries often failed to respect native clergy or to appreciate the positive values of local cultures and customs. However, since Vatican II, the notion of mission has undergone a remarkable transformation. It has changed from a unilateral giving action to a process of mutual exchange. Now missionaries understand themselves as equal partners invited to serve the local church. They are in mission to share their faith and, at the same time, to enrich their own experience of faith by learning from people in the local church.

Because of its isolation from the universal church for nearly three decades, the Catholic church in China has not experienced these recent changes in the understanding of mission. It seems that the missionary enterprise attacked so vigorously by the Chinese church leaders is the old unilateral concept of mission. It seems that Chinese church leaders would likely not object to the new bilateral concept of mission, which respects the dignity and legitimate autonomy of the local church by treating it as an equal partner.

On many occasions the Chinese church has declined help from foreign missionaries and determined to solve its own problems because of its strong sense of national dignity and its unpleasant past experiences. Nevertheless, the rapprochement of the Chinese church with Rome certainly needs assistance from other local churches in the world. At the moment, Rome and the Chinese church have no direct and visible contact or channel of communication. This is the mission of bridge-building that has been initiated by some foreign churches in response to Pope John Paul II's request;[15] it requires patience, understanding, and respect from the bridge-builder. It demands that the churches involved constantly transform themselves in conformity with the gospel of reconciliation. Only those churches that have worked hard for unity and reconciliation within themselves can be effective instruments for bridging the gap between the Chinese church and Rome. St. John says: "Unless a grain of wheat falls into the earth and dies, it remains alone; but if it dies, it bears much fruit" (John 12:24). The mission of bridge building requires one to give not merely material assistance but the person himself or herself. Bridge-builders are genuine missionaries because, following Jesus' example, they are always ready to give themselves up for the new lives of others, as well as for the reconciliation of the whole world.[16]

Conclusion

Perhaps the most difficult problem now facing Chinese church leaders is the internal divisions of that local church. This is a pastoral rather than a theological problem. According to recent news from China (1989), a few Chinese bishops who have been released from prison and who are alleged to have been granted permission by Rome to ordain priests and bishops have secretly become very active in China. They continue to ordain native priests who have not been properly educated in theology. They uphold Pope Pius XII's teachings of the 1950s, and are not aware of recent changes in the universal church since Vatican II, including changes in the church's attitude toward different ideologies.

Foreign visitors who have travelled in China and letters from some Chinese Catholics within China testify that, in some places, these internal conflicts are so strong that Chinese Catholics in those areas are brought into a chaotic situation. Many worry that this chaotic situation may provide a new opportunity for the government to suppress the religious activity of the church. Chinese church leaders, particularly the independent Chinese bishops, blame Rome for this situation because they think that Rome secretly granted authority to these "loyalist" Chinese bishops to ordain unqualified Chinese priests. They believe that the only solution is to make Rome aware of the danger involved, meaning that the government may interfere to suppress the relative freedom of the Chinese church. They suggest that the Vatican should normalize its diplomatic relations with China as soon as possible, and they consider that Rome's recognition of the CCBC and the CCAC may help reestablish order.

Reconciliation between Rome and the Chinese church is an urgent task. The present dispute between Rome and the Chinese church forces the Chinese church to live in isolation. There is fear that this isolation may eventually lead the Chinese church to develop an unsound theology to justify its *status quo*, but not to build up its faith. Besides, in view of the confusion, agony, and anxiety among Chinese Catholics, reconciliation seems to be more urgent now than ever before. However, this is not an easy task. Rome must work very carefully and prudently toward a solution before it is too late, taking every aspect of the problem into consideration.

Notes

1. Chan, Kim-Kwong, *Toward a Contextual Ecclesiology: The Catholic Church in the People's Republic of China (1971-1983), Its Life and Theological Implications* (Hong Kong: Phototech System Ltd, 1987), p. 208.

2. Ibid., p. 208.

3. Linnan, John E., "Toward a Theology of a Particular Church," *China Notes*, Winter 1983-1984 (New York: National Council of Churches China Committee), p. 3.

4. Dulles, Avery, *The Catholicity of the Church* (New York: Oxford, 1986), p. 23.

5. Tu, S.-H., "The International Conference at Montreal," *Catholic Church in China* 4 (March 1982), p. 27.

6. Politi, G., "Interview with Bishop Aloysius Jin Luxian," *Sunday Examiner*, August 5, 1988.

7. Chang, Aloysius B., "Theological-Pastoral Reflections on the Catholic Church in the People's Republic of China," *Tripod* 46 (1988), p. 38.

8. Ibid., p. 38.

9. Ibid., p. 39.

10. Linnan, p. 3.

11. Lau, Maria Goretti, "The Catholic Church in China Today," *Louvain Studies* 11 (1986), pp. 173-175.

12. In September 1992 the fifth national Catholic Representatives' Congress

reversed the order. The CCAC is now a commission placed under the authority of the CCBC. — Eds.

13. Politi, G., "Interview with Bishop Aloysius Jin Luxian."

14. Tu, S.-H., "To Have an Independent, Self-Ruled and Self-Managed Church Is Our Sacred Right," pp. 100-101.

15. Pope John Paul II, "Be a Bridge-Church," *Papal Documents Related to the New China, 1937-1984*, ed. Elmer Wurth (Maryknoll, NY: Orbis Books, 1985, pp. 176-78.

16. The idea of "bridge church" is further developed by Aloysius Chang in Chapter 15. — Eds.

Part III

Looking toward the Future

12

Learning from the Missionary Past

JEAN-PAUL WIEST

A Survey of Encounters between China and Christian Missionaries

The Christian presence in China has a long but broken history, shrouded by the mystery of time. Legend has it that St. Thomas traveled to China from India, converted some Chinese, and then returned to Meliapur on the southeast coast of India, where he died. Studies claiming that Jewish communities already prospered in China during the mid-first century raise the possibility that Christian merchants of Jewish and Syrian extractions traveling to the Far East brought the Christian message to communities along the Silk Road. But legends remain only legends and possibilities do not make history, unless solid evidence can be found to substantiate their claims.[1]

What is beyond doubt is that the Christian message was brought to China by missionaries on more than one occasion. Prior to the nineteenth century, Nestorian and Roman Catholic missionaries made several attempts to establish a lasting and significant presence in China, but each time they failed. The arrival in Chang'an (modern Xi'an) of Nestorian Bishop Alopen in 635 is the first known record of a Christian presence in China. The Nestorian church was officially recognized by Emperor Taizong of the Tang dynasty under the name of the Luminous Religion. It prospered for more than two hundred years. In 845, however, an antiforeign movement resulted in a ban on all foreign religious activity in China. Although the decree was rescinded one year later, it drastically altered the religious climate in China. Buddhism, which had gained a certain degree of political influence before the ban, rebounded rapidly after the ban was lifted, however its force was now that of a popular religious movement. Nestorianism, on the other hand, never recovered from the blow and remained severely diminished.

Outside of China, Nestorianism continued to prosper in Central Asia among the Uighur, Naiman, and Ongut tribes, and gradually spread among the Keraits and the Mongols. In thirteenth-century China, the advent of the Mongol Yuan dynasty marked the beginning of a strong comeback for Nestorian Christianity. Researchers have identified at least twenty-two cities with substantial groups of Nestorian believers. The most compelling sign of the vitality of the Nestorian church in China during the Mongol period is perhaps the fact that in 1280 a Nestorian monk of Uighur descent, born and raised in Shaansi province, was elected patriarch of Baghdad to rule over the entire Nestorian church.

The founding of the indigenous Ming dynasty in 1368 led to the demise of Mongol rule on Chinese soil. The Nestorians lost the protection and favors they had enjoyed for some one hundred years and again disappeared from the public scene. At the same time, the violent persecution endured by the Nestorian church in its Persian and Mesopotamian heartland at the hands of the Muslim conqueror Tamerlane destroyed its vast network as a multi-ethnic organization. The surviving Syro-Persian Nestorian church was so diminished that it was never again able to reach out to China.

The first arrival of Roman Catholic missionaries in China occurred also during the thirteenth century. In 1245, Pope Innocent IV sent a Franciscan friar to the Mongol court at Karakorum to convince the Great Khan Khubilai to stop his advance into Europe. Although the retreat of the Mongol horsemen had no connection with the diplomatic skills of the friar, the papacy continued to dispatch Franciscan led missions to Persia, Mongolia, and China in an attempt to convert the tribes of the vast Mongol empire and to enlist their help against Islam. Again no political alliance was achieved by these envoys, but their missionary efforts led to the establishment of a Roman Catholic outpost in Mongol-occupied China where the Great Khan had founded the Mongol Yuan dynasty in 1271. In 1294 the Franciscan John of Montecorvino became the first Roman Catholic missionary to set foot on Chinese soil. Like the earlier Nestorians, the Franciscan friars enjoyed the protection of the emperor and received a substantial state salary that enabled them to found churches in the capital Beijing (Marco Polo's Cambalic) and some other major cities such as Hangzhou, Yangzhou, and Quanzhou (Marco Polo's Zaitong).

The Franciscan presence in China, however, was small and short-lived. Heavy casualties caused by the perils and privations of the long voyage from Europe to the Far East cut missionary reinforcement to a trickle. John of Montecorvino had to wait eleven years for another friar to help him. After the turn of the century, moreover, the rapid spread of Islam throughout Central Asia further compounded the pope's difficulty in staffing the Chinese missions.

In China, meanwhile, hostility toward the foreign Mongol Yuan dynasty and those associated with it became more widespread and violent after 1340. Like their Nestorian counterparts, Catholic communities were persecuted and their churches destroyed by Chinese patriots. When the Franciscan bishop of Quanzhou was slain in 1362, he was one of the last Catholic missionaries still on Chinese territory.

Under such circumstances, the Holy See eventually lost all contacts with its Chinese missions. Although it continued to send out missionaries from time to time, none seems to have reached China until the time of Matteo Ricci.

When Matteo Ricci and his Jesuit companions entered China two centuries later, they were only vaguely aware that Franciscans and Nestorians had preceded them. Unhampered by the past, the Jesuits saw in Confucian culture an expression of the human spirit worthy of respect, and they searched for ways to adapt Christianity within that context. Their intellectual and moral qualities had considerable positive influence on China's cultivated society and on its emperor. The relationship between the Chinese and the Jesuits was characterized by an absence of rigidity and the possibility of frank discussions.

Meanwhile, in 1633 the Holy See enjoined other European missionary groups to assist in the conversion of China. By the late seventeenth century, it became apparent that some other missionaries considered the Jesuits' accommodations to Chinese culture excessive and inadmissable. The Jesuits, for instance, allowed Chinese Christians to practice Chinese customs in honor of Confucius and deceased ancestors, while most other European missionaries opposed these rituals as superstitious. The dispute worsened into a bitter conflict known as the Chinese rites controversy, involving the papacy and the Qing dynasty.

In the end, European inflexibility prevailed over the Jesuit commitment to adaptation. Between 1704 and 1742, Clement XI and Benedict XIV issued several decrees categorically condemning the Chinese rites. The response of the Kangxi emperor in Beijing gradually shifted from surprise to anger. Finally, in 1724 his son, the Yongzheng emperor, banned all Europeans from China except those employed by the court because of their scientific expertise. What followed was more than a century of persecution against the 300,000 Christians in China.

Despite the ban, foreign missionaries continued to enter the country incognito. Some were able to rejoin their missions and minister in secret. When apprehended by the local authorities, they were usually escorted back to Macao; a few, however, lingered in Chinese jail or were even put to death. It was not until the 1840s that missionaries were allowed to return openly to their missions where, in spite of persecution, they found the number of practicing Catholics had remained constant.

Along with Catholic missionaries came, for the first time, Protestant missionaries. The attitudes of these newcomers, whether Catholic or Protestant, were very different from those of the early Jesuits. They viewed Chinese culture as in conflict with the gospel and sought to rescue their converts from what they considered to be a hostile pagan environment.

The arrival of foreign missionaries in the nineteenth century was unfortunately also associated with the domination of China by Western powers. Through a series of "unequal treaties," these nations forced China to accept foreign influences, including Christianity. Despite this often appallingly imperialistic and culturally insensitive character of both Catholic and Protestant missions in China, in many areas conversions occurred in large numbers.

In the first half of the twentieth century, changes began to appear, indicating that a truly Chinese Christianity might finally emerge. The Protestants were the first to initiate a large-scale process of devolution of authority to Chinese pastors. They also targeted the educated class of Chinese society, creating thirteen Protestant universities and converting high-ranking officials including President Chiang Kaishek.

On the Catholic side, Father Vincent Lebbe, probably the missionary the most sensitive to Chinese culture since Ricci, jolted the missionary community by calling for the church — including its leadership — to become truly Chinese. His stand began a process that, combined with other factors, led to the ordination of six Chinese bishops in 1926, the revocation of the condemnation of the Chinese rites in 1939, and the establishment of a Chinese local church with its own hierarchy in 1946. By the early 1950s, however, these changes had not yet pervaded deeply enough into the Catholic and Protestant churches, which, for the most part, still relied on the Western powers and concentrated the real power in the hands of foreigners.

The victory of the Communist forces of Mao Tsetung in 1949 resulted in the complete rejection of Western imperialism and the departure of all foreign missionaries. They left behind three and a half million Chinese Catholics and one million Protestants, altogether less than one percent of a total population of China that was reaching the half billion mark. Once more, the hope for a strong Chinese Christianity grew dim.

Lessons from the Missionary Experience in China

The repeated failure of Christianity to establish a strong foothold in China is puzzling. Today there are no known actual descendants of the Chinese Christian communities that existed during the Tang dynasty, and few Christians claim that their faith has been handed down in an unbroken tradition since the thirteenth century. Most of what is known about these early Christian settlements comes from a small number of artifacts, carved monuments and tombstones, occasional religious literature, some mention in Chinese historical sources, as well as letters and reports written by Catholic missionaries. Sources that may be in the hands of the Nestorian church, however, still remain for the most part untapped.

By comparison, the stories of Catholic communities converted in the seventeenth century and thereafter are well documented. Yet today Chinese families who can trace their Christian origins to that period are relatively rare. As for the 4.5 million Chinese Christians of 1950, their numbers are far from impressive when put in proper perspective. These Christians amounted to only a very small percentage of the total population, yet they were the meager result of more than one hundred years of conversion efforts by several thousand Protestant and Catholic missionaries.

Many books and articles have attempted to elucidate the underlying reasons for the poor showing of Christianity in China.[2] Much attention has been devoted to the major shortcomings of the Christian churches and their mistakes of the nineteenth and the first half of the twentieth centuries. Suffice it to say that the failure, at least on the part of the Catholic missionaries, was the result of a long association with Western imperialism, a superficial understanding of and a shallow insertion into the Chinese cultural milieu, and a reluctance to let the Chinese clergy assume the direction of the local church.[3]

The lessons from earlier missionary experience in China are much more difficult to determine. The literature on the subject is spotty, and its scholarship stretches from excellent to very poor. The study of the Jesuit period has received the most attention, while other developments are sometimes dismissed as no more than "historical curiosities."[4]

The following overview attempts to take a fresh look at these early expressions of Christianity in China. It emphasizes some of the excellent insights found in many studies, exposes biased or unfounded assumptions, and challenges the reader to search further into yet uncharted grounds.

The Luminous Religion

Among several explanations given for the disappearance of Nestorian Christianity from China, some can be easily discarded and others are more plausible; all, however, point to causes that preexisted the repression of 845 or the collapse of the Yuan dynasty.

In the West, Protestants and Roman Catholics have often implied that the "heretical" foundation of the Nestorian church, compounded by a dubious propensity toward borrowing terms and symbols from other religions, has been the reason for its repeated collapses in China. This assertion runs counter to history, which shows that the Church of the East, as the Nestorian church prefers to call itself, was the most successful church for a long period of time.[5] In fact, until the late twelfth century, it experienced a period of growth unrivaled by any other Christian church of the time and it was actually larger than the Latin church. It survived the change from Arab to Mongol rule and continued to prosper for at least another one hundred years. By the late thirteenth century, the primate of the Nestorian church, the patriarch of Baghdad, headed an international organization composed of twenty-five metropolitan provinces with an average of eight to ten episcopal sees for each province and a total of 200 to 250 dioceses.

Sometimes the disappearance of the Nestorian church from China is attributed to what is seen as a very specific doctrinal weakness. In its most common form, this interpretation faults the Luminous Religion for unduly refraining from stressing the death of Jesus on the cross. This distortion of the Christian message is presented as the flaw that led to its failure to secure a firm foothold in China. Such an interpretation, however, hardly bears up under the facts.

Historians often cite an artifact that is a lengthy description of the religious beliefs of the Luminous Religion on a stone monument erected in 781 near Xi'an. The description of the Messiah "hanging up the bright sun from where he swept away the abodes of darkness" is often construed as a poetic artifice to hide the reality of the crucifixion. It can also be argued to the contrary, however, that it is a very powerful and symbolic description of the resurrection and that the author managed a literary *tour de force* by presenting the reality of the death of Jesus in terms that kept tune with the festive tone of the whole inscription.

There is no lack of Nestorian documents in Chinese clearly presenting Jesus Christ's incarnation and his free choice to be crucified for the salvation of the world. To this category belongs the famous *Jesus Messiah Sutra* as well as several scrolls discovered in Dunhuang by renowned sinologists such as Paul Pelliot.

Furthermore, the display of the cross is the most recurrent symbol found on the carvings and artifacts dating from the Chinese period of Nestorianism. At the apex of the Mongol empire, Nestorian monasteries of Central Asia were known by the name of the "monasteries of the cross." Nonetheless, it is true that Nestorians never had a place in their churches and homes for crucifixes, icons, or images. This is why, in Roman Catholic parlance, they sometimes have been referred to as the "Protestants of the East."

What is really at stake, therefore, is not a question of doctrinal integrity, but a question of difference in liturgical, ritualistic, and artistic expressions between the Latin and Orthodox churches and the Church of the East. The liturgy of the Church of the East is certainly one of the most ancient and appears to be directly related to the first Christian offices celebrated in Jerusalem.[6] Because of their early exclusion from the Christian communion, the Nestorians were not influenced by changes that took place in the liturgies of the other churches and they clung to their original form of worship. The constitutive elements of their rituals convey an atmosphere of simplicity and deep spirituality without the elaborate shape of the later Latin or Orthodox ceremonies.

The absence of a corpus on Nestorian crosses and pictures does not represent a theological breakaway from the other churches; it simply reflects an early Judeo-Christian tradition that preferred to present the cross less as an instrument of death and more as the victorious symbol of the risen Lord. Moreover, it can be argued that the Nestorian approach, far from being an obstacle to its spread, facilitated its acceptance among Chinese people, whose sense of propriety would otherwise have been offended by a religion displaying a naked corpse on a cross.

Another common explanation for the failures of the Luminous Religion in China is the alleged low level of learning among Nestorian monks and clergy. However, this assertion is not supported by the facts. While it certainly cannot be denied that documents connected with the Bishop Alopen period, such as *The Jesus Messiah Sutra* of 638 C.E., are not very polished, yet the exposition of doctrine given throughout this sutra reveals an author with a keen understanding of Chinese culture. For instance, the first part of the document — a kind of exposé of Christian living — reconciles Christian and Chinese ethics by stressing a three fold loyalty to God, the emperor, and one's parents. Along the same line, the section on the Ten Commandments gives prominence to filial piety.

By the eighth century, foreigners such as Jing Jing, the famous scholar-author of the Nestorian monument found in Xi'an, had produced works in Chinese of high quality. As for the bulk of the Nestorian clergy — which may have peaked in China in 845 to around two thousand, there are not many indications of their level of learning. In all probability, many foreign monks knew little of Chinese language and culture; similarly, neither did many Chinese monks have a high intellectual caliber. Yet it is a mistake to generalize that all Nestorian monasteries had the climate of ignorance and spiritual laxity described by the noted Sung poet Su Ziyou.[7] First of all, his description referred to one specific temple rather than to a general pattern. Moreover, Su, who lived in the eleventh century, depicted circumstances of a period when the Nestorian church of China was in an advanced stage of decline. In no way did his poem imply that the same low level of cultural and spiritual attainment had already existed two centuries earlier when the organization was at its apex. What Su witnessed was a pitiful remnant of an organization that, since the edict of 845, had been cut off from its foreign leadership and could not survive without it.

In recent years, research has gone a long way toward clarifying Nestorius' position and toward vindicating his orthodoxy. The Nestorians who went from Persia to China should not be necessarily viewed as heretics or messengers of a lesser form of Christianity. Rather, they represented a very early Christian tradition that developed outside the influence of the Greco-Roman civilization and the control of the church of Rome. The Luminous Religion should, therefore, not be left out of any history of Christianity in China, as was the case in a study published a few years ago in Shanghai.[8] One cannot dismiss the followers of the Church of the East as "non-Catholics." On the contrary, they should be considered as the seeds of further Christian developments in China.

During the Tang as well as the Yuan dynasties, the Luminous Religion was characterized by a heavy reliance on the patronage of the court and high officials. Its chances of establishing a strong foothold in China were spoiled twice by the loss of this protection, and not by any alleged inherent theological flaw or failure to adapt its message to the Chinese context.

Yet the fact that Buddhism also endured the same imperial ban during the Tang dynasty and nonetheless managed to survive, points to a deeper cause for the decline and disappearance of the Luminous Religion. Unlike Buddhism, which from the beginning developed a large native missionary constituency and a Chinese leadership, the Luminous Religion seemed to have been more active among foreign and minority residents and to have kept all major positions of authority among foreign missionaries. The imperial decree of 845, which resulted in the expulsion of these missionaries, had a major impact on Nestorian Christianity. When the ban was lifted one year later, the Church of the East lacked a Christian presence that could act both as a springboard for re-entry into China and a reservoir of missionary enterprise. The oasis of Dunhuang on the far western border was only an isolated outpost, and Samarkand, the nearest Nestorian position of strength, was sixteen hundred miles away across some of the world's most difficult terrain. Baghdad, where the patriarch resided, lay at least another sixteen hundred miles further west. News and people took a long time to travel on the Silk Road between Baghdad and Xi'an. Therefore when its foreign-born bishops and monks failed to return, the Luminous Religion, deprived of a native leadership and a strong Chinese following, rapidly faded away.

The Luminous Religion repeated this mistake in the thirteenth and fourteenth centuries, catering still to foreign communities and concentrating authority in foreign hands. It is quite revealing to find that Chinese official documents of that period classified Christians as "resident aliens." After the ousting of the foreign Mongol Yuan dynasty in 1368, the church again lacked the native leadership and the Chinese following necessary for its survival. In addition, it could no longer count on the support of its parent church in Baghdad. Indeed, since the turn of the fourteenth century, the Church of the East in Persia and Mesopotamia had begun to weaken under violent campaigns from Mongol khans who had embraced Islam. With the ascent of Tamerlane in 1369, the situation got even worse. What followed were thirty-five years of ruthless executions of Christians and the systematic destruction of church properties aimed at eradicating Christianity from Tamerlane's empire. By the dawn of the fifteenth century, the Church of the East no longer existed as a vast multiethnic religious organization. As for the Luminous Religion, without contact with its distant spiritual and magisterial center, it simply vanished.

Faced with such difficulties of communication, one wonders why the Luminous Religion remained oblivious to the need for bringing native Chinese monks into leadership positions. This attitude is a striking contrast with its profound and refreshing attempts to sink roots in Chinese culture. None of the documents available mentions Chinese-born Nestorians of any importance. This is in sharp contrast with Buddhism, which produced illustrious Chinese monks such as Fa Xian in the fifth century and Xuan Zang in the seventh.

The Franciscans under the Mongol Yuan Dynasty

The presence of the Franciscan friars who entered China during the Mongol Yuan dynasty had no significant lasting religious impact. It would certainly be unrealistic to expect that in such a vast country a handful of foreign missionaries could gather a large following in barely seventy years. Yet the shortage of missionaries, lack of time, and persecutions seem to be only external circumstances that do not suffice to explain the disappearance of Catholicism from China in the fourteenth century. As with the Luminous Religion, the real reason for the Franciscan failure lies in its methods.

The Franciscan friars, it seems, considered evangelization of China not as a separate task but rather as part of their overall goal to convert the Mongol empire. As a consequence, Catholicism remained mainly a religion of foreigners who relied on support from a foreign dynasty and failed to recruit a native clergy or a large Chinese congregation.

Since 1245, when the first friar arrived at the Mongol court of Karakorum, the goal of the Franciscans had been to convert the khans of the tribes that composed the Mongol federation. In Europe, the focus of attention had shifted to China in the late 1260s, when the Great Khan Khubilai moved his capital from Karakorum to Cambalic (Beijing) and requested the pope to send one hundred men learned in science and religion to his court. These circumstances led to the dispatch of several unsuccessful papal missions, until John of Montecorvino finally reached Beijing in 1294.

Friar John and the Franciscans who later joined him and continued his work after his death in 1328 enjoyed many privileges. Not only did they benefit from the tax exemption granted by the Mongol Yuan government to monks and priests of all religions, they also received large imperial grants to furnish and decorate their churches. Moreover, as foreign envoys, they received a substantial state salary in the form of an allowance for food and clothing. Friar John was even entitled to an apartment at the court and to regular audiences with the emperor.[9] Under the Great Khan's protection, he preached, built a church, and taught one hundred and fifty choirboys, whose Gregorian chants pleased the imperial ear. By cultivating the khan's favor, the Franciscan missions inevitably linked their destiny to a foreign dynasty that was regarded with hatred by the native Chinese population.

As papal envoy to the Great Khan, John of Montecorvino hoped primarily to convert the emperor and the cosmopolitan non-Chinese court. For that purpose he learned the Mongol language and saw no need to study Chinese. He found a receptive ear among Nestorian civil officials and army officers, including Prince George, son-in-law of the emperor and ruler of the Onguts, and several Alan chiefs who were converted while in Beijing.

Emulating their leaders, many members of the Ongut and Alan tribes sought out Friar John for religious instruction. By 1305, after eleven years in the capital, he had baptized some six thousand people. He even remarked that without false accusations leveled against him by jealous Nestorians, he could have converted five times as many. In fact, Friar John spent much time counteracting the influence of foreign Nestorian religious leaders in the court and trying to bring them and their followers back into the fold of the Roman Catholic church.

John of Montecorvino actively pursued the translation of the New Testament, the liturgy of the mass, and the psalter into Mongol. He also printed illustrations of the Old and New Testament with explanations in Persian and Turkic languages, but he never mentioned doing anything similar in Chinese. Since, according to Friar John's own correspondence, most of his writing, reading, and preaching was carried on in Mongol, it is doubtful that many of his converts could have been Han Chinese people.

What saddened most John of Montecorvino was his failure to baptize the Emperor Timur whom he knew for eleven years. He implied that, had he been helped by a couple of other friars instead of always being alone, he would have succeeded in converting the emperor.

Even after missionary reinforcements arrived in 1308, the Franciscans waited another five years before expanding to other cities. As in Beijing, their apostolate aimed first at the prosperous foreign community who resided in these cities. Roman Catholics, among whom the friars counted rich Italian and Armenian benefactors, received the most attention. The next concern was for those who professed the Nestorian, Jewish, or Muslim faith; however, the Franciscans never raised any converts among the latter two religious groups. Lastly, the solicitude of some Franciscans focused on those whom they referred to as idolaters or pagans. There is little doubt that these terms referred to the Han Chinese. Conversions among them, according to the Franciscans, were ephemeral for many left shortly after baptism.[10]

What could have been the reasons for this lack of perseverance? Many Chinese undoubtedly were attracted by the highly visible presence of the Catholic church in their city. At church gatherings, the opportunity to mingle with influential and well-to-do foreigners was certainly, for a time at least, an important inducement. Yet, if the friars who came after John of Montecorvino also failed to learn Chinese or to produce Christian literature in Chinese, the Chinese people probably had difficulty grasping the Christian doctrine and undoubtedly felt that this foreign religion was not really meant for them. In addition, the fierce bickerings between the Franciscans and the Nestorian leadership, while professing the same Christ, appeared as a petty dispute between foreigners and ran counter to the Chinese value for harmony and conciliation.

Most of all, the Franciscans failed to realize that the time-tested missionary strategy of converting tribes and kingdoms from the top down would not work in the context of early fourteenth-century China. The foreign Mongol rulers and their retinues of foreign advisors were too unpopular among the Chinese to expect the Chinese people to emulate them. Not only did the Franciscans not convert any of the Mongol Yuan emperors, but they soon became targets of rising Chinese antiforeignism because of their close association with the Mongol court.

The final blow came during the 1340s when antiforeign sentiments turned to violence and the number of Han Chinese leaving the Catholic church outpaced those who joined. The religion brought by the Franciscans was a religion of foreigners on the margin of Chinese society and it could not survive the ousting of the Mongol Yuan dynasty in 1368.

From what has already been said, it is clear that the methods of John of Montecorvino and his companions were not conducive to establishing the Catholic church on a firm Chinese base. Although the friars had several opportunities to build a strong Chinese congregation with its own leadership, they did not capitalize on them.

During his eleven years of solitude in the capital, John of Montecorvino bought one hundred and fifty non-Christian Chinese boys between the ages of seven and eleven and housed them on his property. He gave them religious instruction and baptized them. He also taught them Latin and Greek and how to sing the liturgy of the mass and other ceremonies. Although the methods of recruitment used by Friar John do not conform to modern standards of ethics, he had, nonetheless, begun an establishment that could have become a seminary for training of native apostles for the Chinese people. But not even once did John of Montecorvino mention that he had such a long-range plan. He was interested primarily in nurturing a choir of children for the delight of the emperor and the enhancement of the liturgy. This he apparently did to counteract the influence of the Nestorians, whose ceremonies greatly interested the emperor. In any case, Friar John's method with Chinese children is further proof that he was more intent on converting the emperor than in reaching the Chinese masses.

During these same eleven years, John of Montecorvino wrote to the pope asking for missionary reinforcements. This plea, however, did not convey any ambition to better service the vast mission field under his responsibility; it stemmed mostly from his determination to convert the emperor and from the emperor's wish to receive more envoys from Rome. The strategy of the Franciscan missionary seems quite clear. The arrival of papal emissaries would further predispose the emperor toward the Catholic religion and allow Friar John to devote more time to his conversion. Interestingly enough, John of Montecorvino's only other request to the pope was for antiphonariums and hymnals to enhance the liturgical singing that so pleased the emperor. This is further evidence that the boys' choir was indeed an important part of John of Montecorvino's scheme to convert the emperor.

The first and only significant missionary reinforcements arrived in Beijing in 1308. It is not known how large the party was, but it included three bishops. The bishops' initial task was to ordain John of Montecorvino whom the pope had appointed archbishop of Beijing and patriarch of the East. This influx of missionaries signaled the beginning of an earnest attempt to convert the Chinese people. Most of the friars seem to have rapidly moved to other large cities where they preached and built convents and churches. Over the next fifty years, additional reinforcements and replacements from Europe were so few in number that the Franciscan presence in China never amounted to much more than thirty friars.

The advent of the Chinese Ming dynasty and the strong antiforeign persecution that accompanied it were strong blows to Christianity. The young church was deprived of its foreign leadership and did not yet have a native clergy to nurture it. By focusing his work on the emperor and the foreign gathering at the court, John of Montecorvino had no pressing concern for a Chinese leadership: his boys' choir never became a seminary; he never ordained a native priest but did confer minor orders on Prince George, an Ongut; although he had three bishops to help him, he created only one other episcopal seat in Quanzhou.

It is doubtful that, as time went by, the bishops who coordinated the missionary work in Quanzhou and Beijing did not become increasingly aware of the urgency of a native clergy. Yet, obstacles arising from the distance between Beijing and Rome and from the cumbersome pyramidal structure of the church prevented each of them from beginning a seminary or ordaining priests. Because new clergy sent from Rome rarely survived the trip and those who did often died within a short period after assuming their positions, a long-range, sustained policy for the recruitment of native vocations was never implemented.

In fact, the situation never improved. After the death of John of Montecorvino in 1328, there never were more than one or two Franciscan bishops in China at one time. Since all bishops had to be sent by Rome or have their ordination approved by Rome, the leadership of the Catholic church was not able to sustain itself. The tenuous Franciscan presence in China during the thirteenth and fourteenth centuries was, therefore, never conducive to nurturing a native clergy. Persecuted and left to themselves, most of the Chinese Catholic communities disappeared. A few, however, survived without ordained leadership and continued to hand down their faith in an unbroken tradition until they were rediscovered by missionaries during the first half of this century.

The Missionaries of the Late Ming and Early Qing Dynasties

This period, which roughly extends from the end of the seventeenth to the middle of the eighteenth century, has always been a favorite of missionary scholars. In recent years, it has received even more attention at several symposiums and events held to mark occasions such as the four-hundredth anniversary of the arrival of Matteo Ricci in China (1582) and the three-hundredth anniversaries of the birth of Johann Adam Schall and the edict of toleration by the Kangxi emperor (1592). Most readers interested in China probably have a good understanding of this stage of the missionary endeavor and are familiar with the significance of the Jesuit policy of accommodation. I would like to review, however, some aspects of this accommodation that have drawn less attention and yet deserve full consideration because they contain important lessons for the transmission of the Christian faith today.

Accommodation, respect, and friendship characterized the most appropriate Christian missionary approach of that time in China. The archetype of this attitude was the Jesuit Matteo Ricci who, fired by unreserved admiration for Chinese civilization, labored to insert Christianity within the context of Chinese literature, philosophy, and social institutions. His goal was to create a favorable climate for the slow transformation of Chinese society that might lead toward an expanding movement of conversion. Too often, however, the Jesuits are described as the sole promoters of this attitude, while other missionaries are portrayed as detractors whose efforts led to the failure of the enterprise. This simplistic analysis ignores that, in practice, most missionary orders fostered—to the same degree as the Jesuits—a policy of accommodation based on respect and friendship for the Chinese people.

The Franciscan friars, for example, had a long record of flexibility and adaptation to various peoples in America as well as in Central Asia and the Far East. Their program of evangelization did not rely only on the seraphic ardor promoted by their founder; rather it made use of a whole array of human means. Franciscans acted as doctors, civil engineers, architects, jewelers, blacksmiths, painters, sculptors, agricultural experts, and so forth. In the manner of Bartholomé de Las Casas in Central America, the friars acted almost everywhere as advocates of the native population. They absorbed as much as they thought possible from the local cultures, christened it, and put it to use to convert the natives. Where faith and morals were not involved, they sought to preserve these cultures and genuinely adjusted to them.

The Franciscans of the sixteenth and seventeenth centuries attached a great importance to mastering the language of the country where they were sent. The friars, who produced a host of grammars, dictionaries, and vocabularies in Amerindian languages, were no less diligent in the Far East where they applied themselves to the study of languages such as Tagalog, Chinese, and Japanese. While the Jesuits trained in Macao before entering China, so the Franciscans studied Chinese language and culture in Taiwan or among the Chinese community of Manila.[11]

Although early signs seemed to point toward a successful cooperative effort to evangelize China, the reality turned out to be entirely different, primarily because of the deep antagonism between the Jesuits and other missionaries, in particular the mendicant orders.

Since the death of Francis Xavier in 1552 on the small island of Sancian in the South China Sea, the Jesuits had considered China as their mission field. Consequently, they established a strong presence in the Portuguese city of Macao and waited for an opportunity to enter China. In 1576, the bull *Super specula* of Pope Gregory XIII erected Macao as a diocese comprising all of China, Japan, and the surrounding islands, and further reinforced the Jesuit claim to China. They became alarmed, however, when a Franciscan party from the Philippines landed in Canton a few years later. The bishop of Macao complained to Rome of this intrusion in his jurisdiction by missionaries from the diocese of Manila and he asked that such incursions be stopped. In response, in 1585 the pope, in the bull *Ex pastorali officio*, granted the Jesuits from Macao the exclusive right to evangelize China. This monopoly was as bitterly resented by the friars as it was jealously guarded by the Jesuits. It was not until 1633 that other missionary groups finally succeeded in convincing the Holy See to reverse this decision and to allow them to partake in the immense task.

It is not difficult, therefore, to imagine the animosity that existed between the two factions. The Jesuits did not welcome the newcomers; the mendicants, both Franciscans and Dominicans, begrudged the Jesuits for trying to keep them out of China. This antagonism led to a bitter dispute on the methods and conception of mission.

As soon as the Dominican and the Franciscan friars arrived in China, they found themselves differing from the Jesuits in most respects. The main point of controversy revolved around the rites in honor of ancestors and Confucius, which most Jesuits since Ricci regarded merely as civil acts. The friars, on the contrary, considered them superstitious, if not idolatrous, ceremonies. They were equally appalled to find two altars in some Jesuit churches, one for the worship of God and the other apparently for the worship of the ancestors.

Other points of contention involved the preaching of Christ crucified and the major tenants of the Catholic church. The mendicants rebuffed the Jesuits for avoiding open discussions on the passion of Christ and public displays of the crucifix. They were also baffled by Ricci's catechism, which did not mention six of the seven sacraments and completely ignored the commandments of the church.

The two factions had also a different view on how to achieve the conversion of China. The Jesuits gave first priority to the conversion of the ruling and educated classes. They decided that in a rigid hierarchical society like that in China, where education was held in such high regard, converted officials and literati would bring the people along with them into the church. The friars disagreed; they contended that evangelization upward was more likely to succeed because the poor were the most naturally inclined to

Christianity. They maintained that Christian missionaries should live poorly and beg their way through the country instead of riding in sedan chairs and dressing in expensive silk gowns like the Jesuits.

From the beginning, the relationship between the two parties was confrontational instead of trustful. It would have been easy for the Jesuits to come forward and explain to the friars their point of view and any apparent eccentricities or deviations on their part. But this they would not do. Angered by the loss of their monopoly on China, the Jesuits refused to discuss the issues with people whom they considered guilty of condemning what they did not understand. The mendicants, already suspicious of the Jesuits, never had a chance to look upon the China scene with untroubled eyes. They were faced with what seemed to them inexplicable conduct by their fellow missionaries.

It seems that with some dialogue the two factions could have reached a *modus vivendi* and avoided open conflict. After all, the mendicants favored accommodation as much as the Jesuits did and their achievements in other parts of the world proved it. The problem lay in deciding how far to adapt — and this was not insurmountable. A frank exchange from the beginning would have enabled the mendicants to understand, if not to accept, most of the Jesuit approach and methods. Similarly, the Jesuits could have modified ambiguities and corrected excesses in their practices. By the same token, dialogue with another party would have also contributed to solving the malaise within the Jesuit community itself, where some members, in varying degrees, openly shared the views of the friars. On the most crucial question of the Chinese rites, discussion could have led to a more balanced assessment, by allowing a distinction between instances that were only civic ceremonies of respect and those that were tainted with religious superstitions.

Finally, the dialogue could have led the Jesuits and the mendicants to realize that their respective approaches complemented one another. The Jesuits, faithful to Ricci's vision, could have concentrated on appealing to the hierarchical, Confucian aspects of Chinese society; at the other extreme, the Franciscans, faithful to their founder's reverence for nature and paradoxical preaching ("having nothing and yet possessing all things"), could have found a resonance in that part of the society so deeply permeated by Taoism and Buddhism.

Unfortunately, the dialogue never took place. Receiving no explanation for what they considered an unacceptable attitude and afraid that such permissiveness would ultimately imperil the entire Christian mission in China, the friars found themselves with no room to maneuver. They took their case to Rome. Thus began a long series of accusations and counter-accusations between the two factions. In the end, the infighting led to a showdown between the Holy See and the Qing government, which, once more, dashed all hopes for a strong Chinese Christianity.

Conclusion

The preceding overview has revealed two underlying factors that explained in great part the poor results achieved by Christianity in China. All past missionary efforts in China should be evaluated against that background. First, there is the fact that the same foreign missionaries who, from the seventh to the mid-twentieth century, strived to establish branches of the Nestorian, Catholic, or Protestant churches often failed to foster Christian communities solidly anchored in the Chinese cultural context. In other words, they succeeded in planting the church institution, but — deliberately or not — they repeatedly blocked the emergence of the local church. Indeed, by unduly retaining for themselves control over leadership, finances, and forms of religious expression, many foreign missionaries prevented the church from sinking its roots into the surrounding Chinese context and from being nourished by it.

The second underlying cause of the poor result of Christianity in China was the divisions among the groups of missionaries. Not only did disputes and petty differences keep missionaries from different groups apart, fierce competition and rivalries separated competing Christian denominations. This situation prevented missionaries from forming a united front. They were not able to devise a joint approach based on sharing insights regarding the Chinese people and its culture in a way respectful of each group's specific talents and spirituality.

The objective of this overview has been primarily to look at what went wrong in the Christian missionary enterprise in China. The intention has not been to leave the reader without hope, but to avoid repeating past mistakes. In all fairness, it should be acknowledged that within each missionary group, Catholic as well as Protestant, a spirit of cooperation and mutual assistance often prevailed over differences. One must also recognize that genuine displays of ecumenism happened more often in mission fields than in the Christian West. And one cannot deny that over the centuries quite a few missionaries advocated a genuinely contextualized church and left a profound impact on the present-day Chinese Christian church.

The most surprising development of the past forty years is the apparent vigor of this church today, even though the West thought it was not strong enough to survive an oppressive Communist regime. This certainly raises the question as to whether the word "failure" can be an appropriate characterization of the foreign missionary enterprise. It seems that missionaries, with all their imperfections, are the earthen vessels described by Saint Paul. The truth of the gospel was able to shine through them and leave its mark in China.

The advent of communism not only forced out foreign missionaries but it also destroyed, for the most part, the models of Christianity they had brought with them. The recent experience of the church in China has been compared by some to the paschal mystery: through persecutions, it followed Christ into death to reemerge transformed and full of life.

The process, in fact, is still under way. The seeds of the gospel planted by the missionaries have not yet completely shed their Western outer coating, but they have already sunk their roots into the Chinese soil. This inculturation of Christianity in Chinese society cannot happen just by missionary import from the outside, nor by a simple translation of Western theology into Chinese concepts. Rather, it must come from "a reflection and realization of Christian faith from within the sociocultural context of contemporary China and in the framework of an independent (self-supporting, self-administering, self-propagating) church."[12]

Notes

1. For a bird's eye view of the legend of St. Thomas, see Columba Cary Elwes, *China and the Cross, a Survey of Missionary History* (New York: P.J. Kenedy & Sons, 1957), pp. 9-11. A good summary of the studies on early Jewish communities in China can be found in Pan Guandan, "Jews in Ancient China — A Historical Survey, 1953, revised 1983" in Sidney Shapiro, ed., *Jews in Old China* (New York: Hippocrene Books, 1984), pp. 46-102.

2. Two books have been published in recent years: Ralph R. Covell, *Confucius, the Buddha, and Christ* (Maryknoll, NY: Orbis Books, 1986); Hans Küng and Julia Ching, *Christianity and Chinese Religions* (New York: Doubleday, 1989).

3. For a good overview of the impact of the Christian missionaries on China during the nineteenth and early twentieth centuries, see Paul A. Cohen, "Christian Missions and Their Impact to 1900," in John King Fairbank, ed., *The Cambridge History of China* (London: Cambridge University Press, 1978), vol. 10, part 1, pp. 543-590. For more topical studies published within the last fifteen years, see in particular: Thomas A. Breslin, *China, American Catholicism, and the Missionary* (University Park, PA: Pennsylvania State University Press, 1980); Suzanne Wilson Barnett and John King Fairbank, eds., *Christianity in China, Early Protestant Missionary Writings* (Cambridge, MA: Harvard University Press, 1985); Jessie G. Lutz, *Chinese Politics and Christian Missions: The Anti-Christian Movements of 1920-28* (Notre Dame, IN: Cross Roads Books, 1988); Patricia Neils, ed., *United States Attitudes and Policy Toward China: The Impact of American Missionaries* (Armonk, NY: M. E. Sharpe, 1990).

4. Jacques Gernet, *China and the Christian Impact, A Conflict of Cultures* (London: Cambridge University Press, 1985), p. 249.

5. The East Syrian church became known by the West as the Nestorian church when, at the First Ecumenical Council of Ephesus in 431, its bishops refused to go along with the other churches in excommunicating Nestorius, patriarch of Constantinople. On the contrary, they expressed support for Nestorius whose ideas, they claimed, had been misrepresented and were in agreement with the christological doctrine that had always made a distinction between Jesus as a man who suffered and died and the Logos who is God. The other Christian churches rejected this position, which, they contended, created a human person in Jesus and destroyed

the unity of Christ, the God-man. This conflicting point of view sealed the exclusion of the East Syrian church from the communion with the rest of Christianity. From then on, the East Syrian church became known to the other churches as the Nestorian church, even though it chose to call itself the Church of the East.

6. The Church of the East traces its origin to the apostolic age when, following the martyrdom of deacon Stephen, persecuted Christians flew from Jerusalem and arrived in Antioch in Syria. Its liturgical language, Syriac, is a form of Aramaic.

7. Zhao Fushan, *Christianity in China* (Manila: De La Salle University, 1986), p. 15.

8. Gu Yulu, *The Catholic Church in China, Past and Present* (Shanghai: Shanghai Academy of Social Sciences, 1989).

9. Henry Yule, ed., *Cathay and the Way Thither*, rev. ed. by Henri Cordier (London: Hakluyt Society, 1913-16). Book three contains extensive English translations of the correspondence of the Franciscan friars; see in particular pp. 45, 57, 71-73, 100-102.

10. Ibid., pp. 46-48, 50, 71-74, 101-102, 180-83.

11. For a very balanced analysis of the mendicants and Jesuits' methods, see the chapter "Two Missionary Methods in China: Mendicants and Jesuits" in J. S. Cummins, *Jesuit and Friar in the Spanish Expansion to the East* (London: Variorum Reprints, 1986), pp. 33-108.

12. Hans Küng and Julia Ching, *Christianity and Chinese Religions*, p. 252.

13

The Need for Reconciliation

JEROOM HEYNDRICKX

For several years now, I have traveled in China to visit universities and institutions of research and to develop projects of cultural exchange and joint research between these institutes and the Verbiest Foundation of the Catholic University of Leuven. These frequent visits have allowed me to have regular contact with Catholics in China. I have learned to know and admire the Catholic church in China. Each visit to the Chinese church has been a pilgrimage that allowed me to discover the dynamic faith of Chinese Christians and at the same time strengthened me in my own faith.

However, this pilgrimage has also uncovered for me the problems of division within the Chinese Catholic community. Knowing that the Chinese church is strongly divided I have always tried to meet with members of the Chinese Catholic Patriotic Association (CCPA) as well as with Catholics who do not participate in the CCPA and who, in fact, staunchly oppose it. I have also exchanged opinions on the Catholic church in the People's Republic of China with Catholic friends from Taiwan. We all know that it is not easy to give a balanced view of such a complex situation, yet I have always tried to do so. I am, of course, aware that as a foreigner my possibilities for contacts in China are limited and that this may narrow my views. But I also notice that some Chinese friends who now freely travel from Taiwan into China, who, as Chinese, can easily have unlimited contacts with both sides in the Chinese church, limit their contacts to one group, and avoid all contact with the others. This automatically and by their own choice narrows their viewpoint. There is a danger that their opinions are one-sided. Moreover, how can you claim to build a bridge if you refuse to contact the other side?

Jeroom Heyndrickx wrote this personal evaluation of the Catholic church in the People's Republic of China in 1988.

One Chinese Catholic Church

The Catholic church in China is the *una sancta catholica et apostolica ecclesia in Sinis*. When I use these words, I am aware that I use a formula of our Creed that should not be used too freely. Still, I think that, in spite of many controversies and the ambiguous attitudes of a few of its members, one must admit that the church in the People's Republic of China as a whole is a faithful church, not a schismatic one. It is a church of saints, confessors, martyrs, and also of sinners—like any other church. It has recently passed through a very dramatic and traumatic history and is a wounded church.

Although "wounded," this church has surprised the universal church by its faith and by the dynamism with which it has undertaken its reorganization. In ten years over a thousand churches have been restored and reopened and many churches have been rebuilt. Since the early 1980s all these churches are filled with people on Sundays and feast days. Twelve major seminaries, officially recognized by the authorities, have been opened and an additional number of other seminaries exist but without official recognition. More than seven hundred seminarians are preparing themselves for the priesthood in the official seminaries. Sister novitiates are being opened everywhere. The bishops, priests, and lay people who have dedicated themselves to the task of reorganizing the Catholic church in China have, indeed, great merits.

Inner Divisions

No doubt, the creation of the CCPA in 1957 has done great harm to the church community in China. This is true not because it created a schismatic so-called "patriotic church" as some have said, but because it internally split the one Catholic church in China. This split became an open division in 1958 when the CCPA started to consecrate its own bishops without nomination by the Holy See. The split has widened over the years as a few prominent CCPA leaders have voiced much criticism of and opposition to the Holy See. In addition, a few CCPA lay people have obtained positions of authority from which they—and not the bishops—control the church. This situation violates the canon law of the church. At times, these lay persons use their positions of authority to create problems for faithful Catholics who do not cooperate with the CCPA.[1]

All this has caused deep divisions in the Chinese church between those who "chose to collaborate with the CCPA" in order to prove to the government that they were good patriots and those who refused to collaborate with the CCPA because they did not want to put into question their unity with the Holy Father. However, most members of this latter group of Catholics remain at the same time convinced in their hearts that they are also good patriots, and they have proven it by their dedication to the cause of the modernization of the country.

At the same time, it has become clear that many (in fact, I believe that almost all) CCPA members are also faithful Catholics. They have joined the CCPA for the good of the church, while in their hearts and minds remaining faithful to the Holy Father. Many of them also suffered during the Cultural Revolution. As a result, the real meaning of "CCPA" varies from place to place. In many towns, CCPA members do take good care of the church and are respected by the Catholics. In others, they have behaved as enemies of the church. Friends have told me that some persons are even guilty of corruption by taking advantage of their position in the CCPA.

Whatever the personal motivations of CCPA members are or have been in the past, it is a fact that the Chinese church community today still stands internally divided because of the CCPA. Historically speaking and taking into account many facts from the past, one can well understand that during the 1950s authorities wished to stress the importance of patriotic feelings and of "autonomy." On the other hand, we also realize that many Catholics suffered greatly during the Cultural Revolution and that the aftermath of this suffering still lingers on.

On the other hand, it seems that today (1988), more than thirty years later, many of the points of contention and discussion no longer exist. Today all Catholics—CCPA members as well as others—are as much inspired by patriotic feelings as other Chinese. Catholics fully support the country's efforts toward modernization. In many counties Catholic workers have been selected as model workers. Catholics—CCPA members as well as others—state that they want to remain faithful to their faith and to the pope. Even Chinese officials have said that they are in favor of establishing relations with the Holy See. If all this is true, then there are no more objective causes for contention and division, except the human suffering from past events. Apart from that, one could wonder why such divisions should continue to exist.

Some leaders of the Protestant "Three-Self Movement" in China have expressed the opinion that their movement needed revision because the circumstances today are so different from those during the 1950s when the movement was created. One wonders what CCPA members say about their association. Would this also not apply to them?

We realize that the history of the past thirty years has been difficult and complex for Chinese Catholics, who have a hard time explaining the long story of their internal divisions. They expect that we Catholics outside of China, who know so little about their dramatic past, will be understanding, that we will not make judgments about what has happened nor express accusations against individuals. This is surely a time for listening, for doing what Christ did: silently and without judging he wrote with his finger in the sand. Without such an attitude, no bridge formation or reconciliation can happen.

Underground Bishops, Priests, and Catholics

It is a known fact that there are so-called "underground" bishops in China, who have been secretly and validly ordained. They, in turn, have secretly ordained a number of priests. Some of these priests have a good formation, others, perhaps, a deficient preparation for ordination. These priests now say mass privately in houses for those Catholics who suffered during the early 1950s and during the Cultural Revolution and who refuse to attend the masses of any CCPA priests.

In recent years antagonism between this so-called "underground movement" in the church and the CCPA has increased and has deepened the internal divisions. CCPA members often speak as if they alone are the true patriotic Chinese; they unjustly call the others "unpatriotic" Catholics. Underground Catholics give the impression that they alone are faithful to the Holy Father. They accuse CCPA members of being "bad priests" or "men of the devil." True, one must admit that some CCPA members and leaders have caused scandal to the Christian community by what they have said and done. Humanly speaking it is understandable that such attitudes exist. However, from a Christian viewpoint, and so many years after the open policy of normalization in the church, one would hope that more positive steps toward reconciliation would be taken by Catholics from both sides and certainly by church leaders.

Many Catholics are now confused because of the so-called "Thirteen Points" circulated by Catholics in the underground movement, stating that it is a mortal sin to receive sacraments from the hands of a CCPA priest. As a result, many Catholics who are not CCPA members but who publicly attended CCPA masses until recently, have now stopped going to mass. Meanwhile, another document—the "Eight Points," which is said to carry the approval of Rome—is circulating in China. This document expresses different views. It does not approve of CCPA policy, but it shows understanding for those Catholics who go to CCPA masses, receive the sacraments, or even send their sons to CCPA-directed seminaries when other possibilities are not practicable.

The inner split in the one Chinese church has reached a critical point. Because of this division even some seminarians have problems of conscience about staying or not in a CCPA directed seminary, about the validity of their ordinations, and so forth. Recently some seminarians left the seminary because of such doubts and perhaps upon instigation of the "underground movement."

The Difficult Time of Reconciliation

The Chinese church finds itself in a post-persecution period. (I call it "post-persecution" referring to the general trend of developments; it happens that occasionally and locally one still hears about acts of persecution). Throughout church history, from the time of Diocletian, through the French Revolution, Nazism, and until the present, post-persecution periods have always been difficult and delicate times when those who refused to collaborate and those who collaborated must, in spite of mutual accusations and the pain of unhealed wounds, try to join together in one church as they face the difficult challenge of reconciliation.

Pain caused by past events does not allow reconciliation to happen overnight. It often leads people to speak harsh words and mutually accuse each other; the "collaborators" as well as the others, the "sinners" (or "people of the devil") as well as the "faithful." Sometimes, the language spoken by the "faithful" does not sound very Christian; and hard words spoken by so-called "bad priests" or by "sinners" may bring one to believe that they truly are "bad."

As visitors from abroad we feel deeply sympathetic to all Chinese Catholics we meet. We believe that all have suffered much in their own way and that most really wanted to be faithful. Most of the time we are unable to offer pat answers to their many questions. The answers we know are the easy answers from our theology book: but these are insufficient because their situation is very human and, therefore, very complex. It is up to the Catholics who live in China to determine for themselves how to respond in a truly Christian way to their concrete challenge of reconciliation.

It is the Christian duty of Catholics outside China to keep in close communication with all and to exclude no one. We expect from them, of course, that they are faithful to their faith and remain united with the Holy Father. We hope that faith will give them strength to overcome the divisions and sins of the past. We must not take sides; if we do we will be guilty of fostering division. We must speak a language of reconciliation and unity even though we know that it is easier for us to speak that language than for Chinese Catholics to put reconciliation into practice.

More Openness toward Religion in Chinese Society

While the church in China is fully occupied with its reorganization and reunification, China as a country is passing through a period of basic changes, including changes in the official attitude toward religion. Several official documents offer the church an historic opportunity to speak openly about itself and about the gospel. Today official Chinese documents use a different kind of language with regard to religion than in the past. In a

newly edited volume of the *Chinese Encyclopedia* religion is no longer called
"opium for the people," "superstition," "backward," or "against science."
It is now considered to be an important social phenomenon that deserves
special attention and study. Religion is said to have made important contributions to the world of thought and art. Missionaries are said to have
often been pioneers of cultural and scientific exchange and are given credit
for building schools, hospitals, and doing useful social work.

Beijing University and several other universities and institutions have
opened departments for the study of religion. Many scholars show interest
in informing themselves on religion in a more objective way. They are aware
that until now their views on religion have not been based on objective
information.

China is also preparing a new law on religion. An official delegation is
planning to travel to Germany and Belgium to study the relation between
the state and the Catholic church. But change is not only visible among
officials. It is even more evident among young people. Since the Cultural
Revolution many Chinese search for answers to basic questions on life, on
being human, on destiny, and so forth. Young people, who have become
aware that science alone cannot solve all basic questions, show an interest
in religion and in serious reflection upon the meaning of life. Recently a
group of non-Catholic Chinese students who study at a Belgian university
invited me to give a series of lectures on the Catholic faith. They wanted
lectures on: Who is Jesus Christ? What is the content of the gospels? What
is the relation between faith and life? How did the church spread historically through Europe?

Within this changing context inside China, the Catholic church of China
should now be able to come forward as a church inspired by the ideals of
Vatican II—a church in the midst of society, promoting science and progress, yet at the same time pointing to the importance of correct moral
behavior and to the basic spiritual values of life. However, the Chinese
Catholic church has had little time to turn its attention to these important
developments in Chinese society.

Need for Updating of the Church

The Chinese church faces a second and equally important challenge—
the challenge of "aggiornamento," of implementing the changes introduced
by Vatican II. This second challenge is urgent so that the church will be
ready to face important opportunities for direct evangelization within
China. However, the changes introduced by Vatican II that affect the life
of the church, its spirituality, and the practice of pastoral work are so
fundamental that one cannot expect the Chinese church to undertake this
lightly. Chinese Catholics must be well prepared for the renewal of Vatican
II. The Chinese bishops have already discussed this question and agreed

that they want to assure a greater consensus among themselves before pushing ahead with this important change.

Relations with the Holy See

Since the end of 1987, it has become accepted, even by the CCPA, to say openly that diplomatic relations with the Holy See are also wanted by China. Catholics are now permitted and encouraged to pray for the Holy Father. Officially, however, the CCPA still uses ambiguous terms, claiming to set up an "autonomous Chinese church" without making sufficiently clear what this means. It is an age-old practice in the universal church that each bishop runs his diocese autonomously and that each country's conference of bishops runs the national church, also autonomously, yet according to canon law and to the national constitution. The CCPA creates the impression that the Chinese church wants a different kind of autonomy than that practiced by other local Catholic churches and accepted by the governments of their respective countries. Thus Catholic circles inside and outside of China remain confused about the true intentions of the CCPA.

However, the majority of Chinese Catholics — who are not CCPA members — do not use these terms and see no contradiction at all between unity with the universal church and building a truly self-supporting (and, therefore, autonomous) Chinese local church. In fact, it is the Chinese Bishops' Conference, including not only the CCPA bishops but *all* Chinese bishops, which should express itself on how the church should operate in accordance with canon law and also with the Chinese Constitution.

An important issue is the assignment and election of bishops. When will the Chinese church begin to submit to the Holy See names of candidates for assignment as bishops? In the future how will the adopted process of assigning bishops respect the definitions of the Chinese Constitution and the authority of Chinese government?

In the course of its history the church has reached so many agreements with so many governments in such a variety of historical circumstances that one can be sure that a solution to this situation in China is also possible. Over one hundred countries recognize the Vatican. Why not China? Within the scope of such a discussion, a solution to the problem of the secretly ordained priests and the officially — yet illegitimately — ordained CCPA bishops, can surely be found as well.

Equally important from the side of the Holy See will be the answer to the question: Who will direct the church in China? According to canon law the direction of the church belongs to the bishop in each diocese and to the bishops' conference in each country. In China the CCPA has *de facto* directed the church during the past decades. What will be the role of the CCPA in the future? It is normal that the Holy See wants to know that there is an acceptable answer to this crucial question before it moves toward establishing relations with the People's Republic of China and to revising its way of maintaining relations with Taiwan.

In view of recent, more positive official attitudes toward the Holy See, one hopes that Chinese Catholic bishops—CCPA bishops as well as underground bishops—will begin using a language of unity and reconciliation in view of unifying the church with the Holy Father.

Celibacy—Officially Accepted in All Seminaries

The fact that some Chinese bishops and priests are married is a hindrance to church life and to unity in the church. Celibacy is an important church regulation that must be respected in practice. Because of this, Catholics react with indignation to married bishops and priests and do not accept them. Though the percentage of married priests is not high, the issue still causes division and trouble in some Chinese dioceses. It is important though to keep in mind that some priests (not all) were forced to marry by the authorities during the Cultural Revolution and did not marry out of their own free will. It was an event of that time, caused by the course of history.

We must also note that in the meantime celibacy has been officially reintroduced as a rule of life in all Catholic seminaries and for all future priests who unanimously accept this rule. We must not cling to the past but look to the future. The goal remains the same—the unity of the one, holy, catholic, and apostolic church. All obstacles cannot be removed at once; however if we are willing to approach the reality with patience, charity, and magnanimity, they will eventually be removed.

The Chinese Church in Dialogue with Other Local Churches

During the last five years representatives of the Chinese church in the People's Republic of China have traveled abroad to meet with other local churches. Local churches in China are also entering into projects of cooperation with foreign local churches. Projects include a printing press in the Shanghai diocese, and invitations by the diocese of Beijing for agencies to help in projects for physically and mentally handicapped. Other dioceses are following the same line, opening dispensaries, homes for the aged, and small factories.

These are signs of the dynamic faith of the Chinese church, which opens itself to serve the society at large. Here also the entire Chinese church and not only part of it should be involved; for example, not only CCPA members, but other church leaders as well should visit foreign churches. Foreign churches willing to cooperate with the Chinese church should be invited to cooperate not only with CCPA-directed projects, but with all church projects, without distinction. Such distinctions between CCPA and non-CCPA members and activities lead Catholics abroad to believe that there are two Catholic churches in China.

Building a New Type of Relationship

I see the recent developments in China as an historical breakthrough. They invite other local churches to enter into a new type of relationship and a new way of cooperation between the Chinese church and other local churches. Cooperation and exchange must be based upon attitudes of equality and mutual respect. That is new for China and new for the traditionally "giving" or "missionary" churches. The age of missionary work by foreigners is over. Today missionaries go only where they are invited by local bishops. The local church in the People's Republic, however, apparently does not intend to invite foreign missionaries to help in its pastoral work. But, even without active involvement in the pastoral work of the church in China, a fruitful relationship of cooperation may be developed.

It may sound simple to say that the new relationship between the Chinese church and the other churches has to be a relationship based upon attitudes of equality and mutual respect. However, such a relationship can be realized only if churches enter into open *communio* with the Chinese church and if they do so with "both sides," meaning with the so-called underground movement as well as with CCPA members. In the past some CCPA members have tried to monopolize contacts with church visitors from abroad. They have even created the impression that visitors were allowed to meet only members of CCPA. When guests attended services presided over by CCPA members it was interpreted by some CCPA members that their association received full support from the guests and that these guests disapproved of the "underground." The visitors, in fact, did not intend to visit the CCPA but *the* Chinese church. On the other hand, it is also true that other visitors from abroad have been encouraged by the underground to avoid meeting with CCPA members.

This type of discrimination does not foster open dialogue and *communio*. Yet, I believe that to encourage dialogue and to build bridges is precisely the first Christian duty of any Catholic who visits China. A bridge must reach both sides of the river. Any proposal to solve the problem of church division that excludes part of the church is against the spirit of the gospel.

Chinese Catholics—CCPA members and others—have started to pray together in churches and in private homes all over China. From the standpoint of Christian unity this is a very positive evolution. Prayer unites. It is not an act of reconciliation to stop Catholics from praying together or attending mass together, for it is in praying together and breaking bread together that we recognize the Risen Lord who is the only one able to bring true unity that passes beyond all divisions of the past. Therefore, when we visit China we must refuse to discriminate. In the spirit of the gospel we must encourage the unity of the whole Chinese church, excluding no one. Unity grows step by step through a pilgrimage that includes everyone.

Similarly, Catholics from abroad have given different and sometimes conflicting interpretations about the situation in China. Each report contains some elements of truth. Visitors depend, of course, mainly on the testimony of their Chinese counterparts. This is human and is a sign of their genuine interest and love for their Catholic friends in China. Yet, it becomes harmful when visitors spread one-sided and contradictory interpretations. Instead of promoting an objective, balanced Christian understanding of the whole situation, they may cause more division. There is a need for all of us to communicate with each other and to exchange views and opinions openly, yet in a spirit of dialogue and of searching for unity. By "all of us," I mean members of the universal church who are interested in China, including the regular China visitors, but also authorities of foreign local churches and, of course, Roman authorities.

A Chance for the Universal Church To Grow?

Reflecting upon the evolution of the Chinese church can help other local churches to realize that the problems confronted by the local Chinese church are—at least partly—also theirs. Through events in China, history offers the universal church an opportunity to grow to an even more mature type of unity, under the primacy of the Holy Father—a unity characterized by equality, genuine mutual respect for each other's cultural background, and the felt presence of Christ's unifying spiritual leadership through the Holy Father. This invitation coming to us from history may be a sign of our times. A discovery of different characteristics and identities should not hamper unity within the universal church; quite the opposite. A new encounter between various local churches in an awareness of and appreciation for cultural differences can make the universal church grow with mature internal relationships and close unity inspired by the same gospel.

Only an open, undiscriminating *communio* can create an atmosphere in which this can happen and in which the new relationship between the universal Catholic church and the local Chinese church can develop. Only this type of *communio* can help us to deal in the right way with the historical turning point that we are witnessing, namely the emergence of a truly Chinese Catholic local church.

Notes

1. For a different interpretation of the role the laity is called to play in the Chinese church see above, Maria Goretti Lau, pp. 172-73.—Eds.

14

The Language of Reconciliation

ANONYMOUS

According to a brief report on the *ad limina* visit to Rome of the bishops of Taiwan,[1] Pope John Paul II made a strong and earnest appeal for unity and reconciliation among all Chinese Catholics. The words of the Holy Father echoed the desire of Christ, the Good Shepherd, that there should be "only the flock and one shepherd" (John 10:16) and the prayer before His passion: "May they all be one . . . so that the world may believe it was you who sent me" (John 17:21).

In his address the Holy Father made it clear that the unity of the church is not only a gift of God for which Christians must pray but also a task that requires "the humble, hidden, and generous contribution of all concerned."[2] He also pointed out the principal ways and means by which all concerned persons can contribute to the much desired unity: "understanding, good will, forgiveness and the dedication of all to the cause of spreading the kingdom of God."[3] When we hear this plea of the Holy Father, we naturally ask: Why has the promotion of unity and reconciliation become a primary task for the Chinese church?

The Rift in the Catholic Chinese Church

Pope John Paul II made this urgent appeal for unity and reconciliation in view of the fact that, according to an unnamed China church watcher, "Catholics in certain parts of China are bitterly divided, especially about whether and to what degree one should cooperate with the government-

The author of this article wishes to remain anonymous. The article, originally entitled "The Task of Reconciliation in the Chinese Church," appeared in a French translation in *Eglises d'Asie, Supplément à No. 119, Dossiers et Documents 9/91*, October 1991, pp. 108ff. Reprinted with permission.

approved Catholic Patriotic Association."[4] If this opinion is correct we can say that the Chinese Communist government's past and present policy toward the Catholic church is certainly one important factor contributing to the disunity among Catholics in China, but not its primary cause. The reason why Catholics are divided is the diverging position they have taken toward the government's policy and the Chinese Catholic Patriotic Association (CCPA).

Therefore, before we discuss how all concerned persons can contribute to reconciliation and unity in the church of China, we should first try to understand more profoundly the tragic and harmful rift dividing Chinese Catholics. Why can Catholics in good faith—meaning, for at least subjectively good reasons—decide to cooperate with the government-approved church led by the CCPA, while others—also for subjectively good reasons—refuse all cooperation with this part of the Catholic church and the CCPA?

When putting the question in this way we do not deny that in the past some bishops, priests, and faithful may perhaps have failed and seriously harmed their fellow Catholics and the church community. We cannot but deplore such actions and sympathize with all who suffered from them. Asking the question this way, we only try to obey Christ's command: "Do not judge" (Mt. 7:1). We must also remember that in the gospel Christ emphasized the duty to pardon each other and that Pope John in his address to the bishops of Taiwan mentioned forgiveness as a principal way of promoting unity and reconciliation. Furthermore, the Second Vatican Council acknowledges in principle that Catholics can in good faith take different positions regarding the question of how to respond to concrete situations:

Often enough the Christian view of things will itself suggest some specific solution in certain circumstances. Yet it happens rather frequently, and legitimately so, that with equal sincerity some of the faithful will disagree with others on a given matter. Even against the intentions of their proponents, however, solutions proposed on one side or another may be easily confused by many people with the Gospel message. Hence it is necessary for people to remember that no one is allowed in the aforementioned situation to appropriate the Church's authority for his opinion. They should always try to enlighten one another through honest discussion, preserving mutual charity and caring above all for the common good (*Pastoral Constitution*, 43).

This text from the Second Vatican Council can help us to understand the reasons for disunity among Chinese Catholics. Confronted with the government's policy toward their church, Catholics responded to it in diverging ways. Some decided to cooperate—in various degrees—with the government's laws regarding religion. Others rejected all forms of cooperation with the government and the CCPA. In these opposite options we can see the primary cause of the rift between Chinese Catholics. Since the Communist Chinese government acknowledges only the CCPA-led part of the Catholic church and does not recognize groups of other Catholics as legal entities, I will use the expression "public church" for the first group, while the second group of Catholics will be called the "underground church."

The Option for the Public Church

The attitude and actions of advocates for the public church abide by the government's and the CCPA's prohibition of contacts with the Holy See and, therefore, they choose and ordain bishops without papal approval. They use the freedom allowed by the government for practicing the Catholic church's life of worship, of administering and receiving the sacraments, and of training priests in seminaries approved and supervised by the government. These bishops, priests, and faithful Catholics use this possibility not for preaching atheism and materialism, but for doing the work of the church, for preaching and teaching catechism, celebrating the eucharist, training new priests, and supplying the faithful with religious books.

A pragmatic attitude underlies the actions of these Catholics. Under the given circumstances, they wish to do what can be done openly. They probably chose this road because experience taught them that nothing can remain secret and because they prefer the pragmatic approach—no one can do everything, so let's do what we can under the given circumstances.

In order to do what can be done in the open, they put up with the government's supervision and considerable influence on the affairs of the church, such as appointment of bishops, assignment and removal of priests, suppression of the term "martyrs" in liturgical calendars, teaching of politics in the seminaries, and prohibition on administrative contacts with the pope.

This pragmatic approach has produced visible results. Churches have been reopened in which Catholics can worship. This public, government-approved (part of the Catholic) church has established several seminaries in which more than seven hundred young men prepare for the priesthood.[5] Young Catholic women have entered religious life and a printing press can provide reading material for Catholics. On the whole, through these bishops, priests, and faithful, the church has established a legally acknowledged presence in socialist, Communist China.

The members of this public part of the church can point out that, even though they are complying with the government's prohibition on administrative contacts with Rome, they have given signals that they wish to be members of and strengthen their relation to the universal church and its visible head, the pope. In some places they celebrate the eucharist publicly and regularly according to the reformed post-conciliar rite and in Chinese. Both in the Latin mass and in the Chinese eucharist they often pray for the Holy Father. Some houses of the public church conspicuously display photographs of Pope John Paul II. The seminary of Sheshan near Shanghai has invited Jesuits, Salesians, and Dominicans from Hong Kong, Taiwan, the United States, and Canada to teach theology and philosophy.

Critics of this option raise the following questions: Is the Catholic ecclesiology free? Is frequent contact with the universal church and its visible head, the pope, not so essential that it cannot be sacrificed at any price, even for the possibility of supposedly better serving the faithful? Moreover, will not one compromise lead to another, whenever the government yields to the all too human temptation of taking a mile when you give an inch? Furthermore, by operating within the present system, will the church not become part of it, grow interested in its perpetuation, and thus contribute to its continuation? And if the present system is replaced, will not the church be reproached for having compromised itself by its alliance with the system and for having supported it by compliance with its policies?

The Option for the Underground Church

Underground bishops, priests, and faithful reject cooperating with the CCPA, because they regard it as a tool of the Communist government, which, in their opinion, wants to control the Catholic church in China, to tear it away from the universal church and its visible head, the pope. Because the government in returning church property made the CCPA responsible for the administration of the reopened churches, underground Catholics reject attendance at the services of these churches; they view it as a surrender to the CCPA and ultimately to the Communist authorities. For this reason some Catholics regard as sinful reception of the sacraments from priests serving at these churches.

Out of loyalty to the pope they prefer to have no churches and conduct their own services in the homes of Catholics. They put up with an irregular and often shortened training of their priests, secretly ordain priests and bishops, and accept the danger of being imprisoned. They criticize the CCPA, the public bishops, priests, and faithful for (at best) paying lip service to or (at worst) actively supporting an avowedly atheistic government.

Their loyalty to the Holy Father, their courage to risk harassment and even imprisonment, their dedication to serve like-minded Catholics have earned them approval and admiration from many Christians and human rights advocates. For this reason they are sometimes called "church of the Catacombs," "Suffering church," "Loyal church" (literally: faithful like a virgin). Sometimes, it is claimed that these priests outnumber the public church's faithful and newly ordained priests.

Critics of this option raise several questions. First, even if one does not call into doubt the teaching of the First Vatican Council about the authority of the pope, one can and (in accordance with the teaching of the Second

Vatican Council in the *Decree on Ecumenism*, 11) one should ask what place this truth occupies in the "hierarchy of truths." In other words, must we hold on to this truth and emphasize it so strongly even if other and more central Christian truths and features of Christian life cannot be preached and practiced openly?

Second, is the way in which the popes understood and practiced the primacy of the Roman bishop since the First Vatican Council the only way of being the servant of the servants of God? Does the history of the church not provide us with different models for the relation between the local churches and their bishops with the universal church and its head, the pope? In other words, is the way in which the popes practiced the primacy a matter of faith or a matter of discipline that can and sometimes should be revised?

Third, does the emphasis on the role of the pope not all too easily convey to the overwhelmingly non-Christian majority of Chinese people that the Catholic church is allied with a foreign power, because the pope is also head of the Vatican state?

Fourth, does the adamant refusal of all cooperation with the CCPA and the authorities not prove counterproductive? Does it weaken rather than strengthen the relation to the universal church and the pope, if all their actions, especially their relations with outside contacts, are closely watched, with the consequence that they cannot keep in contact with theological and pastoral developments and cannot acquire the reformed liturgical books and invite teachers of theology from outside? Finally, by choosing to remain illegal, do they not pass up many possibilities of preaching, teaching, and administering the sacraments to much larger groups of the faithful?

The Dilemma and the Task Faced by Chinese Catholics

If we look at the situation in which they live, we can see that all Chinese Catholics face a true dilemma. There are good reasons for each of the options, but both are seriously flawed. The tragedy of the situation of Chinese Catholics can be described with the words of the *Pastoral Constitution* (43) quoted above. In China, "some of the faithful" did and still do "and legitimately so" ... "with equal sincerity ... disagree with others" on the most appropriate way to respond to the government's policy toward their church.

If the preceding assessment of the situation is correct, if there are, indeed, good reasons to take legitimately and in good faith one of the opposing stances, we cannot avoid the conclusion that as long as the government's policy toward the Catholic church remains unchanged, the polarization within the church of China will and *can* continue. But if this is so, we must ask what then is the meaning of the Holy Father's appeal for unity in reconciliation? What can and must Catholics do in order to live up to Christ's desire for unity among Christians?

The same text of the *Pastoral Constitution* helps us to answer this question, because it points out the potential danger of such situations. Precisely because there is a *legitimate* disagreement, therefore, "solutions proposed by one side or another may be easily confused with the gospel message" and each side of the dispute will be tempted "to appropriate the church's authority for its opinion." In other words, what is and could remain a legitimate disagreement *within* the church can easily become a definite division *of* the church, and this happens whenever one side claims that its position is the only *legitimate Catholic* response to the given circumstances and consequently treats advocates of the opposite side as traitors and renegades.

We can leave aside the question of whether or not the line between a legitimate disagreement and a definite break between the two groups has been crossed in the dispute between the public and the underground church, because there is at least the danger of such a schism. This is cause for concern, and calls for earnest efforts to prevent such a harmful split by which one or the other or both sides confuse their own opinion with the gospel message and appropriate the church's authority exclusively for themselves.

In the same passage acknowledging the possibility that Catholics might legitimately disagree with one another, the *Pastoral Constitution* also instructs Catholics how, in such situations, they can and should preserve and strengthen their unity: they "must always try to enlighten one another through honest discussion, preserving mutual charity and caring above all for the common good" (43). In the light of this text and the words of the Holy Father in his address to the bishops of Taiwan, we will try to show in a more concrete way how all concerned persons can prevent a definite rift and promote unity and reconciliation among Chinese Catholics despite their opposite stances over and against the government's policy toward their church.

Steps toward Reconciliation

When we try to point out what can be done in order to promote unity, we should keep in mind the words of the Holy Father that reconciliation requires the *"humble, hidden, and generous* contribution of all concerned." Although unity cannot be expected from some spectacular gesture or action of one person, we wish to identify those humble and hidden actions which in hope have already been made by some Catholics. We wish to point out what common sense and especially the desire to be a genuine disciple of Christ can do to heal the deplorable rift between the Catholics in China. We want to point out actions that may be incompatible with Christ's desire for unity. Likewise, we want to describe actions that can contribute to unity and reconciliation.

Actions for Unity and Reconciliation

1. All concerned persons must be convinced about the importance of striving for reconciliation. The desire for the unity of the disciples was and is living in the heart of Jesus, and reconciliation among Chinese Catholics is a profound concern of the Holy Father. Moreover, all concerned persons must be convinced that the division among Catholics is a grave scandal that seriously harms the church. We must apply the Chinese proverb to the ugly infighting of the Catholics and say that only the enemies of the church can gain from the bitter division and mutual accusations of Catholics, which must be repugnant even to good-willed non-Christians. For this reason, both sides should remember and comply with what both Chinese and Westerners advise—one should not wash one's dirty linen in public.

2. All concerned persons should constantly keep in mind the words of our Lord: "Do not judge, and you will not be judged" (Mt. 7:1). Even if their own conscience forbids them to do what public Catholics do, underground Catholics have no right to condemn their Catholic brothers and sisters who attend mass and receive the sacraments in the public church. Even less may they call public Catholics, their priests, and bishops "traitors" or "Judases." Similarly, public Catholics should never pass judgment on underground Catholics, charging them with being unwilling to forgive, stubborn, narrow-minded, bad citizens, or unrealistic fanatics.

3. All concerned persons should be critical about their own motives, put away all self-righteousness and ask themselves: "Is our dispute only about the pope and about a realistic acceptance of the social and political situation and the possibility to do pastoral and missionary work under the given circumstances? Are not questions of power, prestige, and property playing a hidden and, therefore, disastrous role? Is our quarrel not conditioned by personal, factional, and regional rivalries?

4. All concerned persons should realize that personal factors can also play a constructive role. Membership in the same religious community, attendance at the same school or seminary, and friendships can help in understanding the viewpoint of the opposite "camp" and thus lessen harmful animosity; they can also open up channels of communication, of sharing precious material, and of experiencing the special circumstances of the Chinese church. Therefore, wherever bonds of friendship, trust, and common experience exist, they should be strengthened in order to promote mutual tolerance, understanding, and reconciliation.

5. All concerned persons should be extremely careful about the expressions they use when referring to advocates of the opposite option and to themselves. For the sake of promoting unity, they should give up convenient and customary ways of speaking and thoroughly revise their language so it is not inaccurate, unjust, or harmful. More than two thousand years ago the Chinese sage Confucius stressed the importance of using correct language. His teaching still holds true in the bitter dispute dividing Chinese

Catholics, because some words confuse the issues, create and uphold prejudices, prevent reasonable dialogue, and widen the existing rift. The revision of language is certainly one of the humble and hidden steps toward reconciliation; nevertheless it is of great importance and, therefore, rightly demands attention and generous efforts. For this reason, we shall discuss some of the expressions often used and suggest other ways of speaking that seem less harmful and more helpful on the road to unity.

Language for Unity and Reconciliation

Both in Chinese and in Western languages one can frequently hear and read the expression "patriotic church." This expression is inaccurate if it refers to "Ai Gwo Hui," which is more correctly translated by "Patriotic Association" of Chinese Catholics. It is a harmfully misleading expression when it is used to designate those bishops, priests, and faithful who worship and/or minister at churches reopened by the government with the cooperation of the CCPA, because it easily suggests that all the faithful are members of the CCPA, or are at least supporters of its policy. Just as in other parts of the world faithful Catholics who regularly attend mass at a church served by Franciscans do not become a Franciscan church or members of the Franciscan order, in a similar way, Catholics attending mass at churches under the administration of the CCPA do not become members of the CCPA or a patriotic church. If "patriotic" is taken in its literal sense of loving and being loyal to one's country and when this expression is reserved for members of the public church, this name becomes an insult to underground Catholics because it brands them as "unpatriotic" and traitors to their nation. Thus, all who wish to promote reconciliation and unity in the church of China should delete forever the expression "patriotic church" from their language.

What term could be used to designate those bishops, priests, and faithful Catholics who do comply with directives of the government and the CCPA? Some people use "official church" and correspondingly call the underground Catholics the "unofficial church." However, since "official" often has the meaning of "approved, acknowledged by the competent authorities," this pair of expressions might be offensive for the underground Catholics, who certainly reject the idea that the Communist and atheistic government is a competent arbiter in the matter of which persons represent the genuine Catholic church.

Since the expressions "government-approved church" and "government-acknowledged church" leave this question about competence open and simply state the fact that this group of Catholics is approved by the government, they seem more objective and less offensive to underground Catholics. Therefore, to designate communities attending services at officially reopened churches, one should use expressions like "public church," "open church," or "government-approved church" and keep in mind that these names should never designate a separate entity, but only one part of the Catholic church, namely, that which operates in the public and complies with the present government's prohibition on administrative contacts with the Holy See.

Sometimes underground Catholics are called the "loyal or faithful (like a virgin) church." No matter by whom this name is used, this expression seems inappropriate. When underground Catholics use it themselves, it smacks of pharisaic self-righteousness. It also makes faithfulness to the pope the only criterion of true Catholic life. By implication it brands the Catholics of the public church as unfaithful and forgets the teaching of the Fathers and the Second Vatican Council that the whole church is in constant need of conversion, because it is always stained by sin.

Sometimes the underground Catholics are called the "suffering church." Indeed, the underground bishops, priests, and faithful do suffer. Some of their bishops are in jail and their priests ministering to the faithful risk imprisonment. Nevertheless, the expression "suffering church" seems inappropriate. When underground Catholics use it for themselves, they assume the pose of martyrs, of the persecuted just, which is hardly in accordance with the spirit of Christ. Furthermore, the expression "suffering church" all too easily suggests that Catholics of the open church joined the public church in order to escape suffering; it also conveys the idea that members of the public church are exempt from suffering. Certainly, they are spared some hardships that are sustained by or threatening underground Catholics, but the members of the public church also suffer from painful restrictions and from the rejection, suspicion, and accusations from the side of the underground Catholics.

Therefore, in the interest of unity and reconciliation the terms "faithful, loyal church" and "suffering church" should be deleted from our vocabulary; due to the lack of better expressions, terms like "underground church," "clandestine church," or "secret church" can be used *provided* we keep in mind that these expressions do not designate a separate entity, but only one part of the Catholic church, namely, those who refuse to join the government-approved church led by the CCPA.

The Public Church

The members of the public church can contribute to reconciliation through the following attitudes, actions, and omissions.

1. They should respect the option of underground Catholics who, in order to uphold a Catholic truth and in order to defend the right to freely practice religion, renounce the use of CCPA-administered churches and risk imprisonment.

2. For this reason, they should never make or cooperate in any attempt to solve the problem of reconciliation by force, never make denunciations,

or cooperate in confiscation and closure of places of worship, or in the arresting of underground Catholics.

3. They should provide—whenever possible—some sort of legality to underground Catholics in ways similar to that where in some Moslem countries legal Catholic church buildings are lent to Protestant Christians. They should also use their channels of communication to the government to provide legal assistance to imprisoned underground bishops and priests.

4. They should provide underground Catholics with liturgical books, Bibles, and information about the universal church, which paradoxically can sometimes be more easily obtained by the public church through legal channels or through printing in Shanghai.

5. They should provide underground Catholics with information about the public church, its pastoral work, its training of priests in accordance with the guidelines of the universal church, its frequent and public prayer for the pope, and its use of the reformed liturgy.

6. They should assign new priests to places where they are accepted by the majority of both sides and where they can minister to most of the Catholics. This will spare Catholics on both sides the agony of being rejected by fellow Catholics, of being torn apart, and becoming discouraged by ugly infighting.

7. The Catholics of the public church should regard the attitude of underground Catholics as a challenge. They should ask themselves: Do we live up to Christ's command to be the salt (not the sugar or the honey) of the world? Do we heed the admonition of St. Paul: "Do not model yourselves on the behavior of the world around you" (Rom. 12:2)? Are we only conformists and never witnesses to the word of St. Peter before the Sanhedrin, that we owe obedience more to God than to humans (cf. Acts 4:19)?

8. Finally, they should be willing to learn from underground Catholics that large congregations, spacious churches, regular administration of the sacraments, and fully trained priests are not an absolute necessity, because Christ promised that He will be in the midst of two or three persons assembled in His name (Mt. 18:19). They should also be reminded that according to classical Catholic theology God is not bound to the sacraments.

Underground Catholics

Underground Catholics should contribute to the task of reconciliation through the following attitudes and actions.

1. They should not fix their attention on the past. The policies of both the government and the CCPA have undergone significant changes in the direction of more tolerance of religion in general and of the Catholic church in particular. If they refuse to forget true injustices done in the past, as Christians they must keep in mind that in the gospels Christ's command to forgive is much more clearly expressed than the truth about the primacy of St. Peter and his successors. As Catholics who want to be obedient to the

pope, they cannot be disobedient to him and turn a deaf ear to his words spoken to the bishops of Taiwan—that unity and reconciliation must be sustained by forgiveness.

2. They should not fix their attention on the statutes of the CCPA and some public statements of some members of the public church. Rather they should look at what the bishops, priests, and faithful Catholics of the public church do: teaching catechism, hearing confessions, visiting the sick, establishing seminaries, training priests and sisters. Although in their seminaries there are lectures on politics, the much larger part of the teaching is devoted to the classical themes of Catholic theology, God, Christ, creation, sacraments, Mary. Most of their teachers use their old textbooks and try to obtain and use post-conciliar books and articles. In their liturgy, even when government representatives are present, they often pray for the universal church and the pope. In some places they celebrate the eucharist according to the reformed rite and in Chinese. If underground Catholics look at the actions of the public church, they can perhaps come to believe that the majority of the faithful and many of their priests and bishops do wish to be members of the universal Catholic church, although for the time being they do not have any official contact with the pope.

3. Underground Catholics should without suspicion welcome the new priests trained in the seminaries of the public church. Most of these men come from devout Catholic families. They entered the seminaries of the open church with the hope of getting a more adequate spiritual, intellectual, theological, and pastoral training. Their life in the seminary followed the traditional rules of Catholic seminaries before the Second Vatican Council. Their teachers used mainly their own textbooks or books written by Catholic authors from abroad. Some students from Sheshan seminary had as teachers Jesuits, Salesians, Dominicans, priests, and sisters (from Hong Kong, Taiwan, and overseas) who are faithful to the universal church and its head, the pope. Before ordination they are not required to join the CCPA.[6] If they do so their motive is probably to be able to serve the Christians in a more open and freer way. Catholic respect for the priesthood, Christian understanding, and ordinary fairness demand that they are accepted without prejudice and suspicion by genuine Catholic Christians.

4. Underground Catholics should regard their disagreement with the public church about its compliance with the directives of the government as a challenge to rethink their attitudes toward the society in which they live. At the least, they must realize that Christians are obliged to obey all just laws and devote themselves to the upbuilding of a just society. They must also realize that the church as a community normally must operate within the given framework of a society. When the Second Vatican Council teaches that "in virtue of her mission and nature, the church is bound to no particular form of human culture, nor to any political, economic or social system" (*Pastoral Constitution*, 42) it does not intend to say that the church lives outside concrete societies; rather it says indirectly that the church can

live and can fulfill its mission of being the salt of the earth and the light of the world not only in past forms of society but in all circumstances.

Outsiders

1. Friends and visitors from Hong Kong, Macao, Taiwan, and abroad should be convinced, first of all, that they cannot fully understand the complexity of the situation in which the Chinese Catholics live. Therefore, they should abstain from passing judgment on either side of the dispute and resist all attempts to make them partisans of one camp. Naturally, their contacts will often be mainly with one side or the other and the help they give will mainly benefit one side. But visitors should make it clear that, above all, they wish to help all Christian faithful, not an (ecclesiastical) party or clique. Whatever help they give to whichever side, they should clearly express the wish that the recipients work for greater unity and reconciliation.

2. Visitors from the outside should not deceive themselves into believing that they are not carefully watched by all sides. Neither should they play heroes by breaking the rules and silent understandings which, when observed, avoid renewed confrontation and even some degree of tolerance from the government toward the secret church. Truly, those visitors may get away with their "courageous" actions, but their behavior may very easily prevent them from visiting China again to render more humble but — in the long run — more effective help to all sides. Furthermore, they easily might create new difficulties with the government for all Catholics and thus aggravate the tension between the public and the secret church.

Rome

Without progress toward reconciliation on the local level between the different communities, priests, and bishops in China, measures taken by Rome will not significantly — if at all — contribute to the desired reconciliation. Nevertheless, Rome can assist Chinese Catholics in the following ways:

1. Whenever any help is given it should be made clear that the Holy Father above all wants all Catholics united and dedicated to the task of evangelization in China, that he regards dedication to this task and striving for unity as *the* proof of loyalty to the universal church and the pope.

2. Rome should encourage the young priests who were trained in the seminaries established and conducted by the public church to devote themselves wholeheartedly to their ministry. Just as in other parts of the world, the fact that a bishop is secretly married or even lives in open concubinage or holds certain political views is never a reason for urging priests to abandon the faithful. In a similar way, Rome should let these young priests know that the sacraments they administer are not only valid but fruitful

and that pastoral work is their holy duty, whatever the political position or status (married or celibate) of their bishop might be.

3. Rome should encourage young underground priests to take notice of the post-conciliar developments in theology, pastoral ministry, and spirituality and thus compensate for their perhaps deficient theological training. It is important to avoid the formation of an anachronistic ghetto-like mentality in the communities they serve as priests.

These steps toward greater unity recommended above accord with the Holy Father's words to the bishops of Taiwan: The promotion of reconciliation among Catholic groups requires "humble" and "hidden" contributions from all concerned. No sweeping measures, no actions for which anyone might get the papal order "Pro Ecclesia et Pontifice" were mentioned. Significantly enough, Pope John Paul II called the humble and hidden contributions also "generous" contributions. Indeed, mutual forgiveness, tolerance of attitudes one cannot approve of for oneself, and the extension of help to those who criticize cannot be practiced without a high degree of generosity. Thus, promotion of unity among Catholics in China is similar to the practice of ecumenism, which constantly requires "a change of heart. For it is from newness of attitudes (cf. Eph. 4:23), from self-denial and unstinted love, that yearnings for unity take their rise and grow toward maturity" (Ecumenism, 7). To actively seek greater unity and reconciliation is thus not confined to some particular actions, nor does it consist only in praying for the gift of unity; it is often nothing else in the concrete circumstances of the Chinese Catholic church than to follow Christ who taught us by word and deed: Do not judge (Mt. 7:1); forgive each other, not only seven times, but seventy seven times (Mt. 18:22); be like the Father in Heaven, who causes the sun to rise on bad people as well as on good, and his rain to fall on honest and dishonest alike (Mt. 5:45). Thus the task of promoting unity and reconciliation is no more than that of following Christ and no less than responding fully to His special gift, His daily call to be and become His disciple.

Notes

1. *Asia Focus*, January 2, 1991, pp. 1-6.
2. Ibid., p. 6.
3. Ibid.
4. Ibid.
5. *Tripod*, no. 59. p. 40.
6. Ibid., p. 43.

15

Fundamental Attitude of the Bridge Church

ALOYSIUS B. CHANG[1]

People of faith observe, analyze, and judge situations within the context of their faith. I do not claim that the following essay has absolute objectivity. None such exists. China is very vast. The church there, quite naturally, is spread throughout an immense area and its situation differs in the various regions. It is important to keep this fundamental fact in mind. To make sweeping statements that would be true for the church as a whole in China, especially after only one trip, would be quite foolhardy. Such opinions could only be superficial and erroneous. What follows is an evaluation of what I myself have seen, or what I have heard from others or what I have gleaned from materials I have read.

The Environment

The church of the nineties in China lives under a Communist regime that is different from the one of forty years ago. There is freedom of religious belief but this freedom, at best, is tolerated by a Communist and socialist government whose understanding of religion is limited by its own ideology. It permits religion to have a community organization, liturgical expression, and a religious discipline. Presently this is the only kind of freedom religious organizations can enjoy.

China's Constitution gives a very narrow interpretation of freedom of religious belief. It strictly prohibits any foreign interference by those religions having worldwide connections, such as Buddhism, Islam, Protestantism, and Catholicism. Religion is solely a matter for China's internal administration, and foreign powers are forbidden to intervene in any way. Because of its universal and international character as well as its admin-

This essay was expanded by Aloysius B. Chang from a speech he gave in Taiwan in 1991.

istrative organization and structure, the Catholic church is in a worse situation than other religious bodies that do not have such centralized leadership. The primacy of the pope and the Vatican with its apparent political organization makes the Communist government extremely suspicious.

Under the Communist regime, religion exists for the good of the country and society. In the present atmosphere of religious toleration, the United Front department of the Communist party and the Bureau of Religious Affairs of the central government are two related organizations whose duty is to implement religious policies and govern religious bodies. Under the United Front department and the Religious Affairs Bureau is the Catholic Patriotic Association. The Protestant church has the Three-Self Movement and its role is similar to that played by the Catholic Patriotic Association. The Buddhists, Taoists, and Muslims also have parallel associations.

The United Front and Religious Affairs Bureau use the Patriotic Association as a liaison unit between the party and government on the one side and the church on the other. It is responsible for transmitting government and party directives and policies to the church. In turn it also lets government officials know the church's needs.

The Chinese Catholic Patriotic Association has a chairperson and a vice-chairperson; its membership consists of bishops, priests, sisters, and lay Catholics. It is divided into national, provincial, urban, and local associations, and it adjusts its policies and their implementation to fit the needs of the United Front department. During its early years the Patriotic Association's way of working differed considerably from that of today. It has, however, made several contributions to the church. Owing to the association's mediation with the government, many churches have been rebuilt. Overall, it is a pliant organization apt at adapting its actions and communications to the party's policies. In itself it is not an ecclesial organization nor a community.

The Situation

We must bear in mind that the environment in which the church on the Chinese mainland today finds itself is not favorable to religious freedom. This situation is something that all of us should realize and always keep in mind. The church is split into two factions: the public and the underground church.

The Public Church

The church exists by following party and government regulations and brooks no foreign interference. It implements the policy of independence and autonomy in church administration. It is noted especially for choosing and consecrating its own bishops. This causes an incomplete communion between the local church and the Holy See, especially on the level of law. In the past, owing to government pressure, the public church expressed a certain hostility toward Rome. Lately, however, this attitude has gradually mellowed. Today the public church openly recognizes that the pope's pastoral primacy belongs to the content of faith. It even prays for him.

Noting this relaxation of tension, some people who do not live in China have overrated the public church, disregarding the fact that many problems still exist. We cannot deny that the public church's communion with Rome is truncated. This is true at least on the legal level, even though there is still a many-sided communion in faith. There is the communion, for example, of a shared faith in the Father, of a shared life in the Son and the Holy Spirit as well as common scriptures.

Some will ask, "Why speak of the lack of communion on the legal level? Is not reality more important than law?" This may sound reasonable at first, but since law is indispensable for social order and unity, our attitude toward it should be more positive. Many voices in today's society vying to bring solutions to the myriad problems facing our world lack guidance and direction. The pope, representing the entire church, makes use of his encyclical letters and speaks to the whole world. He wants the church to have one voice. This is the pope's unifying function, a role not found among Protestant churches.

The incomplete communion of the public church in China with the pope is, I maintain, at the least, a legal question that hopefully one day will be resolved. An indication of this possibility lies in the fact that some bishops in China have already been legalized.

The Underground Church

The underground church does not accept the Communist party's demands that it be independent and self-governing. It firmly maintains complete union with the pope in order to safeguard the hierarchical nature of the church and loyalty to his primacy. There is an antagonism, even conflict, between the public and underground church. Both, however, despite their differences, are influenced by the special circumstances in which the church in China exists.

Analysis of the Present Situation

An analysis of the situation described above involves making judgments. My aim is to make these judgments within the spirit of the gospels, our faith values, and the church's tradition.

According to traditional theology (which still has value today) the individual church is a faith community of the people of God. It consists of the bishop, the clergy, and the laity. The bishop holds the office of chief pastor in his diocese, safeguarding the church's unity and catholicity. In other words, the bishop as head represents the individual church community and guides its life and activities while also being closely linked with the other pastors. He must also be in communion with the pope and under his leadership pastor his individual flock, otherwise his church cannot keep its unity and catholicity intact. He must have the permission of the pope for his ordination and appointment to his individual diocese. Church law demands this. To be elected, ordained, and installed as bishop without papal authority is not only illegal, but it also breaks communion with the pope.

The Illegality of the Public Church

Today's ecclesiology and canon law both state that without papal approval the election, ordination, or appointment as bishop to a diocese is illegal. The ecclesial community under his pastorship is also illegal. This illegality breaks the communion of the individual diocese with other bishops and the pope and also with the entire church. Allow me to state clearly at this point that illegality and communion established by law should not be straightaway confused with the fundamental issue of salvation.

Any action that is illegal involves the question of choice, which, in turn, is linked with the "responsibility of law" and "responsibility of conscience." Let us analyze these two terms. Very many elements obviously bear on the question of responsibility in the present special situation of the Chinese church. (Here we can make only a general analysis of the situation without touching on particular details governing the cases of various bishops.) On the negative side, there is the external environment that creates fears, intimidation, and the temptation to gain personal advantage. On the more positive side, there is the possibility of making an illegal decision based on pastoral needs. Unless one is personally involved in such a situation, it is impossible to understand the situation of one who is helpless, lacks viable alternatives, and finds it impossible to have acted otherwise.

We must admit that, even given this situation, the person who makes illegal choices cannot entirely escape all responsibility. Nonetheless a bishop who accepts ordination within the public church in order to provide for the sacramental and liturgical life and moral guidance of the faithful makes a contribution to the church of this particular time and place even though his action is illegal. In a word, we cannot deny the existence of the illegal act or the legal responsibility of the bishop concerned, yet this responsibility differs with individuals. We must, by all means, try to understand the situation.

Although we have said that individuals bear responsibility for their illegal actions, we have no way of judging the state of their conscience or their moral responsibility. Only the person in question can answer for this before God. It is better that we do not discuss a person's moral responsibility and refrain from judging whether he or she is culpable or not.

It is very important that we not try to judge the culpability of any member of the public church; rather we must try to understand the circumstances behind their illegal acts. For example, priests who work in the diocese of an illegal bishop act illegally, but they share in the illegality in varying degrees. Some priests who have never joined the Patriotic Association have suffered very much for the faith. Some are now cooperating with an illegal bishop purely for the sacramental and spiritual life of the faithful. Other priests who have joined the Patriotic Association and are cooperating with the illegal bishop may do so for personal gain. Nonetheless they also render genuine service to the faithful. Some priests have married. Obviously, their responsibility for cooperating with an illegal bishop is very different from the former two classes of priests.

Many of the laity who take part in the services of the public church know nothing about the legality or illegality of church matters. They are leading a life of faith and are receiving valid sacraments. It is useless to speak of responsibility as far as they are concerned. Summing up:

1. Priests, sisters, and the laity who belong to the public church share in the illegality of the bishop who has been illegally consecrated and bear legal responsibility in varying degrees.

2. As far as moral responsibility is concerned only those persons directly and personally involved have the answer.

3. Persons, especially those who do not live in the People's Republic of China, should refrain from openly discussing, analyzing, and judging these matters of conscience.

The Legality of the Underground Church

The underground church is the one not recognized by the Communist party and government. Since the bishops in this church maintain full union with the pope, they are legal in terms of canon law. At great cost to themselves, they face constant dangers but remain faithful to their belief in order to safeguard the church's orthodoxy. They are loyal to the primacy of the pope and continue the church's long tradition of martyrdom under persecution. The church, in its long history, has never encouraged its members to compromise or deny their faith during times of persecution. We must acknowledge that, as a matter of fact, the underground church has, for the past forty years, remained loyal to the universal church and preserved Catholic unity.

Naturally, the priests, sisters, and laity who are under the leadership of these legal bishops are also legal. Considering the circumstances in which they live and the difficulties they endure, we can understand why the underground church does not readily understand the public church and why they even maintain an attitude of hostility toward it. Obviously, all the members of the underground church are not saints. Furthermore, those bishops in the public church whose status has been legalized now also enjoy complete communion with the pope and the universal church. We must emphasize that communion with Rome is not just limited to matters of law. There are other links as well, such as prayer, scriptures, and sacraments. In saying this, I do not wish to minimize the importance of maintaining legitimate ties with Rome. Because the mass is at the center of the church's liturgical life and symbolizes its unity, church officials have forbidden legitimate priests from concelebrating with illegitimate clergy. The public church, for its part, knows that such concelebrations would also be against national policies.

Finally, it is not our place for us to pass moral judgment on some of the actions undertaken by some members of the underground church now facing so many difficulties.

Theological Reflections

The church in China today is under the guidance of the Holy Spirit who permits a pluralism to exist within the church. We have seen this from the various phenomena described above and from our analysis. The Spirit permits illegal bishops, acting under the principle of the "lesser evil," to be active in an atmosphere entirely hostile to a life of faith. The underground church, too, under the guidance of the Spirit has safeguarded ecclesial orthodoxy and Catholic unity. Both sides are concerned about the faith and moral life of the Christian community and both, in varying degrees, have to bear the pressures inflicted on the church by the Communist regime.

In light of this most complex situation, interactions between the public and underground church are of utmost importance. I would like briefly to propose three possible ways in which these interactions can take place: a) mutual communion, b) peaceful co-existence, and c) mutual antagonism.

In the October issue of *Clergy Review* (1990, No. 299) an article by John Baptist Jiang states that in a certain area in China a bishop of the public church and a bishop of the underground church live together in one house. Although it is not too clear from the article just how far this "mutual communion" has gone, we can say that such a situation does exist. We must ask, however, what does this "mutual communion" really mean? Is it limited solely to the love that Christians must have for one another? From the negative angle, this could mean avoiding conflicts at all costs; on the positive side, it could mean taking preliminary steps to cooperate along certain lines. As a matter of fact, there are many levels of communion already existing within the Christian community. Both the public and the underground church belong to the same church of Jesus Christ, both share the same trinitarian life of grace; both have received the same baptism and read the same scriptures.

There is a difference, however, in terms of hierarchical communion. As far as the church's hierarchy is concerned, "mutual communion" means more than just saying that Jesus Christ is the Head of the church. It also requires accepting the pope's primacy. In the case of those bishops living in the same house, some might say that "mutual communion" already exists as far as they are concerned. We also have to ask, however, does hierarchical communion also exist? Would not hierarchical communion require the bishop of the public church to renounce the policy of independence and autonomy and let the bishop of the underground church take over leadership of the local church?

The second mode of interaction is peaceful co-existence, with each church doing its own work without interference or conflict and working in the same area. This can be considered a viable, commendable, and even ideal form given the present situation of the church in China and the difficulty of achieving a hierarchical communion at the present moment.

The third possibility, from an ecclesial viewpoint, mutual antagonism, is certainly not an ideal situation. Recrimination and discord do not accord at all with Christian love. The fact that each party has chosen to walk a different path is no reason for antagonism. Articles, biased on either side, which report these conflicts do not help the situation; they actually cause harm. Such matters can be reported but the "bridge church" should blame no one. If there must be blame, it should be laid on the environment hostile to religious freedom.

We have mentioned that the Patriotic Association has national, provincial, and local structures. Its influence and operations differ. In some places it has little influence and in others, some maintain, it does not even exist. Where the Association has little or no influence, or where it does not exist, there is no difference between the public and the underground church. There is only one church — the legitimate one. This does not mean, however, that the life of faith in those places is free from intimidation and fear.

Principles and Activities of the Bridge Church

The analysis of the situation on the Chinese mainland can help us chart a course which we, who live outside the Chinese mainland but who are called to be the bridge church, can follow.

The pope, knowing the situation in the People's Republic of China, has appealed to us living outside that country to bear the responsibility of being the "bridge church." He has called us to action. We cannot stand by disinterested in what is happening in China as though helpless, devoid of concern or feeling. God is speaking to us through this situation and through the church's chief pastor who asks us to be the "bridge church." We must respond actively to this call.

Whether we are praying for the church on the Chinese mainland or are offering it any form of assistance, our attitudes should be in conformity with the following five points:

1. Compassion for both sides should be our hallmark. Although certain elements of the church may enjoy some modicum of freedom, both are living under conditions that are not favorable to religious life and progress in faith.

2. We regret the public church's independent way of acting—at least on the level of law—and its break in hierarchical union with the successor of Peter. We are also aware that the public church is to some degree responsible for this state of affairs and as such cannot escape all blame. We hasten to add that the church's independence, self-government, and self-support can be implemented while remaining within the bounds of church law. These three aims are an ideal for the church and should in no way constitute a reason for breaking hierarchical communion.

3. The loyal orthodoxy of the underground church should encourage us.

4. Hopefully both sides are maintaining the bond of love that holds Christians together. If we visit China, we must, while making our point of view clear, avoid entering into individual quarrels or doing anything that could exacerbate conflicts existing among different parties. If we, as the bridge church, act in this way, we will not only assist our brothers and sisters in China, but we may also be called upon to share in their suffering.

5. We believe that the Holy Spirit is at work in the church on the Chinese mainland. The Spirit is the one who preserves and develops the faith of the Christian community. We maintain that this holds true for both the underground and the public churches. Some Catholics from the underground church, owing to the humiliations and sufferings they have had to endure, do not understand why we have anything to do with the public church. We take this opportunity to exercise our function as a bridge church and offer them our analysis of the situation. The Catholic laity may not experience the problems discussed in this article, but priests and sisters often do. It is our duty to acquaint them with our position.

During the years of the Cultural Revolution all religions suffered tremendous losses. Temples, churches, and sacred writings need to be replaced. The church in the People's Republic of China is in urgent need of all kinds of assistance. We of the bridge church must offer a helping hand. The attitude we manifest in doing so and the way we extend this help require both wisdom and prudence.

Our desire is to help both the public and the underground churches. When we extend help to the public church we are not saying that we agree with or support their position. Our assistance is aimed at preserving and fostering the faith. Illegality is a matter of law that does not necessarily deny the presence of Jesus in the church. When we see their real needs, we cannot simply say: "You are an illegal church; we will have nothing to do with you." How would this manifest the love of Christ? The underground church, of course, needs even greater assistance, especially in the remote countryside.

We hope both sides will understand why we desire to help them. We also hope that the bishops and priests in China will explain our motives for helping them to their faithful. Bringing in books and other daily necessities is, of course, a good thing, but what is more important is to make use of these occasions to explain that our assisting both sides is part of the integrative nature of a bridge church. We are aware that we cannot resolve their fundamental problems but our explanation may help build a new psychological climate. At the present moment, this is a very important task. The existing legal problems can one day be resolved. However, the psychological knot still needs to be untied. As we prepare for the task ahead, we need to be farsighted and supportive.

The training of leaders is one of the most urgent needs of the church in the People's Republic of China. This holds true both for the public and underground churches. The public church already has twelve major seminaries with approximately seven hundred seminarians. While we emphasize that this is the age of the laity, we cannot deny that, at the present stage, China is in dire need of church leaders from among the priests and sisters. Seminarians must be offered the best formation possible.

The bridge church must be very careful in handing out information about the church in China. Some reports originating in Taiwan are, at times, erroneous. This is bad for the church in Taiwan as well as for the church on the Chinese mainland. It is also blameworthy. Those who write reports on the church on the Chinese mainland should give their readers a sound, truly catholic, constructive, and reconciling point of view. We need healthy and accurate reporting written in charity. Sensitive questions should be avoided. Sound reporting should be the work and hallmark of the bridge church.

The service of the bridge church to the church of the People's Republic of China cannot be limited solely to material support. Christ's work is never accomplished without the cross. Therefore, the bridge church must also be willing to share in the experience of suffering of the Chinese mainland. The members of the bridge church will certainly experience misunderstanding and reproach but such sufferings are an integral part of being the bridge church.

Notes

1. Recently, the Directresses of Novices in Taiwan invited me to talk to them on the proper attitudes the "bridge churches" should have. With some daring, I offered them my thoughts in a systematic manner. After that, a Sister laboriously put them in the form of a paper which I asked some of my colleagues to read. They thought that it would be worthwhile to publish these insights. Of course, we agreed that as a paper it was not complete in all aspects. Besides, I had not considered the reaction that the attitudes expressed in it would produce among the people in mainland China. Nor had I made sufficient use of the experiences of other collaborators of the bridge churches who had visited the church there. Yet, I have decided to publish it because I think that the theoretical elements contained in this paper have a positive value as a reference for concrete actions.

16

China and the Future of Hong Kong

Risk and Responsibilities

LUKE TSUI

One Country, Two Systems

Situated at the South of China, the island of Hong Kong was ceded to Britain by China after the First Opium War in 1842. While trading with China, British traders needed cash badly to balance the trade deficit [1] They sold opium, which was harmful to the Chinese people and illegal according to Chinese law, to pay for the tea, silk, and Chinaware they exported to England. Confronted by China's determination to stamp out the flourishing opium trade, Britain attacked Canton (Guangzhou) in 1840. So began the First Opium War, which resulted in the signing of the first of a long series of unequal treaties. China was, for the first time, forced to open five coastal ports to British trade, and the island of Hong Kong was handed over to Britain.

The Kowloon peninsula was added to the colony in 1860 after the Second Opium War (1856-60). In 1898, a 99-year lease was signed for the New Territories, a much bigger area north of Kowloon peninsula. Today these three areas along with a number of outlying islands make up what is known as "Hong Kong."

Since the island of Hong Kong and Kowloon peninsula cannot survive practically without the New Territories, all of "Hong Kong" will be returned to China after the end of the New Territories lease on June 30, 1997.

Back in 1979, after the Hong Kong Governor Murray McLehose came back from his visit to Beijing, preparation was made for the final withdrawal of Britain from the colony. The visit of Prime Minister Margaret Thatcher to Beijing in 1982 and the following negotiations that led to the signing of the Sino-British Joint Declaration in 1984 formally marked the beginning of the transition of Hong Kong from a British colony to becoming a "special administrative region" of the socialist People's Republic of China.

And so the international problem of unequal treaties, always regarded by most Chinese people as a great humiliation, is now settled. Hong Kong will return to Chinese sovereignty on July 1, 1997. Under the "One Country, Two Systems" concept devised by the Chinese leader Deng Xiaoping, the destiny of Hong Kong will be tied very closely to that of China. After the visit of Prime Minister John Major to China and the subsequent signing of the Sino-British Memorandum of Understanding in 1991,[2] Hong Kong entered the final phase of the transitional period. This means that Hong Kong's relationship with China is further increased. According to Governor David Wilson in his fifth policy address in 1991, cooperation and partnership are the two main concepts that the people of the two places (Hong Kong and China) will always bear in mind.[3]

But despite assurances repeatedly made from Beijing that Hong Kong's capitalist way of life, especially its tradition of personal freedom, will continue for fifty years after 1997, many Hong Kong people are uncertain of what the future will hold. This uncertainty escalated to fear and disenchantment and even disappointment after the suppression of the student movement in Beijing in June 1989 and the subsequent crackdown on dissent in China.

Emigration and "brain drain" have become one of the greatest problems ever since. The rapid increase in emigration since 1985 is one indication of peoples' lack of confidence in post-1997 Hong Kong. This, coupled with the active recruitment of professionals and investors by Western countries, has led to an exodus of the "brain" in Hong Kong. In 1988 alone, some 45,000 people left the colony, an increase of 50 percent from the previous year, and more than double the average for the preceding five years.[4] More than 60,000 are expected to leave Hong Kong in 1991.

Church-State Relationship

Facing all the problems of the society, the Catholic church of Hong Kong must respond positively in her own way as a sign and instrument of salvation. The church had come to Hong Kong almost at the same time as the British expeditionary force. Ever since that time, the church has remained a faithful and useful partner of the colonial government, which is basically sympathetic and supportive to Christianity. Some even regard the church, whether Catholic or Protestant, as a useful tool of the government to control and serve the community, especially through educational and social welfare enterprises operated by the latter, particularly since the 1950s. In education, for instance, one quarter of primary and secondary pupils in Hong Kong study in Catholic schools. Although the government subsidizes a major portion of education and other social services, the church has to contribute a large portion of its resources in terms of personnel, buildings, and finances. In fact, among the three main tasks of the church in Hong Kong in terms of personnel, education occupies the most important place. Then come social services. Pastoral works take third place.[5]

To date, the church of Hong Kong has contributed greatly to the success of the colonial government and until now, its role has been mainly servant rather than prophet. The church has always cooperated with the government as a faithful partner, rather than taking a critical stand toward it.

With 1997 approaching, the basic nature of the Hong Kong government will change. It will be directly responsible to a state that is atheistic and socialist, and a state that has historical suspicions of Christianity and hostile memories of the West. The complicated problems between the Vatican and Taiwan and Beijing, and the highly sensitive relation between the underground church and the Patriotic Association in China all contribute to the difficulties that lie ahead for church-state relationships after 1997.

People are asking questions. Will church members be free to meet and evangelize? Will the government continue to subsidize Catholic schools, hospitals, and other social services? Will the church continue to be tax exempt on its income for charitable purposes? Will the church be allowed to use government properties (such as rooms in government-subsidized Catholic schools) for Sunday masses? Will the Catholic religion remain a compulsory subject in the Catholic schools?

In 1984, John Baptist Wu, the bishop of Hong Kong, sent to the government of the People's Republic of China, through the Hong Kong branch of the Xinhua News Agency, a statement of the Catholic position on the future of Hong Kong. In this statement, he enumerated the kind of religious freedom that the church has enjoyed until now, and express his hope that these freedoms can remain unaltered after 1997.

The statement says:

Religious freedom as we enjoy it in Hong Kong includes the following rights:

a. The right to have or to adopt a religion or belief of one's choice, and to manifest it in worship, observance, practice and teaching.
b. The right of the individual to worship in private and public, alone and with fellow believers.
c. The right to make one's religion known to others, and to instruct those who are interested in this religion by the spoken and written word.
d. The right of parents to provide religious instruction in bringing up their children.
e. The right of religious communities and associations to hold meet-

ings and to promote educational, cultural, charitable and social activities.

f. The right to appoint personnel, to train them and to send them abroad for specialized studies and at the same time the right to utilize, if and when necessary, the services of personnel from abroad.

g. The right to erect and/or use buildings for religious purposes and to acquire such property if necessary.

h. For Catholics, in particular, the right to maintain their existing links and unity with the universal church, through union with the pope and also with the bishops and Catholic communities in other parts of the world. This unity is basic to the Catholic church's belief.[6]

It is very difficult to predict whether the church can get all that it wants. There seems to be a deep mutual misunderstanding and distrust between Hong Kong and China, and especially between Christianity and socialism, for two main reasons. First, most of our parents were refugees escaping from the socialist Chinese regime after 1949. Second, Catholics are inclined to believe that God-fearing Christianity cannot coexist with atheistic socialism. And so neither Hong Kong and China, nor Christians and socialists, can build up a kind of genuine partnership. The consequences are grim. Most Catholics will be very reluctant to live under socialist China, and China will lose a good portion of its citizens who are Christians and at the same time a useful building force in temporal and spiritual, technological, and moral areas. Therefore, it is vital to readjust our attitudes toward China and socialism, and to be ready to tie up our destiny with that of China.

A Glance at History

China and Christianity have never been good bed fellows in Chinese history. Unlike Buddhism, the church in China has been labeled by most Chinese as foreign and Western, although it has been in China under various forms for more than one thousand years. The Nestorian Christians came to China during the Tang Dynasty in 636-845. This was a total failure, with only a stone monument remaining. The Franciscan friars came to China during the Yuan dynasty in 1245-1370 with no greater success. Only John of Montecorvino is now still in our memory. The Jesuits, with Matteo Ricci and his colleagues, led the China mission for the third time. It came to a halt after the dispute on the question of whether Catholics could honor their ancestors and Confucius according to Chinese rituals and tradition. Christianity had a fourth opportunity to evangelize the Chinese people along with the "gunboat" policy of the Western powers.[7] Many misunderstandings, tensions, hatreds, conflicts, and persecutions have happened ever since. After the Opium War, many Chinese scholars and ordinary people regarded Christianity as linked with colonialism and imperialism. There was a period in modern Chinese history when people would say: "If there is one more Christian, there will be one less Chinese." This type of Christianity cannot flourish in China. After the takeover of China by Mao Zedong, Christianity once again experienced failure—its fourth.

The problem is not with the gospel. It is with the way one spreads the gospel. Buddhism was successful because it was like a seed buried quietly in the Chinese soil. It sprouted, took root, and grew to be an indigenous Chinese plant. Catholicism, however, is genuinely imported goods, only a plant transplanted in Chinese soil.

John Paul II has stated clearly in his encyclical *Centesimus Annus* that "Man is the Way of the Church," "the primary route that the Church must travel in fulfilling her mission," and that this "man" is not a "man in the abstract," but a "real, concrete, historical man," an "individual."[8]

But in the history of mission in China, the Chinese people and Chinese culture have rarely been treated seriously. To many Catholic missionaries, China is not an "individual," different from others. To many Westerners, China is simply a backward country, and the Chinese simply a package of objects to be saved. Chinese culture has rarely been integrated into the liturgy of the church, its catechetics and theology, or its life.

In his 1984 statement Cardinal John B. Wu emphasized: "As Chinese, we are proud of our heritage—of our long history and our rich culture, which we treasure. Its high moral values and noble ideals have been repeatedly admired and praised by the Catholic Church which respects and embraces all the positive elements present in every culture."[9] Even so, the majority of Catholics in Hong Kong remain unfamiliar with this "heritage" and "rich culture." Or they simply ignore it.

On the whole, the church in China has not really "walked the way of the Chinese people" and is not yet rooted and immersed in the Chinese culture and way of living. Perhaps this is the basic reason why it has failed repeatedly in bringing the good news to the Chinese.

Real Partners

Both Hong Kong and the church of Hong Kong are to "walk the way of the Chinese people." The future of Hong Kong lies in its willingness and capability to be real partners with China. Similarly the future of the Hong Kong church lies in its willingness and capability to be real partners with the Chinese people.

As a result of continuous experimentation for over a hundred years, the Catholic church learned how to cooperate with capitalism as working partners, sometimes even as faithful allies. In Hong Kong, the society at large, as well as the church, has also learned how to live with capitalism. And the church, whether in supporting the good of the government and the society or in rejecting what is not good in government and society, has become both a constructive and a moral force that cannot be neglected.

Cardinal John B. Wu thus exhorted the Catholic church in 1989: "In the future, social service organizations ought to pay greater attention to the servant and prophetic roles and see that both develop in a more balanced way."[10] Nevertheless, the church of Hong Kong, both in the past and at present, vis-à-vis government and society, mainly plays the role of servant, and seldom if ever assumes the role of prophet. This is because right from the start the church has been in alliance with capitalism, most of the time cooperating with it and rarely criticizing it.

On the contrary, confronted with the fact that Hong Kong will be returned to socialist China, the people in Hong Kong and the church of Hong Kong appear very helpless, desperate, even frightened, not knowing how to cope with the situation. A great deal of time is spent in criticizing the Chinese government and finding the country backward, to the extent that when Eastern Europe and the Soviet Union were experiencing drastic changes, many zealously expected that socialist China would meet the same fate. Many people in Hong Kong directly resisted the expressed upholding of socialism by the Chinese authorities. Not wanting to be part of China as it is today is the immediate reason cited by Hong Kong people who emigrate to other countries.

In matters of ideology, people in Hong Kong have been greatly influenced by the West, so much so that all the success and positive contributions of China in the past forty years can be readily wiped away by the knowledge of the mistakes China commits. The result of this endless opposition is the birth of mutual distrust, which makes cooperation, mutual influence, and mutual transformation difficult. This self-afflicted insulation from China causes the people of Hong Kong to pay the price of having no positive influence on the future of China.

The anti-Communist stance of the church has been made prominent by the public manifestation of Father Louis Ha, director of the Hong Kong Catholic social communications office. Father Ha wrote an article in which he openly described the pope's encyclical *Centesimus Annus* as anti-Communist. He exhorted the faithful of Hong Kong "to stand up bravely" even to the point of sharing the fate of those Catholics of the 1950s who, because of their anti-Communist stance, were persecuted by the Chinese Communists.[11] In the same article it was insinuated that in the 1960s and 1970s, the church's post-Vatican II spirit of openness in forebearing socialism, which led to the birth of liberation theology, was, in fact, a softening of the church's stance on the truth. Afterward, two other priests wrote in the Chinese Catholic weekly *Kung Kao Po*, pointing out that the anti-Communist stance of the church is correct. But, at the same time, two directors of the Catholic Institute for Religion and Society, Peter Cheung and myself, wrote in the *Hong Kong Economic Journal*, showing that the focal point of the encyclical *Centesimus Annus* is not anti-communism, and that lay people in conscience can have the freedom of different political options or inclinations.[12] The anti-Communist tendency of the Catholic church, mingled with that of the Hong Kong people, has become what the Beijing authorities describe as a "general atmosphere" of anti-communism.

The demonstration of one million people in June 1989, the popular acceptance of the "H.K. Alliance in support of the Democratic Movement in China," and the landslide victory of the United Democrats, in contrast to the all-round failure of the pro-Beijing candidates during the first Hong Kong Legislative Council election in September 1991, prove that Hong Kong people in general are afraid of and opposed to communism.

In such an anti-Communist "general atmosphere," the Catholic church has always been regarded as an important moving force by the leftists. One of the pro-Beijing Chinese newspapers, *Wen Wei Po*, published an article by a certain Mr. Chung entitled "Political Persons Getting the Votes of Christians." It openly stated:

> The fact that a certain group of candidates (meaning the United Democrats) managed to have a landslide victory in the present election is certainly related to the help given by certain people of the Church as well as by the social service organizations run by the Church ... Certain Church organizations (Catholic and Christian included) have become the basic cells of these political groups.[13]

It is a very unfortunate development in Hong Kong in recent years that democracy is equated with anti-communism and that anti-communism, and anti-China have become synonymous. A church that sides with anti-Communist (and anti-China) groups will not be regarded by the Chinese regime as a purely religious body. The Chinese government does not mind too much when people contradict certain of its policies. Yet it definitely minds when others are "anti-Communist," for this means that they oppose its existence.

I am not saying that what we do should be conditioned by what Beijing thinks about us. But we certainly need to be clear about our own intentions. Do we want to get involved in a political battle to overthrow the Communist regime in China? Is that the calling of a Christian *per se*? Or do we want to stay close to our gospel values, and be free enough to take a firm stand on these values, in criticism of policies and practices of both capitalist Hong Kong and socialist China?

Right after the events of June 4, 1989 I gave a homily at a eucharistic celebration in memorial of the dead at the Hong Kong stadium. In it I openly reproached Beijing's suppression of the peaceful democratic movement. The entire content of the homily was published a few days later in four Chinese newspapers.[14] In December of the same year, however, I was invited to have an exchange with the teaching staff and student body of several seminaries in China, just as the year before. This was possible because I objected only to certain policies that I thought were mistakes made by the Chinese authorities. I was not anti-Communist.

In the 1950s when China was surrounded, isolated, boycotted, and ruthlessly suppressed by the countries of the West, the Vatican sided with these countries. The Vatican thus justified what the West did to China as the liberation of the Chinese people. Religion can be muddled with politics. Today what Beijing minds most is whether the people of Hong Kong will unite themselves with and seek the support of the West to put pressure on China to accept the ideology and political aspirations of the West, even to the point of dictating to China both the content and speed of reforms.

Pressure coming from the people of Hong Kong may be tolerated. But pressure coming from the same people allying themselves with the Western powers will not be tolerated. People in Hong Kong may criticize China point by point, but these same people may not adopt an anti-Communist attitude, entirely negating the Chinese government. The Catholic church in Hong Kong must be very clear about this. In criticizing China, there must be sympathy, understanding, and a willingness to take the whole situation in the People's Republic into consideration, thus recognizing all the difficulties that any large nation has to meet: it is not easy to eliminate — or to revive it.

In order to win the confidence of China, the church in Hong Kong must identify itself with Chinese culture and enhance it, accept China's weaknesses, her slow pace and capriciousness in making reforms, her growing "old, big, and difficult." We must accept the fact that, for the time being, in the People's Republic there is little democracy, only limited freedom, and that China is very suspicious of the outside world. We must also accept the fact that as an economically developing country, there is corruption, a habit such as going by the "back door," not treating everyone on the same basis, not always sticking to the rule of law. There is inefficiency and widespread ignorance or illiteracy.

We accept these factors not because we are passive but because we recognize this is the *terminus a quo*, the reality from which we actively and positively commit ourselves. More important still, we accept these factors because we love our country and we would like to be with her, to grow with her, and as Chinese, to be willing to dedicate ourselves for China. In face of all the restrictions we might encounter, of all the obscurities and uncertainties we might find, we still want to develop a *modus convivendi*, a way of living peacefully together with our mainland brothers and sisters. Only then can we find space in which to live and move and opportunities to expand this space. And only then mutual trust will become a reality — trust that is vital for cooperation and mutual influence. With greater mutual trust, even mutual criticism may be welcomed or at least tolerated.

At a conference organized for lay representatives from China, Hong Kong, Taiwan, and Macau, which took place in Hong Kong on April 12,

1991, in which I emphasized the necessity of "carrying the burden of the Chinese society, the Chinese nation, and the Chinese people," and "walking with China . . . trying to know, meet, understand, and accept this country which seems far yet so close, and being willing to cooperate with her."[15]

In July 1991 a large group of secondary-school students took part in a seminar on China. At the end of three days they made a declaration in which they stated: "We are willing to cultivate national sentiments, and to show solicitude for the future of China. We are not afraid to face a China that is unscientific, undemocratic, insufficient in many ways, and full of miseries. We are willing to understand her political and economic situations, carrying in ourselves our identity as Chinese."[16] It is only with such an attitude that the church in Hong Kong can assume its "historical mission of reconciliation" in China so that the differences of the two places can "lead to communion on a higher level."[17] This attitude toward China is different from that of many people in Hong Kong, Christians included. Among the latter, many are seeking to find fault with China, hoping China will soon collapse.

Rosemary Radford Ruether has something to say about that which deserves our attention:

A key element in this move toward a genuine new world order of justice and peace must be a new international culture. We must categorically refuse to allow governments, media, preachers or any other public leaders to continue to exploit the culture of Manichaean conflict between good and evil, identified with one side of any conflict against the other, to claim that one group of people are the people of God and their opponents are the brood of Satan.[18]

Start from Basic Christian Communities

The church is a community that has received salvation and brings this salvation to others, that has received the gospel and proclaims the same everywhere; it is both an evangelized and evangelizing community. It must, under all circumstances, live out its dynamism, work positively, witness the gospel, commit itself to building a better and more humane place.[19]

The church has lived with capitalism, and has succeeded in giving it life, and making it more humane. Similarly, the church can do the same with socialism, revitalizing it, and enabling it to perfect itself. To attain this, besides engaging in dialogue and being partners with socialism, there must be a new model of being church. The basic Christian community, a church model of living faith, can liberate the inner force of every single person and also enable these persons to insert themselves into society. The basic Christian community is such a model; it is the lowest level of the church inserted and inculturated in society.

The basic Christian community is the grassroots church because it is located in every social milieu. This can be an apartment building, a factory, a school, an office. It is present in every single profession, in every single social group. It is the "capillary church," because it carries the blood — the good news of the gospel, the dynamism of faith — from the hearts (the universal church) through the arteries (the dioceses, the parishes) to every single cell. This is the "nerve-ending church," because it lives at the lowest level of society, can sense the changes and needs of this society, and effectively sends this news to other parts of the central nerve system (parishes, dioceses, universal church).

The raison d'être of a basic Christian community is to elevate and enhance the quality of life, particularly in improving the family, work place, and environment. Its dynamism comes from faith, particularly from the scriptures and the eucharist. The basic Christian community has a broad mind and huge heart. Horizontally it is in communion with the whole church and the whole human race; vertically it is in union with God and history. It must carry out the mission of the church and society, simply because it is a missionary and liberating community.

In this view, a basic Christian community is made up of a group of people who are rooted in faith, committed in society, have the nation close to their hearts, and show concern for the whole world. Members are genuinely citizens of society and an important force in building a better society and nation. Such a church can definitely be more easily accepted by socialists, who proclaim that the ordinary people are the masters of the nation.

To build such a model, the church must make a few changes.

First, the church must be de-clericalized and decentralized, so that lay people have the power to take part in and administer church matters. They must be encouraged to search for their own way of leading their spiritual life and living out the ideals of their faith. Lay persons must realize that they have the Spirit too. They can and should study scripture by themselves, look for the revelation of God, and share their own convictions, passing on to others the faith that has its origin in the gospel. Then, together with those who have the same ideals, they will search for ways and opportunities to give corporate witness to Christ.

Second, we must emphasize the integration of faith and life, religion and society, scripture and Chinese culture, so that faith affected by life becomes "flesh and blood," and life affected by faith is deepened every day.

Third, the parish must be restructured. In the present model of the parish, lay people exist for the parish. Be they individual lay persons or associations, they are alive only in the parish. The parish, in turn, tries its best to attract all the lay people to meet, to organize activities, and to celebrate within the parish circle. When Christians do not go to the parish, they do not feel the vibration of the church, or do not even feel that it exists.

In the new parish model, which is based on basic Christian communities

(BCCs), the parish exists for the laity. The parish is the place where lay people "meet in order to be dispersed"; the parish is the communion of communities. It must guarantee that the church exists in each neighborhood and social milieu. It must encourage lay people to be salt, light, and yeast in their own environment, bringing joy and hope to their beloved, filling the society with the resonance of prayers and hymns, and allowing Christian actions of care, love, and service to be promoted in the neighborhood. When other people stop going to church, the church must go to the people.

The mission of the parish is to proclaim the gospel. The responsibility of the BCC is to mediate, digest, and share the messages of the gospel, applying them in different situations. It is only with this life as the base that one can go to the parish to celebrate, make contrition for omissions, give thanks for successes, and beseech on behalf of all.

The principal work of the parish then is to create BCCs on a large scale, to train leaders, and to provide material for meetings. In brief, the parish is to inspire and encourage, to unify and coordinate, letting each BCC have its own life and characteristics, making all the BCCs one in the Catholic family.

Right from the start Cardinal John B. Wu realized the importance of the BCC. Thus in his pastoral letter *March into the Bright Decade* he strongly stressed the objective "to develop Small Faith Communities (BCCs) throughout the Diocese."[20] He commissioned the Catholic Institute for Religion and Society, a new organization specifically established in 1986 to help the laity cope with the 1997 situation, to devise a three-year plan for two purposes: first, to create BCCs at all levels in an experimental parish; second, to try to create one or more BCCs in each of the fifty or more parishes in the diocese. It is hoped that these BCCs can have an effect in Hong Kong, and that through them the energy and life force of the 260,000 Catholics will be released in order to meet the challenges of proclaiming the gospel after 1997.

The relationship between the church of Hong Kong and the People's Republic is at stake. It is similar to a person walking on a tightrope. On the one hand, by cooperating too eagerly with the future political authorities, the church could lose its identity and abandon its principles. On the other hand, it could also commit itself wholeheartedly in the society, genuinely be the yeast of the world. In the end, a church that is filled with the Spirit and has the good will to take life seriously will surely find space for its existence and development. This is its risk and also its responsibility.

Notes

1. Asia Partnership for Human Development, *Hong Kong Profile*, 1989, p. 1.
2. About a multi-billion dollar project on the Hong Kong port and airport scheme.
3. Editorial, *Ming Pao Daily News*, October 11, 1991.

4. *Hong Kong Profile*, p. 3.

5. *Hong Kong Catholic Church Annual Directories, 1960–1991*.

6. John B. Wu, "Statement on the Catholic Church and the Future of Hong Kong," *Sunday Examiner*, Hong Kong, August 24, 1984.

7. Luke Tsui, *Facing the Demands of the Faith for Life — Manual for Catechumens*, 1989, p. 280.

8. John Paul II, *Centesimus Annus*, 1991, 53 and 54.

9. *Sunday Examiner*, August 24, 1984.

10. John B. Wu, *March into the Bright Decade*, 1989, p. 10.

11. Louis Ha, "Inspiration of *Centesimus Annus*," *Hong Kong Economic Journal*, July 1991, p. 10.

12. *Hong Kong Economic Journal*, August 18 and September 15, 1991.

13. *Wen Wei Po*, October 9, 1991.

14. *Ming Bao Daily News, Wen Wei Po, Hong Kong Economic Journal*, and *Hong Kong Daily News*, June 15, 1989.

15. Luke Tsui, *Hand in Hand towards the Future with the People in Christ*, 1991.

16. *Kung Kao Po*, August 2, 1991.

17. John B. Wu, *March into the Bright Decade*, p. 11.

18. Centre Oecuménique de Liaisons Internationales, *Religion and War in the Middle East* (Brussels, Summer 1991), p. 7.

19. John B. Wu, "Statement on the Catholic Church and the Future of Hong Kong," p. 3.

20. Ibid., pp. 5-8.

17

Contextualization of the Chinese Church

EDMOND TANG

Very few countries have gone through as much upheaval as China—from the Opium Wars to the Boxer Rebellion, from the first Republic to Liberation, from the Cultural Revolution to today's economic reforms and the pro-democracy movement in 1989. China has been at the center of world attention for most of this time and yet its destiny seems always to lie at the periphery, except for the foundation of the People's Republic in 1949, which generated so much hope and at the same time so much suffering.

A Look at China Today

Before examining the question of if, and how, the church may have changed in responding to changes in China, I would like to look at some of these changes. When today's visitors descend in cities like Shanghai or Guangzhou (Canton), they see much that they would not have seen in the late 1970s. The road from Hongcao airport leading into Shanghai was formerly a dusty dirt road flanked by small villages and huts. Today it is lined with multi-storey apartments and grandiose international hotels. Formerly the streets of Guangzhou were quiet and dark after seven o'clock at night and it was difficult to find a public place for a meal. In the early 1990s they are lit up with advertisements throughout the night and sidewalk stalls serve the latest delicacies until dawn.

All over China empty shelves are now full, and the most popular topic of conversation is what one can or cannot afford to buy. In other words, the austere, ideologically dominated society of China of the 1970s has made a U-turn and become a consumer-oriented if not yet a consumer society.

The tragic events of June 1989 struck fear in the hearts of many intellectuals, but for the general public the biggest fear today is something new called inflation, which the generation born after 1949 has never experienced. In China prices of essential goods had always been controlled and subsidized by the state until it decided to liberalize the economy. In some cities inflation has reached double digits. A dissident Chinese writer, Liu Binyan, wondered if the Chinese people would once again exchange their freedom and dignity for a guaranteed standard of living and stability, as they did in 1949. If one travels around the countryside, the answer is inevitably "yes."

On the other hand, the intellectual landscape has also changed radically. Although writers, artists, and intellectuals today live under the cloud of June 1989 and many have decided not to write or publish, the door opened by ten years of reform cannot be instantly closed. Freedom of thought, if not expression, is deeply cherished. At the time of the liberation of China, this freedom was given to the state in return for a new society, which never came about; since retrieved, this freedom has become a cause to live for.

The encounter with Western thinking is part of this new freedom. Some of the richest people in China are not writers but translators, and serious tomes on philosophy, psychology, sociology, and especially religion are selling well.[1] This encounter with the West is quite different from that of the May Fourth Movement in 1919. The May Fourth intellectuals started out by destroying the old, corrupt culture as they welcomed "Mr. Science and Mr. Democracy" to save China. The intellectuals of April Fifth (referring to the start of the first pro-democracy movement in April 1976 (also in Tiananmen Square and also violently put down) had very little culture left to destroy. "Mr. Science" of the 1920s was replaced by "Mr. Economy."

The search of the new generation of thinkers, however, goes beyond the social or cultural salvation of China to enter the realm of the ontological — the burning question underlying novels, philosophical treatises, political theories on human rights, and so forth is: What is the basis of and what constitutes the human person — the *humanum*? This is true of the novels of Dai Houying, of the philosophical works of Wang Juoshui, of the religious quest of Liu Xiaofeng.

However, in China today, this willingness to call the most sacred traditions into question is not limited to scientists and intellectuals. Even popular media such as television participate in the most radical soul-searching that China has known since the days of the May Fourth Movement of 1919. Only this time it goes deeper and is participated in by a larger sector of the population. This picture of China's cultural climate will not be complete without mention of the television series "River Elegy." Following its debut in June 1988 this television series stimulated a furious debate among its TV audience of six hundred million. By any standards the six-part series entitled "He Shang" or "River Elegy" cannot be called a literary success, except in one regard: it dares to attack the most sacred monuments of Chinese tradition and culture, such as the Great Wall and the Yellow River, which are symbols of the origin and uniqueness of the Chinese empire.

China has always been proud of its Yellow River. It takes pride in the last great and continuous "river civilization" of the world, as the ancient civilizations of the Nile, the Tigris, and the Euphrates have all disappeared. China is equally proud of its Great Wall, a unique monument of humanity, the only human construction that could be observed by astronauts from the moon. But the Great Wall is also a symbol of a closed kingdom. By protecting the integrity of its civilization, the Great Wall also signs the warrant of its decline. And is the Yellow River always a blessing? Lost soil from the western mountains is deposited as the river flows down the great plains. As a result it changes its course every seventy years, flooding several provinces and causing enormous loss of life and widespread famine. The authors of the TV series compare the Yellow River to the feudal dynasties of China and recurrent civil wars. Will China ever be rid of its turbulence if it remains a "river civilization" closed in on itself?

By juxtaposing symbolic images with those of war and destruction, the progress of industrial civilization, and interviews with critical scholars, the authors dealt a heavy blow to Chinese confidence in its past. For some this "river civilization" has been the last rampart against the disintegration of China, faced as China is with the onslaught of Western values; for others it is the last vestige of conservatism, the last myth holding China back from embracing the hopes of a brave new world. The authors of "River Elegy" conclude that the Yellow River must finally flow into the ocean, that China must break down its own barriers in order to become a nation of the world.

Christianity Fever

There is a consensus among researchers that one of the fastest growing areas in China is not the economy but religion. In 1991 at a small conference in London on religion in China, an anthropologist from the City University of New York used the term "quantum leap" in describing the increase of religious practice along the southeast China coast. Another researcher did not hesitate to describe the province of Henan as being gripped by a "Christianity fever."

Although the general increase in religious activities is by no means limited to Christianity, the phenomenal growth of Christian churches in China is a fact that defies the imagination of many. This is particularly applicable to Protestant Christianity, which has increased from an estimated 700,000 in 1949 to today's official figure of 6.5 million or more.[2] Unofficial statistics put the figure significantly higher. The Catholic church has also witnessed a substantial growth in the period since the Cultural Revolution.

Given the scope of this increase in conversions, is it justifiable to talk about a "Christianity fever"? Some government publications seem to suggest this. As early as January 1989 an article in the magazine, Liaowang, used the term in its analysis of the new phenomenon. Since then a series of internal documents, as well as scholarly articles, have been devoted to the question.[3] In a number of cases government cadres complained that illegal groups, seminaries, and Koranic schools were springing up like mushrooms after the rain. One report says that a recent survey conducted in ten poor villages in Xiangshui county of Jiangsu province revealed that religious believers outnumbered Communist party members by 29.7 percent. The report further noted that while religious believers were enthusiastic about regular gatherings, party members rarely called a meeting.[4]

Three reasons were given for this phenomenon:

1. The sense of helplessness fostered by social and health problems, including poverty, backwardness, and a high rate of disease, has caused people to turn to religion for support.

2. The lack of contribution toward economic uplift by Communist party leaders in these villages is behind the gap between the increase of religious believers and the decline of the party.

3. Low educational standards and geographical isolation contribute as well.

These explanations, typical of the Chinese press, were probably put forth by more liberal-minded cadres. Orthodox Marxist views were not quoted. Rather, there seemed to be an underlying conviction that economic reform and greater openness to the outside world would change the situation.

Other researchers have not been convinced by these superficial explanations. A number of more sociological motifs have been put forward, such as the attraction to the practice of healing in Christianity, the search for a surrogate family, the sense of inferiority of the traditional culture, rural isolation, breakdown of kinship, the policy of one-child families, and so on.

There are other observations that are important as well. The first is that most new Christians are not converts from atheism. It is more often a question of transferring one's beliefs from an existing popular religion to another religion, in this case Christianity. A second observation is that religious revival is a direct result of the decentralization policy of the last ten years, in which provinces and local places were given an economic identity. This has led to the recreating of a social identity, and religion plays an important role in the creation of new social fabrics. If these explanations are viable, which seems to be the case from available evidence, they add an entirely new dimension to our understanding of the growth of Christian groups and the new tensions between centralized and local forms of religious organization (in this case the spread of Protestant "house churches" and the Catholic underground church).

Reflections

In examining the growth of Christianity in China, I have observed that there is a great interest in religion, especially Christianity, among intellectuals. There is also a "Christianity fever" at the grassroots, especially in the countryside. The first, however, does not usually interact with the latter.

Chinese intellectuals seem interested in Christianity as a philosophy or a cultural system but not in Christianity as a church, at least not in the Chinese church. Liu Xiaofeng, much discussed in the West for his intellectual adoption of Christianity, has declared himself a Christian (*Jidutu*), but not a "church Christian" (*Jidujiaotu*). In their search for a universal understanding of the "human" as the ground for human values and relations following the collapse of the class theory of Marxism, Chinese intellectuals are attracted to the universal, the abstract, and the ideal. Consequently there is an impatience with the limitations of the concrete, and dissatisfaction with the imperfections of the Christian church, be it Chinese or Western.

This intellectual interest is generally not grounded in any religious experience, at least not an experience mediated by a Christian community or a church.[5] Without this religious experience, Christian philosophy is seen as an answer to a conjunctural question, either existential or national or both. Yet, without a first-hand experience of the mystery of death and resurrection in Christ, will this "culture Christianity" develop and take root on Chinese soil?

This leads to the question of to what extent the Chinese churches today, public or underground, "three-self" or "house-based," are a conducive environment for this experience to take place. Are the Chinese churches competent partners in the dialogue on the existential as well as on the socio-political level? What will be the role of the Chinese churches in the urgent task of China's search for a new identity? What is the future of the church, or churches, that remain on the margin of the unique movement of cultural transformation taking place in Chinese society?

Changes in the Chinese Church

Chinese Christians have gone through a difficult period in their recent history and rejoice in finding a new sense of faith and a vibrant movement. They are now in a period of reconstructing their beliefs as well as their communities. Questions about the inculturation of Christianity on Chinese soil at this unique moment in Chinese history are being asked by Christians and non-Christians as well. Professor Tang Yi, a non-Christian who is head of the Christianity Department in the Institute of World Religions at the Chinese Academy of Social Sciences in Beijing, wonders if the Chinese churches are capable of taking up both political and cultural challenges. If not, he writes, the danger is that Christianity will remain outside the mainstream of Chinese life and "settle down to be a sub-cultural minority religion in China."[6]

According to Professor Tang Yi, Chinese Christianity after 1949 can be divided into two periods. The first phase (1949 to the 1960s), in his opinion, was characterized by a movement of patriotism and collaboration with the new Chinese government. The argument goes like this: thanks to the leadership of the Communist movement and the sufferings of its members, the new Chinese nation is now free from the colonial control of the Western powers. Christians, like all other citizens, should therefore support the Communist government in all spheres of social life, cut off relations of foreign domination, and build an independent church. Theological reflection was comprised of efforts to find support for the stand of the churches in the Bible and the early church.

In the second phase, which began in the early 1980s, Professor Tang observes a shift of emphasis in the Catholic church. Instead of seeking proof for its claims to autonomy, Chinese Catholics now put the emphasis on the concrete experience of Catholic contributions to society. The legitimacy of the Chinese Catholic church is thus built upon the many examples of model workers and other exemplary citizens who contribute to the country's modernization. There is also an attempt to break out of the churches' confines to be of service in society. This is an important new development. However, Professor Tang also notes a "survivalist overtone" in both periods. As to the consequences of this approach, his comments are controversial: "In stressing the absolute importance of patriotism, both the Catholic and Protestant churches have either overlooked or suppressed the prophetic traditions of Christianity which uphold the spirit of the Gospel and the Kingdom of God as a challenge to the secular world."

Besides political adaptation, which was the subject of Professor Tang Yi's paper, there have been other adaptations and consequences as well. In the case of Protestant Christianity, in order to maintain the unity between different denominational traditions in what is called the "post-denominational" phase of the church, their common core of beliefs as well as the curriculum of theological education is restricted to a minimalist understanding of the Christian experience. One Christian leader regretted that in order to preserve unity, theological creativity is being sacrificed.[7] Another theological educator said that the theology and mentality of the majority of Christian Protestants and pastors remain "pietistic, conservatively dogmatic (or fundamentalist), seeking individual salvation of the soul and (tend to be) other worldly."[8]

The Underground Catholic Church

While the previous discussion applies equally to Protestant and Catholic Christianity, I would like to give some special attention to the Catholic situation, which is not entirely encouraging. Definitions of and distinctions between the so-called "underground" church and the "public" church abound and will not be taken up here. In trying to understand the underground church, it is perhaps useful to distinguish between two moments of its unusual history.

In the 1950s, there were Catholics who, following the instruction of the

Holy See, refused to join or recognize the leadership of the Chinese Patriotic Association. They refused to go to the open churches or to accept the sacraments administered by pastors who had joined the association. These Catholics practiced their faith privately in homes and were served by itinerant priests. Although hostile to the open churches, their attitude was more defensive in character.

The underground church that is often discussed nowadays has a different character. More organized and more aggressive, the concerns of its leaders go beyond the pastoral—of seeking alternative ways of serving Catholics who do not want to worship in the open churches. Their activities become more and more daring and seem to suggest that they are seeking a confrontation with the existing authorities. Secretly ordained priests are sent throughout China to denounce those who have joined the Patriotic Association and to instruct Catholics not to receive sacraments from the CCPA priests since they are considered to be invalid. Many communities have become confused and divided by these actions.

Reflections

The division within a church is always a source of scandal rather than witness. The first result is that the conflicting parties retreat into protective ghettos. Theology then becomes a weapon to settle political or social differences. Belief—and not faith—is turned into a monolithic ideology. How do these exclusive belief systems appear to a Chinese society that is starting to breathe the first fresh air of freedom and plurality?

The price for political legitimacy and stability in the church is high. It was perhaps justifiable in the period immediately after 1949, but a more relaxed international atmosphere since then should be able to provide some space for experimentation. Some persons have suggested ways to bring the churches in China up to date with the reforms of Vatican II. It is a necessary task, but what is more important is to create an atmosphere in which the Chinese church can *itself* feel free to invent and be creative.

On the other hand, how will these churches, preoccupied as they are with internal tensions, respond to the queries of Chinese intellectuals, especially those of young students after the events of June 1989? Many young persons have approached pastors or gone to the churches and left in disappointment after being told that their concerns are "philosophical and political" questions that have nothing to do with religion.

As for the underground church, it is hazardous to make too many comments. Although the strong faith and loyalty of these Catholic Christians is impressive, little is known about the qualities of their leaders in other ecclesial matters. There may be a parallel, however, with a common experience of resistance fighters who come to govern: most often, the transition from the stage of resistance to the stage of reconciliation and reconstruction is not without obstacles. Attitudes of confrontation do not easily become attitudes of reconciliation.

The experience of the situation in former Eastern Europe is a useful case in comparison. The churches were united under the authoritarian governments of the Warsaw Pact. Once the lid was removed, however, the old rivalries in the churches reappeared. Personal and regional interests were put before unity, and vindication and revenge before reconciliation. Worst of all, the churches, which had gained their strength through suffering and opposition, are now completely helpless as they are faced with the onslaught of a new consumer society. Younger people are no longer listening to the churches.

Contextualization — The World Church and the Chinese Church

There is no real doubt that for the last two decades the world church has greatly benefited from the rich experience of other local churches — not only churches in the so-called third world but also churches in North America and some parts of Europe. Some theologians believe that an important shift in the Catholic church took place at the Second Vatican Council when, for the first time in history, a significant number of the world's bishops came from outside Europe. It was pointed out that this shift was not only of a geographical or demographic character, but was also a change from a Hellenistic worldview in theology and a monarchical institutional view of the church to a new multicultural and polycentric Christianity. In 1979 Karl Rahner reflected that the greatest achievement of Vatican II was that it was the first self-realization of Catholicism as a world church.[9]

Following this insight, some theologians now divide the history of Christianity into three main periods: 1) the brief period of Jewish Christianity; 2) the bonding of Christianity with the mainstream of European culture; and 3) the beginning of the world church.[10] The passing of the old eurocentric model was perhaps due as much to the crumbling of the old colonial empires as to the work of theologians and the leaders of the Second Vatican Council. It was pointed out by Walbert Bühlmann that "if the values enshrined in these cultures are now at last being given practical recognition instead of being shunned, this is due less to Papal documents from Rome than to nationalist movements arising in the countries in question."[11]

The consequence of this change is evident. The old model of the eurocentric church, based on a concept of empire, can no longer operate once the political empire has disintegrated. The church that was once at the center of this empire is now relegated to the periphery.

How long can the Catholic church resist making changes in its ways of operation? The women's movement in North America and Europe, the spread of basic Christian communities in Latin America, and the grassroots cooperation between Catholics and Protestants are all instances that are stretching the old model to its limits. Bishops from Latin America, Africa, or Asia as well as in Europe and North America are requesting changes. In fact the universal church today is already multi-centered.

In this period of transition, while the old is not yet dead and the new is only in travail, there is naturally much confusion. Two sets of values are operating at the same time, creating division and inconsistency. This has happened in Holland, Switzerland, Germany, and Belgium where churches are divided by the introduction of conservative bishops. It has also happened in North America and in Brazil.

But what about China? If there were not a deep division among Chinese Catholics or if there were no Communist government, where would our sympathies lie? Whom would our ecclesiological arguments favor? There are two reasons for asking these questions. The first reason is to show that in this period of transition we do *not* have one model of the church that is acceptable to all. Current ecclesiological models are only of a relative nature and cannot be normative for all situations. Second, and following from the first reason, often those working with China do not seem to have a consistent ecclesiology. One ecclesiology can be applied to Latin America and a different one to China. Is this acceptable?

An integral part of the new ecclesiological experience is the emergence of local churches. It appears that they were waiting in the wings before Vatican II and suddenly were thrust to the center of the stage.

The present code of canon law equates a "particular" church with the diocese, while the local church is described as a "grouping of particular churches." In practical usage, however, the term is used to describe anything from a parish or a basic Christian community to a national church led by an episcopal conference. Maria Goretti Lau identified four basic elements in the primitive *ecclesia* that she considers essential to a local church: 1) the teaching of the apostles, 2) the breaking of bread, 3) fellowship, and 4) prayer and the presence of the Holy Spirit.[12]

The catholicity of the local church is, of course, an important element that can be interpreted on various spiritual and temporal levels, one of which is its structural link with the see of Rome. In this case, the Catholic church in China is essentially a respectable local church, although there are certain defects in terms of full communion with Rome.

Life, however, comes before definitions. What is of concern here is more the experience of a local church coming into being rather than its systematic definition. In the recent history of the church, most of the local churches have emerged from countries that have passed from colonialism to national independence. In most instances the local church is first an experience of liberation from all forms of domination—colonial as well as ecclesiastical. But above all it is an experience of freedom to be true to a calling: to develop a more relevant Christian experience in liturgy, community, ministry, theology, and spirituality; and to become more relevant in its life of witness and mission. In Asia, the local church has unique problems. Christian churches are constantly faced with a demand to justify themselves before a non-Christian majority: Why is your church so Western, your rituals so esoteric, your beliefs so alien? Where does your sympathy lie in building our nation? Can we trust you as partners in social struggles?

A local church emerges out of a demand for greater relevance. In other words, the local church is essentially missionary in nature. It exists to bear witness to the Kingdom of God that is present and that is to come. Its life in community is supposed to be a foretaste of that heavenly community to be fulfilled at the Second Coming. The experiences of many local churches from different continents all affirm this central role of the community in the mission of the church, whether it is concerned with the problem of inculturation or the struggle for justice and liberation.[13] The faith of the community forms the heart of the evangelizing process, and the process of evangelization in turn strengthens and confirms the community. As it confronts different social and cultural milieus, the community constantly renews itself.

It is important to point out the essential condition of freedom if this dialectical process is to take place. In the case of the Chinese church this dynamic seems to be inhibited by both political pressure from within China and ecclesiastical pressure from without. The church in China is not free. It is not free from political authorities, it is not free from Vatican authorities, and it is not free from its past.

The role of the local church vis-à-vis its sociocultural milieu is understandably not neutral. What attitude should it take faced with the dilemma of respect for a culture, including the predominant political culture, and any transformation that might result from the Christian message? In analyzing the dynamics of communication and transformation, Robert Schreiter suggests three guiding principles taken from the preaching and mission of Jesus: inclusion, judgment, and service.[14]

The principle of inclusion comes from Jesus' preaching of the Kingdom. It departs from the ethnic interpretation of the "chosen" people to include people from other tribes as well as social classes (prostitutes, the poor, the dissenting Zealots). Following from the concept of the Kingdom is the call for repentance and conversion. Any relationship of injustice and enslavement needs to be identified and changed. However, this principle of judgment cannot be drawn from the culture identified with the evangelizing church, or from abstract "universal" concepts. The internal logic of the receiving culture and the historical juncture in its evolution must be taken into account in identifying the central values of a particular society. Finally the principle of service as *diakonia* must accompany the principle of judgment. Without the spirit of humble and devoted service, the inclusive principle becomes paternalistic, and judgments become self-righteous.

How do we compare these principles with the situation in China? The government-approved Chinese church has fully embraced the principle of inclusion and it is beginning to venture into the mission of service. What is found wanting, however, is the exercise of judgment. And what about the churches outside China, including the central authority of the Catholic church? Have they not too often judged from abstract principles without taking into account the history of domination still so vivid in the Chinese memory? Are judgments of the government-approved Chinese church and its leaders accompanied by a genuine sense of service? One may even ask if we and our churches do have a clear and convincing vision of service we are offering to the Chinese people.

Reflections

It seems clear that unless the Chinese church is inculturated or contextualized it will not be able to enter into the mainstream of Chinese life and contribute to needed transformation. But is inculturation (or contextualization) a condition for Christian witness, or is it in itself the witness? This question of evangelization seems to be paramount yet it is often overlooked in debates on the Chinese church. What kind of a church is needed in China and for what purpose? The characteristics of the ideal church model, issues of authority and communion, or relationships between local and universal are, of course, very important. But they have only half their meaning unless they also respond to the needs of evangelization.

What service can we offer the Chinese church? The rich heritage of Catholic humanism could be of use in philosophical dialogues, Catholic social teaching could be a resource in political debates, and Catholic spiritual and liturgical traditions could help provide new space for encountering the mystery of life that is often hidden or banished by a materialist ideology. Yet this is not taking place, and often for reasons that become insignificant in the face of challenges offered within China.

By the same token the interests and activities of Western churches in China must be judged on the same principles. How does concern for full communion relate to the need for the contextualization of the local church? Is the universal always a guarantee of the viability of the local? How can this tension become creative of something new and enriching instead of falling into the trap of sterile power struggles?

How do we define the relationship between the universal and the particular? Can a universal model of church remain superior to its actual implementation in human society? Can concrete models of the church — local churches — rise above or escape their destiny as imperfect models within human society? (In this respect, one needs only to look at how churches sometimes treat each other.) Perhaps the church is an ideal of brotherhood and sisterhood that is best realized in small communities rather than in large institutions with great cultural and political diversity.

Although we should be guided by ideal principles, such as those of the Kingdom of God, we should also be looking for a workable model, especially one that can be revised and improved as the world evolves. What will it be like? An empire with a vassal, a multinational company with a subsidiary, the Warsaw Pact, the United Nations, American federalism, or Swiss federalism? Examples are not lacking.

From a different perspective, I can also see a political role for local churches. A church cannot be limited to giving understanding and spiritual or material support. These latter services are automatically understood. However, I believe that local churches also have a role to play in creating an alternative space where past controversies, present hopes, as well as murky hidden agendas, can be debated in the open. Some people will be hurt — the "underground," the "patriotic," the Vatican — but the problem of the majority of Catholics in China today is not only their suffering but their confusion. Suffering must have meaning, but its meaning today is confused. The local church in China must be resistant to pressures, concerned with but detached from its emotional suffering and — above all — clear in its own faith and discernment. This is a tall order, but without these qualities it will be paralyzed in inaction and, even worse, in a self-gratifying feeling of having done its best. And so much confusion, dissension, and fear remain. Human analysis is always prone to error and misjudgment and often fails to comprehend the work of the Spirit. Fortunately, however, the Spirit remains at work.

Notes

1. Religious works such as Augustine's *Confessions*, Paul Tillich's *Theology of Culture* and *The Courage to Be*, and MacQuarrie's *Principles of Theology* were recently translated and published by secular publishing houses. Liu Xiaofeng has just completed a two-volume introduction to Western philosophical and theological writers with more than one thousand pages of translations from their works.

2. *Tianfeng*, the official organ of the China Christian Council, and *Bridge*, a Hong Kong magazine reporting on the Protestant church.

3. See Xiao Jitian, "Further Reflections on the Long-term Nature of Religion: Revelations on Christianity Fever" in *Religion* 2, Nanjing (1990); Wang Weifan, "An Evaluation and Analysis of the Present Situation of Religion in Our Country" in *Contemporary Religious Studies Review* 1, Shanghai (1991). See also Tony Lambert's reference to the situation in northern Jiangsu in his book *The Resurrection of the Chinese Church* (London: Hodder & Stoughton, 1991), p. 142.

4. *Baoding Ribao Weekly Digest* 7059 (June/July 1991).

5. Cf. Tan Xing, "Culture Christians on the China Mainland," *China Notes*, New York (Spring Summer 1991):628-633.

6. Tang Yi, "Chinese Christianity in Development," *China Study Journal*, London (August 1991):8.

7. Verbal communication of Bishop Ding Guangxun in London, July 22, 1991.

8. "These Ten Years," a paper delivered at the Mission Department, Hamburg University, November 1991, p. 7 (mimeographed).

9. Karl Rahner, "Towards a Fundamental Theological Interpretation of Vatican II," *Theological Studies*, Princeton, 40 (1979):716-726.

10. See, for example, Richard McBrien, *Catholicism* II (New York: Harper & Row, 1980; London: Geoffrey Chapman, 1980), chapters XVIII-XX.

11. Walbert Bühlmann, *Courage Church* (Maryknoll, NY: Orbis Books, 1978), p. 45.

12. Maria Goretti Lau, *Towards a Theology of the Local Church* (Leuven: Catholic University, 1989), p. 296.

13. See the various country reports in Mary Motte and Joseph Lang, eds., *Mission in Dialogue* (Maryknoll, NY: Orbis Books, 1982).

14. Robert Schreiter, "A Framework for a Discussion of Inculturation," *Mission in Dialogue,* p. 546.

Selected Bibliography

Books in Western Languages on the Church in Modern China

Breslin, Thomas A. *China, American Catholicism, and the Missionary* (University Park, PA: The Pennsylvania University Press, 1980).

Brown, G. Thompson. *Christianity in the People's Republic of China* (Atlanta: John Knox Press, 1986).

Carino, Theresa C., ed. *Christianity in China: Three Lectures by Zhao Fusan* (Manila: China Studies Program of De La Salle University, 1986).

Chan, Kim-Kwong. *Towards a Contextual Ecclesiology: The Catholic Church in the People's Republic of China (1979-1983)* (Hong Kong: China Church Research Centre, 1987).

Charbonnier, Jean. *La Chine sans muraille: Héritage culturel et modernité* (Paris: Le Sarment Fayard, 1988).

―――. *La Forêt des Stèles: Scènes de la vie chinoise depuis Mao* (Paris: Le Sarment Fayard, 1989).

―――. *Guide to the Catholic Church in China*, 2nd ed. (Singapore: China Catholic Communication, 1986).

―――. *Histoire des Chrétiens de Chine* (Tournai: Desclée, 1992).

Chu, Theresa and Christopher Lind, eds. *A New Beginning. An International Dialogue with the Chinese Church* (Montreal: Canada-China Programme of the Canadian Council of Churches, 1983).

Covell, Ralph R. *Confucius, the Buddha and Christ: A History of the Gospel in Chinese* (Maryknoll, NY: Orbis Books, 1986).

Crouch, Archie R. et al., eds. *Christianity in China: A Scholar's Guide to Resources in Libraries and Archives of the United States* (Armonk, NY: M. E. Sharpe, Inc., 1989).

Fung, Raymond. *Households of God on China's Soil* (Geneva: WCC Publications and Maryknoll, NY: Orbis Books, 1982).

Gernet, Jacques. *China and the Christian Impact* (Cambridge: Cambridge University Press and Paris: Editions de la Maison des Sciences de l'Homme, 1985).

Hanson, Eric O. *Catholic Politics in China and Korea* (Maryknoll, NY: Orbis Books, 1980).

Hunter, Alan and Don Rimmington, eds. *All Under Heaven: Chinese Tradition and Christian Life in the People's Republic of China* (Kampen: Kok Pharos, 1992).

Küng, Hans and Julia Ching. *Christianity and Chinese Religions* (New York: Doubleday, 1989).

Ladany, Laszlo. *The Catholic Church in China* (New York: Freedom House, 1987).

Lambert, Tony. *The Resurrection of the Chinese Church* (London: Hodder & Stoughton, 1991).

Lau, Maria Goretti Choi Mei. "Towards a Theology of the Local Church," doctoral dissertation (Belgium: Leuven Catholic University, 1989).

Lazzarotto, Angelo S. *The Catholic Church in Post-Mao China* (Hong Kong: Holy Spirit Study Centre, 1982).

Lyall, Leslye T. *New Spring in China?* (London: Hodder & Stoughton, 1979).

MacInnis, Donald E. *Religion in China Today: Policy and Practice* (Maryknoll, N.Y.: Orbis Books, 1989).

MacInnis, Donald and Zheng Xi'an, trans. *Religion under Socialism in China* (Armonk, NY: M. E. Sharpe, 1991).

Malek, Roman and Manfred Plate. *Chinas Katholiken suchen neue Wege* (Freiburg, Basel, Vienna: Herder, 1987).

Myers, James T. *Enemies without Guns: The Catholic Church in the People's Republic of China* (New York: Paragon House, 1991).

Nanjing 86—Ecumenical Sharing: A New Agenda (New York: National Council of Churches, 1986).

Spae, Joseph J. *Church and China: Towards Reconciliation?* (Chicago: The Chicago Institute of Theology and Culture, 1980).

Tang, Dominic. *How Inscrutable His Ways! Memoirs 1951-81* (Hong Kong: Aidan Publicities and Printing, 1987).

Towery, Britt E. *The Churches of China* (Hong Kong: Long Dragon Books, 1987).

Van Houten, Richard, ed. *Wise as Serpents, Harmless as Doves: Christians in China Tell Their Story—Interviews by Jonathan Chao* (Hong Kong: China Church Research Centre, 1988).

Whyte, Bob. *Unfinished Encounter: China and Christianity* (London: Collins, 1988).

Wickeri, Philip. *Seeking the Common Ground: Protestant Christianity, The Three-Self Movement, and China's United Front* (Maryknoll, NY: Orbis Books, 1988).

Wiest, Jean-Paul. *Maryknoll In China* (Armonk, NY: M. E. Sharpe, 1988).

Wurth, Elmer, ed. *Papal Documents Related to the New China* (Maryknoll, NY: Orbis Books and Hong Kong: Holy Spirit Study Centre, 1985).

Periodicals

Bridge (bimonthly in Chinese and English by the Christian Study Centre of Chinese Religion and Culture in Hong Kong).

Catholic Church in China (quarterly in Chinese by the Chinese Catholic Patriotic Association in Beijing).

China and the Church Today (in Chinese and English by the China Church Research Centre, in Shatin, Hong Kong).

China News and Church Report (weekly in English only by the China Church Research Centre in Shatin, Hong Kong).

China Notes (in English only by the National Council of Churches, New York).

China Study Journal (in English only by the Council of Churches of Britain and Ireland, London).

Ching Feng, A Jornal on Christianity and Chinese Religion and Culture (quarterly in English by the Christian Study Centre on Chinese Religion and Culture in Hong Kong).

Kung Kao Po (Catholic Newspaper) (published in Hong Kong, esp. "God Loves China" monthly supplement).

Tian Feng (monthly in Chinese by the China Christian Council, Shanghai).

Tripod (bimonthly in Chinese and English by the Holy Spirit Study Centre in Hong Kong).

Yi-China Message (in Chinese and English in Hong Kong).

Zhonglian (in English biannually and Chinese bimonthly in Singapore by China Catholic Communication; in French quarterly by Relais France-Chine in Paris).

Contributors

Aloysius B. Chang is currently provincial superior of the Chinese province of the Society of Jesus and professor of theology at Fujen Catholic University in Taiwan. Recent publications include *The Church of Christ* (Taipei: Kuangchi Press, 1990) and *The Mysteries of Jesus* (Taipei: Kuangchi Press, 1991).

Jean Charbonnier, a member of the Missions Etrangères de Paris, is director of China Catholic Communication in Singapore. His most recent publications include *La Chine sans muraille* (Paris: Le Sarment Fayard, 1988) and *Histoire des Chrétiens de Chine* (Paris: Desclée, 1992).

Julia Ching describes herself as an ecumenical Catholic. She is professor of religious studies, philosophy, and East Asian studies at the University of Toronto, and author of *Probing China's Soul: Religion, Politics, Protest in the People's Republic of China* (Harper & Row, 1990) and co-author with Hans Küng of *Christianity and Chinese Religions* (Doubleday, 1989). Professor Ching is a fellow of the Royal Society of Canada.

Thomas Gahan is the pen name of an expert on the Catholic church in China who writes from Hong Kong.

Jeroom Heyndrickx is a member of the CICM (Scheut) Mission Institute. A former missionary in Taiwan, he is director of the Ferdinand Verbiest Foundation and the China-Europe Institute at Leuven Catholic University in Belgium.

Geoffrey King, a member of the Australian province of the Society of Jesus, is director of the East Asian Pastoral Institute in Manila, where he also teaches ecclesiology. He has recently published articles on decision-making in the church, formation for ministry, and religious fundamentalism.

Maria Goretti Lau, a Catholic sister, completed her doctorate at Leuven Catholic University in Belgium. She is presently on the faculty at the Holy Spirit Seminary College of Theology and Philosophy in Hong Kong.

Edward J. Malatesta, a member of the California province of the Society of Jesus, taught biblical spirituality at the Gregorian University in Rome. Since its founding in 1984 he has directed the Ricci Institute for Chinese-Western Cultural History at the University of San Francisco.

Edmond Tang, formerly of Pro Mundi Vita, is currently director of the China Study Project of the Council of Churches of Britain and Ireland.

John Tong, a diocesan priest, is the director of the Holy Spirit Study Centre in Hong Kong.

Luke Tsui, a diocesan priest, is executive director of the Catholic Institute for Religion and Society in Hong Kong. He is the author of many catechetical and parish materials.

Hans Waldenfels, a member of the Society of Jesus, is presently dean of theology and professor of fundamental theology at Bonn University in Germany. He is also chairman of the Catholic China Commission in Germany.

Jean-Paul Wiest is research director of the Society History Program and the Center for Mission Research at the Maryknoll School of Theology in Ossining, New York. A specialist in the history of the Catholic church in China, he is the author of *Maryknoll in China* (Armonk, NY: M. E. Sharpe, 1988).